the Optimal Diet

THE OFFICIAL CHIP COOKBOOK

Dedication

To the memory of Denis P. Burkitt, MD, medical pioneer, prevention-oriented visionary, physician role model, loyal CHIP supporter, personal mentor, and dear friend.

To the 50,000 CHIP graduates who have demonstrated in their daily lives that lifestyle medicine principles can indeed reverse and arrest many disease processes and often dramatically improve their health and the quality of their lives.

To Residential Lifestyle Centers that demonstrate month by month with real people, that the principles presented in this book really work. Such live-in centers include the NEWSTART Lifestyle Center (800-525-9192), the Lifestyle Center of America (800-213-8955), the Silver Hills Guesthouse (866-304-7060) and the Rocky Mount Lifestyle Health Center (540-483-7775).

To order *The Optimal Diet Cookbook,* call 1-800-765-6955.

Visit us at **www.AutumnHousePublishing.com** for information on other Autumn House® products.

Copyright © 2011 by Lifestyle Medicine Institute LLC.

Published by Autumn House® Publishing, a division of Review and Herald® Publishing, Hagerstown, MD 21741-1119

"Coronary Health Improvement Project"®, and CHIP® and 🛡 are trademarks used under license from Lifestyle Medicine Institute LLC.

Content Editors: Hans Diehl, DrHSc, MPH; Dena Guthrie, RN, NP
Recipes: Darlene Blaney, MSc, NCP; Hans Diehl, DrHSc, MPH
Recipe Consultants: Heather Reseck, RD, author of *Fix-It-Fast Vegetarian Cookbook;* Julianne Aranda, RD
Nutritional Analysis: Darlene Blaney, MSc, NCP
Analysis Programs used: "Clinical NutriBase IV" and "Living Cookbook"
Photography: Lasting Memories Digital Photography, Calgary, Alberta, Canada
Food design: Darlene Blaney, MSc, NCP, and Lasting Memories Digital Photography
Cover design: Patricia Wegh
Interior book design: Darryl Ludington
Copysetting: Ron Blaney
Typeset: Times New Roman 11/14

PRINTED IN U.S.A.

15 14 13 12 11   5 4 3

Library of Congress Cataloging-in-Publication Data
Blaney, Darlene P.
      The optimal diet cookbook, by Darlene P. Blaney and Hans A. Diehl.

      1. Vegetarian cookery.   2. CHIP (Coronary Health Improvement Project).
I. Diehl, Hans A.
             641.5636

ISBN 978-0-8127-0437-2

RECIPES TO REVERSE AND PREVENT:
Obesity · High Blood Pressure
High Cholesterol · Diabetes · Heart Disease

the Optimal Diet

THE OFFICIAL CHIP COOKBOOK

Darlene Blaney, MSc, NCP

Hans Diehl, DrHSc, MPH, FACN

Autumn House® Publishing
www.autumnhousepublishing.com
A Division of **REVIEW AND HERALD® PUBLISHING**
Since 1861

Before you go further . . .

The Optimal Diet Cookbook is for people who know of the power of the plate. They know that what we eat can promote health or fuel disease; it can undermine health or prevent, arrest, and reverse common Western killer diseases. It can shorten our life or lengthen it.

The Optimal Diet Cookbook is for people who want to eat well and be well. It is for people who eat meat but who would like to eat less meat. It is for people who are caught in the crinkly bag eating pattern, but who want to break out of the engineered food trap and decrease their dependence on refined foods, such as doughuts, Quarter Pounders, potato chips, and presweetened cereals. It's for people who want to be well.

The Optimal Diet Cookbook is for people who want to leave a softer footprint on the earth. They know that a meat-centered diet is ecologically and economically unsustainable. They know that it takes 2,500 gallons of water to produce one pound of beef but only 25 gallons of water to produce one pound of wheat. They have heard that one acre of arable land can produce 20,000 pounds of potatoes but can yield only 200 pounds of beef. And they want to move toward a more plant-food-centered diet because they are tuned in to ecological and economic issues.

The Optimal Diet Cookbook is for people who want to lower their medical bills and their food budget. They have seen statistics showing that one pound of wheat as found in some of the presweetened cereals may cost 10 times more than one pound of grain found in a seven-grain hot cereal. They have seen the Coronary Health Improvement Project (CHIP) data showing that a more optimal diet, centered more on plant foods and whole foods, can reduce food bills by up to 40 percent and reduce medical bills also. And they want to take advantage of that.

This *Optimal Diet Cookbook* promises to facilitate many of these desirable transitions by helping you to increase the foods that are grown and are still intact—the whole foods. At the same time, it will help you decrease those refined, fractured, hydrogenated, bleached foods that have been reengineered to stay on the shelf for another 20 years thanks to stabilizers, preservatives, and chemicals with names few people can read or pronounce.

And this *Optimal Diet Cookbook* is also for more than 40,000 graduates of our 40-hour educational CHIP lifestyle-intervention program who have asked for an official CHIP cookbook to help them sustain their new lifestyle. Their often dramatic clinical improvements within weeks have provided them with powerful object lessons for the fundamental difference between living to eat and eating to live.

In response to so many requests, we are delighted to place this cookbook into your hands. Enjoy these mouthwatering recipes that make your taste buds smile. They are simple, practical, economical, nutritionally sound, and delicious. These recipes were designed for you to eat well and to be well.

About the Authors

Darlene P. Blaney,
MSc, NCP

Darlene Blaney, born and raised in Calgary, Alberta, Canada, was working as a certified ophthalmic technician when she met her husband, Ron. Together they left their careers and opened a health food store focusing on education and information through cooking classes and seminars.

Darlene obtained her diploma in nutritional consulting and opened her own practice helping others to achieve their personal health goals. During this time Darlene and Ron were introduced to the CHIP (Coronary Health Improvement Project) program. Darlene is now a corporate CHIP director in Calgary. Thousands of CHIP participants have enjoyed her recipes and the many health benefits derived from wiser and more deliberate lifestyle choices.

After obtaining her Master of Science degree in nutrition, Darlene opened the Total Health School of Nutrition, licensed and registered federally across Canada. The college has been offering a one-and-a-half-year diploma program in nutritional consulting (www.totalhealthschoolofnutrition.com). Darlene is currently completing her PhD degree in nutrition.

Ron and Darlene are raising four active, healthy sons following the CHIP lifestyle. As a family, their focus and mission is not only to enjoy healthy, long lives, but to help others to enjoy the same benefits.

Hans Diehl,
DrHSc, MPH, FACN

Chosen by *Vegetarian Times* as "one of America's superheroes of health," Hans Diehl directs the Lifestyle Medicine Institute in Loma Linda, California, and lectures at the College of Medicine at the University of Illinois at Rockford. Offering more than 25 years of leadership in the emerging field of lifestyle medicine, he has shown, through his pioneering efforts as an epidemiologically trained lifestyle interventionist with the Coronary Health Improvement Project (CHIP), how simple lifestyle changes can prevent, arrest, and reverse many of our largely lifestyle-related diseases. With more than 50,000 graduates, the results of the recently conducted and government-funded Randomized Clinical CHIP Trial have been released via 13 articles published in peer-reviewed medical journals.

His book *Health Power* (coauthored with Aileen Ludington, MD) has more than 2 million copies in 16 languages in circulation. He most recently addressed the World Congress on Weight Management.

He earned his doctorate in health science and an MPH in public health nutrition from Loma Linda University, where he also worked as a research fellow in cardiovascular epidemiology, supported by the National Institutes of Health. Before assisting in the establishment of the Center for Health Enhancement and Research at the University of California at Los Angeles, he was the director of research and education at the Pritikin Longevity Institute.

Hans has been married to Dr. Lily Pan for 38 years. Together they have two children: Byron, an orthodontist, and Carmen, a clinical psychologist.

His greatest joy is "to know that my life has significance because of the God I found and cherish."

Table of Contents

About the Authors 5
The Importance of the Optimal Diet 6
Implementing the Optimal Diet. 11
Stocking a Healthy Pantry. 12
Specialty Items Glossary. 13
Focus on
    Beans 15
    Grains 16
Nutrition Terms 17
    Fats and Oils. 18
    Flax. 19
    Protein 19
    Soy 20
    Sugar. 21
    Carob 21
    Vitamin B_{12} 22
    Yeast. 23
Food Additives 24
Calcium Content in Food Sources. 25
Breakfasts and Brunches 27
Breads and Muffins 39
Breadmaking 40
Spreads, Sauces, and Condiments. 53
Soups and Stews 69
Salads and Dressings. 85
Sprouting 100
Vegetables 103
Main Dishes. 115
Desserts 141
Drinks and Party Foods. 157
Two-Week Menu Plan. 166
Recipes:
    Sectional Index. 168
    Alphabetical Index 169

The Importance of the Optimal Diet

The accomplishments of modern medicine have been prodigious. We have seen the development of proton accelerators that can zap cancers, surgical robots that can be employed in performing coronary bypass surgeries, and advances in molecular biology and genetics that can open doors to amazing new worlds. And yet these advances in high-tech medicine have not altered the advances of our modern killer diseases.

Western Diseases Boom

Virtually unknown less than 100 years ago, coronary artery disease and cancers of the breast, prostate, colon, and lungs are now claiming every third and fourth American life, respectively.

In spite of newer and refined forms of insulin and a plethora of bioengineered medications, the incidence rate of the common form of diabetes has gone up 700 percent since World War II, with one in three children born today now developing diabetes before they die.

Concurrently, we have seen an enormous rise in the prevalence of excess weight, making it necessary for manufacturers to supersize everything from shirts to pants and from gurneys to coffins. At present more than 45 percent of American adults are overweight, and another 36 percent are obese. By the year 2010 obesity is expected to increase to 50 percent.

The Myth of an Extra 30 Years

For years we have cherished the belief that we are the world's healthiest society and that this new epidemic of Western diseases was related to our extended life expectancy. After all, over the past 100 years the life expectancy at birth has gone up 28 years—from 49 to 77 years of age. Our ancestors just didn't live long enough to die of the Western diseases of "old age."

The often-overlooked fact is that 100 years ago every sixth baby died before reaching the first year of life, while today this number has been dramatically reduced thanks to improvements in public health, sanitation, and maternal health. The high mortality rate of newborns and children 100 years ago greatly shortened the average life span. With this in mind, it's sad to see that 65-year-old Americans today may have gained only six or seven years of life expectancy over their counterparts of 100 years ago. Once people survived these early-childhood diseases, they had a reasonably good chance of living almost as long as today's seniors, and that in an era when very few medical interventions were available and when less than 1 percent of the country's gross domestic product (GDP) was devoted to the cost of health care.

Health-care Costs

In contrast, we are now devoting 18 percent of our GDP, or $2.5 trillion, annually to health care. This amounts to $8,300 for every man, woman, and child. By 2013, growing at the current rate, health costs are expected to constitute 19 percent of the GDP.

It is obvious: the current system is unsustainable.

The Interventional Imperative

Ever since the estrogen dilemma—in which Premarin, the number one prescription drug in America, was shown to cause more morbidity and death than benefit—other interventions, such as bypass surgery (400,000 per year at $150,000 each) and angioplasty (900,000 per year at $35,000 each), have been questioned.

Many physicians and patients don't know—or don't want to believe—that:
- only 10 percent of heart attack patients have their life extended with bypass surgery,
- 15 to 30 percent of grafted vessels close within 12 months after bypass surgery,
- some 30 to 45 percent of angioplasty procedures are no longer functional within six months.

Surgical interventions for heart disease provide only limited sustainable clinical benefit, but they often generate 50 to 70 percent of a hospital's revenues. Pharmaceuticals, plagued by side effects, result in some 150,000 deaths per year, making prescription drugs the fourth-leading cause of death in America. No wonder many health policy analysts have felt that medical care has become largely a business-driven enterprise. They are increasingly aware of the tremendous pressures that pharmaceutical lobbies and massive marketing efforts exert on researchers, physicians, journal editors, government agencies, and the general public. And they are keenly aware of how, tragically, numerous procedures and medications are often accepted and widely used by many without adequate research to assess their effectiveness, safety, and long-term impact.

Medical Care Versus Health Care

It is clear that the medical-industrial complex offers silver bullets that are all too readily picked up by health-care providers and consumers alike. Many mistakenly have been sold on the idea that medical care is synonymous with health care. Health, however, is largely a matter of personal responsibility that must be exercised within the limits of genetic endowment. With more than 70 percent of our well-being determined by lifestyle factors, medical care actually has little impact on health.

Health, then, is largely a function of how people take responsibility for their own actions. Promoting health, therefore, has to do with causes, not with symptomatic or palliative treatment, as helpful as this may be at the time. It has to do with education, motivation, and cultural transformation.

Let's take a look at the nation's number one killer, heart disease, and its underlying disease process—atherosclerosis.

Atherosclerosis: The Silent Killer

We were born with clean, flexible arteries, and they should stay that way until we die of old age. The arteries of most Americans, however, are clogging up with cholesterol, fats, and calcium. This creates unstable, soft plaques—they can rupture and clog up suddenly, causing most heart attacks and strokes—and stable, hard plaques that can gradually clog up, causing progressive angina and degenerative diseases.

This buildup of atherosclerotic plaques affects the circulatory system in different critical areas. While the clinical expressions of atherosclerosis may carry different disease names, the main underlying pathologic process is the same. It is atherosclerosis, which reduces tissue oxygenation and leads to degenerative changes, associated with angina pectoris, myocardial infarction (heart attack), intermittent claudication (peripheral vascular disease), gangrene, impotence, hypertension, cerebral infarction (stroke), senility, hearing loss, visual loss, and possibly some of the common adult cancers. In our society this narrowing process commonly begins early in life and can be demonstrated in teenagers by way of autopsies.

With so many deaths taking place every year, one would expect more than a murmur of protest from the public, the press, or government agencies. Such a rash of killings by any other means would mobilize the country! Atherosclerosis is not a "natural" way to go. It's not the inevitable result of the aging process. Large populations in the world are unaffected by it. After World War II, the University of Tokyo's medical school had to import

atherosclerosed coronary arteries from the United States to be able to show its medical students what was killing every second American, since the disease was so rare in Japan at that time. With the importation of the rich Western diet, however, came the Western diseases. After only 20 years, Japan became totally "self-sufficient" in creating narrowed coronary arteries.

With more than 4,000 heart attacks a day in the United States, and with sudden death often being the first symptom of underlying coronary artery disease, what are the predisposing conditions? The first solid evidence came during World War II, when coronary disease rates in industrialized European countries dropped dramatically, with coronary arteries beginning to open up again, apparently in response to a simple, spartan diet. Some 15 years later these plaques, however, returned, as the typical affluent American lifestyle (with cigarettes, automobiles, and a rich diet) gradually became the hallmark of many European countries.

Research with monkeys has consistently demonstrated that atherosclerotic plaques can be created and promoted by feeding the animals a Western diet very high in fat and cholesterol. But they can also be reversed by removing these atherogenic dietary stimuli.

The Framingham Heart Study

Initiated in 1949, this monumental research conducted for almost 60 years now in Framingham, Massachusetts, led to the discovery of "risk factors" for heart disease and its underlying atherosclerotic disease process. This risk factor concept has become as important to heart disease as the germ

Figure 1

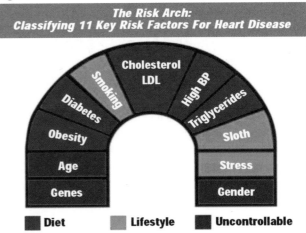

The higher on the arch, the higher the contribution of the risk factor to heart disease and its underlying atherosclerosis. The more risk factors, the greater the risk, whereby these risk factors are not additive but multiplicative. Five of the eight controllable risk factors are largely under the control of diet.

concept has become to infectious disease.

Multimillion-dollar studies funded by the National Institutes of Health have shown that 63 to 80 percent of all major coronary events before age 65 could be prevented if Americans would lower their cholesterol (to less than 180) and their systolic blood pressure (to less than 125), and quit smoking. These simple changes in lifestyle would do more to improve the nation's health, productivity, and vitality than all hospitals, surgeries, and medical procedures combined.

The Connection Between GDP and Western Diseases

Examining the global distribution of Western diseases (with many prominently related to atherosclerosis), a strong economic gradient emerges: the higher the national income (gross domestic product), the greater the prevalence of Western diseases.

The China Study

The massive China study, masterminded by T. Colin Campbell, PhD, of Cornell University, for instance, clearly showed two clusters of diseases in China. Populations surveyed near metropolitan centers displayed high rates of "diseases of affluence," such as coronary artery disease, stroke, hypertension, diabetes, osteoporosis, and cancer of the breast, prostate, lung, and blood. Rural populations, in contrast, suffered from "diseases of poverty," such as pneumonia and tuberculosis, digestive diseases, cancer of the stomach and liver, and infectious and parasitic diseases. While the diseases of affluence correlated closely with the level of economic development and the abundance of processed foods, fast foods, and animal products high in fat and protein (eating meat in China has become a status symbol and a sign of prestige), the diseases of poverty were predominantly intertwined with poor sanitation, nutritional deficiencies, and poor food quality because of a lack of refrigeration.

The researchers concluded that "Chinese counties with a more affluent lifestyle (a richer diet, more smoking, and less exercise) showed a clear shift from diseases of poverty to diseases of affluence." But, they said, "diseases of affluence are not inevitable. Societies that can afford sanitation, refrigeration, and abundant food may yet conquer these diseases of affluence by simplifying their diet and by eating more foods as grown."

Changes in Diet Composition

Developing countries have to rely predominantly on foods as grown. They rely basically on corn and beans, potatoes and yams, wheat and rice, and plenty of fruits and vegetables. These inexpensive yet nutritionally rich plant foods provide more than enough protein, modest amounts of fat and sugar, and plenty of complex carbohydrates, the body's preferred and clean-burning fuel to meet energy requirements.

As the GDP increases, however, dietary energy sources change drastically (see Figure 2). Developing countries rely mostly on unrefined complex carbohydrate foods high in starch, which account for 70 percent of total calories (shown in green), with very few calories coming from fats, oils, sugars, and ani-

mal products. On the other hand, the diet of affluent countries is largely composed of fats and oils (36 percent of calories) and sugars (24 percent), shown in red and yellow, respectively. And their complex carbohydrates are usually refined, white flour products, such as pies, pastries, pastas, and pizzas, crowding out the nutritionally rich unrefined complex carbohydrates (now accounting for only 6 percent of total calories).

Diets incorporating foods as grown are naturally very low in fat, oil, grease, salt, and sugar, and usually very low in animal protein. Thus they are almost devoid of cholesterol and saturated fat, yet are high in fiber.

As these countries become more affluent, however, potatoes are turning into Pringles, corn into Doritos, wheat into Zingers, and beans and grains into sirloin steaks. With food technology being able to create new taste sensations on one hand, and with advertising being able to create a mass market on the other, the diet composition undergoes a major overhaul—the largely unrefined complex carbohydrates become a minority player. In their stead, calorie-dense, processed foods—usually high in sugar (simple carbohydrates) and fats—as well as meats, sausages, eggs, and cheese high in fat, calories, and cholesterol, become the dominant energy carriers.

The Food Revolution

Even in our country, food just isn't the same as it was some 100 years ago. Back then the American diet consisted largely of foods as grown, coming mostly from local gardens and nearby farms. It was supplemented with a few staples from the general store and some meat from range-fed cattle. Our great-grandparents didn't have 30,000 slickly packaged, cleverly promoted products waiting at the local supermarket, or 85,000 fast-food restaurants spending billions of dollars advertising take-out service. Families in those days sat at their own tables and ate their freshly cooked food and home-baked bread. But times and tastes and serving sizes

have changed. Many of us spend 60 percent of our food dollars "eating out." Our livestock is fattened in feedlots in which lack of exercise, antibiotics, and "growth enhancers" produce bigger cattle faster, and juicier meat with about twice as much fat as range-fed cattle. Farm produce is processed, refined, concentrated, sugared, salted, and chemically engineered to produce taste sensations that are rich in calories but poor in nutritional value. Advertising and marketing have created a demand that produces big profits and big bodies.

Food as grown is nutritionally balanced. It doesn't need nutrition labels. Refinement, however, strips these foods of most of their fiber and nutrients. Processing adds calories, subtracts nutrition, and contributes myriads of chemical additives. Strip seven pounds of sugar beets of their bulk, fiber, and nutrients, for instance, and you get one pound of "pure" sugar! Some 50 percent of the calories eaten are now empty calories, almost totally devoid of any significant nutritional value. No wonder many Americans are overfed and undernourished!

Cooked whole-grain cereals, rich in fiber, expand in your stomach, creating satiety, a feeling of fullness; and they save you money. On the other hand, presweetened cereals crumble and shrink to almost nothing, and they cost you, pound for pound of grain, eight to 10 times more.

The least nutritious foods with the most sugar are the most widely advertised. Enormous resources of advertising go far toward the destruction of our more sensible eating habits. And don't forget that meat is the single largest source of fat in the U.S. diet, and its excess protein may contribute to kidney disease, gout, and osteoporosis. But even more serious is the heavy load of saturated fat that most animal protein foods carry, and the trans fats found in crackers, cakes, pies, and crinkly bags, causing the liver to go into overdrive in making excessive cholesterol.

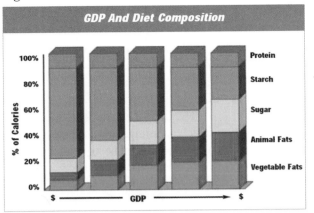

Figure 2

GDP And Diet Composition

As the GDP increases from developing countries on the far left to the affluent countries on the far right, the dietary energy sources change drastically.

No wonder the surgeon general warned in *Nutrition and Health*: "For the two out of three adult Americans who do not smoke or drink excessively, one personal choice seems to influence long-term health prospects more than any other: what we eat."

Making the Change

Today, more than ever, we have become victims of our own lifestyle. The contribution of the medical-care system to the health status of Western nations is marginal, since it can do little more than serve as a catchment net for those who have become victims of their own choices. The greatest health benefits are likely to accrue from efforts to improve the health habits of the American people instead of further medicalization of society.

Lifestyle Medicine Approach

So what would happen if people really simplified their diet, did something about their smoking, and started an exercise program? Since 1975 the Pritikin Longevity Center has had more than 75,000 people attend its residential one- to four-week lifestyle-change program. More than 90 clinical reports sponsored by the Pritikin Research Foundation have been published in peer-reviewed journals demonstrating some of the advantages of a lifestyle medicine approach over the high-tech and pharmaceutical approaches, both in clinical outcomes and in cost-effectiveness.

Building on Pritikin's work, Dean Ornish, MD, a young Harvard-trained cardiologist, published in 1990 the results of his randomized clinical trial with coronary patients. Employing a very simple, very low-fat, unrefined vegetarian diet coupled with exercise, stress management, and group support, he demonstrated with PET scans and angiography that the "majority of atherosclerotic lesions were indeed subject to regression regardless of the patient's age." They begin to melt down.

Since then, his pioneering work has been duplicated, established, and extended in many clinical research centers around the world. For instance, Caldwell Esselstyn, Jr., MD, demonstrated at the Cleveland clinic, in a 20-year study, that diet alone (a simple, natural, vegetarian diet, very low in fat, sugar, and salt, yet high in fiber) could reverse coronary artery disease and reduce the incidence of subsequent coronary events to zero! And Neal Barnard, MD, demonstrated recently that a similar simple diet devoid of animal products was very effective in reversing diabetes.

The Birthing of CHIP

Concerned with how best to bring these concepts to society at large, I learned that advocated lifestyle changes without thorough education, skill development, and a supportive infrastructure would be doomed to failure. I also learned that it was necessary to find a way to integrate the medical and public health models and to take advantage of an ecological-social concept in which people would learn in a social setting as a group and feel supported by communal infrastructures.

Our first CHIP program, conducted in the small Canadian town of Creston, British Columbia, attracted more than 400 people in the midst of winter.

The clinical results were so compelling that the program leapfrogged—largely by word of mouth—from one town to the next, ultimately ending up in Ottawa, Canada's capital, where it was presented to the Canadian Parliament.

In an effort to meet the demands, the CHIP program was later videotaped, and training and certification programs for facilitators were established.

The CHIP Program

CHIP is an educationally intensive lifestyle intervention program with more than 50,000 graduates worldwide. It is currently conducted in more than 300 cities and is offered in faith-based communities, corporations, and hospitals through certified and licensed CHIP leaders. Endorsed by the Physicians Committee for Responsible Medicine (PCRM) and the Center for Science in the Public Interest (CSPI) (both headquartered in Washington, D.C.), the CHIP program focuses on developing a greater measure of intelligent self-care involving a clearer understanding of the nature and etiology of heart disease, its epidemiology, and its risk factors.

The program aims at a marked reduction of coronary risk factor levels through the adoption of better health habits and lifestyle choices. The goal is to facilitate disease reversal by lowering blood cholesterol, triglycerides, and blood sugar levels; by reducing excess weight; by lowering high blood pressure; by enhancing daily exercise; and by eliminating smoking.

Conducted in communities, churches, and corporations, the CHIP program works closely with referring physicians, restaurants and cafeterias, and the media. Local chapters are strongly encouraged to have active alumni support groups to sustain adherence to the program guidelines.

The CHIP curriculum is carefully structured and emphasizes the prominent role that diet plays in the etiology and reversal of many chronic diseases.

Risk factor levels are carefully assessed before the educational intervention begins (immediately following the completion of the 40-hour educational program) and again after 12 months.

The clinical results released in 13 articles have been published in many peer-reviewed medical journals, among them the *Journal of Preventive Medicine, American Journal of Cardiology, Journal of Occupational and Environmental Medicine,* and *Journal of the American Dietetic Association.*

Wherever CHIP—the flagship of the emerging lifestyle medicine approach—is conducted, the clinical feedback is consistent: if people take charge of their lifestyle, especially how they eat, their healthy lifestyle will take care of them!

Dietary Lifestyle

The CHIP *Optimal Diet* emphasizes largely unrefined foods as grown. These foods (grains, legumes, vegeta-

EAT FOR HEALTH!
Basic Guidelines for a Lifetime of Good Eating

EAT LESS:

Fats and Oils
Strictly limit fatty meats, cooking and salad oils, sauces, dressings, and shortening. Use margarine and nuts sparingly. Avoid frying (sauté instead with a little water in nonstick pans). Especially avoid saturated and trans fats (cookies and crackers).

Sugars
Limit sugar, honey, molasses, syrups, pies, cakes, pastries, candy, cookies, soft drinks, and sugar-rich desserts, such as pudding and ice cream. Save these foods for special occasions.

Cholesterol Foods
Progressively eliminate meat, sausages, egg yolks, and liver. If used, limit dairy products to low-fat cheeses and nonfat milk products. If you eat fish and poultry, use them sparingly.

Salt
Use minimal salt during cooking. Banish the saltshaker. Strictly limit highly salted products, such as pickles, crackers, soy sauce, salted popcorn, nuts, chips, pretzels, and garlic salt.

Alcohol
Avoid alcohol in all forms, as well as caffeinated beverages, such as coffee, colas, and black tea.

EAT MORE:

Whole Grains
Freely use brown rice, millet, barley, corn, wheat, and rye. Also eat freely of whole-grain products, such as breads, pastas, shredded wheat, and tortillas.

Tubers and Legumes
Freely use all kinds of potatoes and yams (without high-fat toppings). Enjoy peas, lentils, chickpeas, and beans of every kind.

Fruits and Vegetables
Eat several fresh whole fruits every day. Limit fruits canned in syrup. Limit fiber-poor fruit juices. Eat a variety of vegetables daily. Enjoy fresh salads with low-calorie, low-salt dressings.

Water
Drink eight glasses of water a day. Vary the routine with a twist of lemon and occasional herb teas.

Hearty Breakfasts
Enjoy hot multigrain cereals, fresh fruit, and whole-wheat toast. Jumpstart your day.

DIET COMPARISON

	U.S. Diet	CHIP Optimal Diet
Fats and Oils	80-120 g	under 45 g
Sugar	35 tsp	under 10 tsp
Cholesterol	400 mg	under 50 mg
Salt	10-15 g	under 5 g
Fiber	12 g	40+ g
Water (fluids)	minimal	8 glasses

bles, and fresh fruits), usually high in unrefined complex carbohydrates, are encouraged to be eaten freely without concern for serving size.

Such a natural whole-food diet—very low in fat, animal protein, sugar, and salt, yet high in fiber, antioxidants, and micronutrients, and virtually free of cholesterol—is in stark contrast to the typically rich Western diet (see chart on previous page). Please note that the arrows pointing to a decrease and increase for certain foods are dynamic in nature, indicated by the broken and progressive arrow design. CHIP, then, does not follow an ideo-logically prescribed dietary dogma. On the contrary, while it offers some optimal dietary reference points, it allows people to choose their level of implementation based on their motivation, clinical status, and readiness. CHIP participants in greatest need of clinical improvement do best by making the greatest dietary changes. For them, implementing a diet of simple whole foods (lots of fresh fruits, vegetables, whole-grain products, and legumes, and some seeds and nuts), devoid of any animal products, offers the greatest clinical benefit and the potential to reverse disease.

Many people, as they begin to understand the cause-and-effect relationship between their dietary and lifestyle choices and the effects on their health and disease, give up the "good life's" excesses. Instead, they opt for the best life possible with its elegant simplicity. Church people, employees, executives, and administrators everywhere are making new commitments toward health, because while they realize that health may not be everything, they also recognize that without health, everything is nothing.

Implementing the Optimal Diet

It is our joy to share with you some of our favorite recipes that will hopefully inspire and motivate you to incorporate a more plant-food-centered diet into your own lifestyle.

When making changes in diet, some have to do it all at once because of a life-threatening event, such as a heart attack or the diagnosis of diabetes. Most people, however, should make these dietary changes more gradually. Dr. Michael Klaper said it well: "Every time you substitute spaghetti for steak, your new habit becomes reinforced, and you are actually decreasing your risk for disease, step by step."

If you are a typical meat eater, you may wish to decrease your meat intake from five to seven times per week to perhaps three times per week. Of course, you can find nowadays many meat analogs in almost any supermarket. These meat substitutes can serve as "stepping-stones." They are transition foods that help you to cross the bridge to the other side. But be sure to read the ingredient list and nutrition labels. To help you, we have selected a couple of brand names we recommend in our Special Items Glossary. Stay away from those analogs that contain high amounts of fat, sodium, preservatives, and artificial colors or flavors, because these ingredients can be just as detrimental to your health.

If you are new to the idea of a non-dairy milk, you may want to begin by substituting a low-fat milk for whole milk. Eventually, you can begin mixing this low-fat milk with a soy, rice, or nut milk, until you become "weaned off" cow's milk and ready to settle in for a plant-based milk.

Since plant oils are very concentrated in calories and devoid of much nutritional value, most people may want to use them sparingly. Instead, obtain your essential fats from some nuts, seeds, and avocados, and even from beans and grains.

The Special Items Glossary will show you the oils we recommend to use in your baking and salad dressings. It is probably best if you can make your own dressings: you can eliminate many of the hydrogenated oils, trans fats, salts, and sugars commonly found in these prefabricated slurries.

Each recipe has a preparation time and a level of complexity listed. The preparation time does not include the cooking or baking time. It's the time it will take to prepare the dish. The complexity has three levels: easy, intermediate, and advanced. Every dish in this cookbook is quite simple to prepare. We have rated these recipes, however, according to the number of steps each recipe has, and the machinery required, such as a blender or food processor.

To establish healthy menus for this CHIP cookbook, the following dietary guidelines have been used. We have tried to achieve these goals for a complete meal.

	Per Meal
Cholesterol	0 milligrams
Sodium	<600 milligrams
Refined Sugar	<5 teaspoons*
Fat	<20 grams
Fiber	>10 grams

*1 teaspoon of sugar is 4 grams

While we have tried our best to make each dish flavorful, every person's taste buds are different, and therefore you may need to add your own "personal touch" to please your family.

Some recipes will include italicized names directing you to special items that you will find in the cookbook or that can be served as a side dish.

Most of all, have fun, and enjoy experiencing the benefits of a pure, natural diet while making your taste buds smile!

Stocking a Healthy Kitchen Pantry

Restock your pantry a little at a time. You may find it will cost you a little extra money at first, but look at it as an investment. Before you know it, you will be saving an average of 40 percent on your food bill and enjoying good health to go along with it!

Grains

Barley, pearl

Barley, whole

Millet

Multigrain cereal, seven- or nine-grain mixture

Oats, whole

Oats, rolled (old-fashioned, slow-cooking)

Oats, quick-cooking

Quinoa, whole

Rice, brown, short- or long-grain

Rice, red

Rice, wild

Spelt, whole

Wheat, bulgur

Wheat, hard red

Flours

Barley

Brown rice

Cornmeal

Rye

Soy

Spelt

Wheat bran

Wheat germ

Wheat, gluten

Whole wheat, 100 percent

Whole wheat, pastry

Wheat, unbleached white

Whole-grain pastas (brown rice, whole wheat, etc., in a variety of shapes and sizes)

Legumes (dry, canned, or frozen)

Black beans

Black-eyed peas

Garbanzos (chickpeas)

Kidney beans

Lentils, brown and red

Navy beans

Pinto beans

Soybeans

White navy beans (for more beans, see p.15)

Raw Nuts and Seeds

Almonds, whole, sliced, slivered

Cashew pieces

Coconut, unsweetened, shredded

Flaxseeds, whole

Peanuts, dry-roasted

Pecan, halves, chopped

Sesame seeds

Sunflower seeds

Walnuts, chopped

Nut Butters

Almond

Peanut

Tahini

Dried Fruits, Frozen Fruits, and Juices

Apricots, dried

Cranberries, dried

Dates, whole, pieces

Figs, dried

Mango, dried

Papaya, dried

Pineapple tidbits, dried

Prunes

Raisins, golden

Raisins, sultana

Raisins, Thompson

Blackberries, frozen

Blueberries, frozen

Peaches, frozen

Raspberries, frozen

Strawberries, frozen

Apple juice, unsweetened

Lemon juice

Orange juice, unsweetened

Orange juice, frozen concentrated, unsweetened

Pineapple juice, unsweetened

Baking Ingredients

Agar agar, powdered or granulated

Arrowroot powder

Baking powder, aluminum-free

Baking soda

Bragg's All-Purpose Seasoning

Cane sugar, granulated

Carob chips (barley-malt sweetened, nonhydrogenated oils)

Carob powder, roasted

Coffee substitute (Caf-Lib, Inka, Roma, Pero)

Cornstarch

Ener-G Egg Replacer

Flaxseed oil

Flavoring, maple extract

Flavoring, vanilla extract

Honey, liquid

Instant ClearJel powder

Lecithin granules

Maple syrup, pure

Molasses, blackstrap

Nonstick cooking spray

Olive oil

Soy milk (Silk)

Tapioca, minute

Tofu, tetrapak (silken), firm and extra-firm

Tofu, fresh, waterpacked

Yeast, baking (active, quick-rise)

Dried Herbs and Spices

Allspice

Basil, crushed

Basil, whole dried leaf

Cardamom

Celery seed

Cinnamon, ground

Cinnamon, sticks

Cloves, ground

Cloves, whole

Coriander, ground

Cumin, ground

Dill weed

Chickenlike seasoning

Beeflike seasoning

Garlic powder, granulated

Herbamere

Italian seasoning

Marjoram

Mrs. Dash herbal seasoning

Nutmeg

Nutritional yeast flakes

Onion, flakes

Onion powder, granulated

Oregano

Paprika

Parsley

Poultry seasoning

Rosemary

Sage

Salt

Spike, regular and salt-free

Thyme

Turmeric

Specialty Items Glossary

Meat Analogs

Vegeburger

Soy curls

TVP *(textured vegetable protein),* granulated

You will want to have a refrigerator filled with fresh vegetables and fruits. Stock up your pantry with lots of squash, onions, potatoes, yams, and other items. They don't spoil easily. They last, especially when they are in season. Some canned items you may wish to have on hand include:

Canned Items

Applesauce, unsweetened

Mandarin oranges (light syrup)

Olives

Pimentos, unpickled (or roasted red peppers)

Pineapple tidbits, *unsweetened*

Tomatoes, *diced, whole, stewed, or pureed*

Tomato sauce, low-sodium

Tomato paste, low-sodium

Equipment

Blender

Crock-Pot

Food processor

Frying pans, nonstick

Rice cooker

Waffle iron, nonstick

Agar Powder

A gelatinous product made from seaweed used in place of animal gelatin. One tsp agar powder equals 1 tbsp agar flakes.

Aluminum-free Baking Powder

A baking powder containing no aluminum.

Arrowroot

Derived from the starch of a tropical tuber native to the West Indies, used for thickening. (Usually less processed than cornstarch.)

Blackstrap Molasses, unsulfured

The final residue of the sugar cane. In contrast to regular cane sugar, it still contains some of the nutrients of calcium, zinc, copper, and chromium.

Bob's Red Mill

We highly recommend the use of whole grains and legumes. Bob's Red Mill is one good product line with a wide variety. (See pages 170-173.)

Bragg's All Purpose Seasoning ("liquid aminos")

An unfermented soy sauce made from organic soybeans and distilled water, much lower in sodium than other commercial-brand soy sauces.

Barley Malt or Brown Rice Syrup

These syrups are rich in sugar, and can be used interchangeably with honey. Barley malt is from the grain barley, and rice syrup is from the grain rice.

Cane Sugar

Made by evaporating the water from sugar cane juice and allowing it to solidify and granulate.

Carob Powder

A more natural replacement for cocoa powder. Made from the locust bean pod, the powder is inherently sweet, containing some calcium, phosphorus, magnesium, potassium, and iron. Because of its natural sweetness, recipes with cocoa powder need to be cut in half when using carob powder.

Carob Chips

Carob chips can be used in recipes in place of chocolate chips. Choose carob chips that are free of trans fats and dairy, and sweetened with malted barley.

Cedar Lake-MGM Foods

A brand name for frozen and canned meat analogs. Free from preservatives and additives, Cedar Lake-MGM foods are often considerably lower in fat and sodium compared to other brand-name meat analogs. For more information: www.cedarlakefoods. com.

Coriander or Cardamom

Coriander may be used in combination with cardamon to replace cinnamon. Cardamon may be used as a substitute for nutmeg.

Chickenlike or Beeflike Seasoning

Used often in this book, these seasonings vary in saltiness and flavor. Good low-sodium choices: Blaney's (settepublishing.com/totalhealth/) (forms the basis of the nutritional analysis for sodium content); Bill's Best (billsbest.net); La Chikky Seasonings (thevegetarianexpress.com). A higher sodium option is Mckay's Chicken Style or Beef Style Instant Broth and Seasoning (Vegan Special) (mckays-seasoning.com).

Ener-G Egg Replacer

A nondairy powdered leavening and binding agent used as an egg substitute in many baked goods. It is made from tapioca flour, potato starch, and leavening.

Flaxseed Gel

Used as an egg substitute for binding loaves or patties. Made from flaxseeds and water.

Flaxseed Oil

High in omega 3 fat. Use in a cold-pressed form. Don't cook with this oil.

Gluten Flour

Made from the protein (gluten) of the wheat kernel. This flour is used to make meat substitutes (gluten) as a binder in recipes, and in bread recipes to promote elasticity to enhance the raising of the bread.

Herbamere Seasoning

A mixture of dried herbs and vegetables.

Instant ClearJel Powder

A thickening agent made from corn. Does not require cooking. Blend in blender with ingredients to thicken and prevent lumping.

Lecithin

Comes in a thick, oily liquid or granulated form derived from soy. Can be used in baked goods such as breads to prevent crumbling.

Mori-Nu Silken Tofu

A smooth-textured tofu made from soybeans. Vacuum-packed, with a long shelf life, it comes in soft, firm, or extra-firm texture. Also available in a low-fat version.

MorningStar Farms

A brand name for soy-based meat analogs offered by Kellogg's Foods. www.kellogg.com.

Mrs. Dash

A blend of natural seasonings. No salt added. Comes in many varieties of flavor.

Nasoya Nayonaise

A commercial soy-based sandwich spread or salad dressing.

Nutritional Yeast Flakes

Different from the yeast used in raising bread, this great-tasting nutritional yeast is grown on molasses. It has a "cheese-like" flavor. The Red Star brand is particularly rich in B_{12} and other B vitamins.

Soy Curls

A dehydrated product made from the whole soybean. Great for stir-frys, pasta, soups, or stews, or made into "chicken" salad. www.butlerfoods.com.

Soy Milk

A milk substitute usually made from organic soybeans. The Silk brand, among many, is a favorite.

Spike Seasoning

A special blend of 39 herbs, vegetables, and nonirritating exotic spices. Available salt-free or with salt.

Tahini

A calorie-rich smooth butter made from sesame seeds. Use sparingly.

Textured Vegetable Protein

TVP is a meat substitute made from defatted soy flour that is compressed until the protein fibers change in structure. Sold in dehydrated granular form.

Tofu

Fresh soybean curd containing concentrated protein and often high in fat. Comes as silken (vacuum-packed) or fresh (water-packed), and in soft, medium, firm, and extra-firm textures.

Tofutti Brand Products

Soy-based products free of casein, the milk protein found in most soy cheeses. Tofutti products include: sour cream, ice cream, cream cheese, and cheese slices. Choose from the nonhydrogenated variety. Use for special occasions!

Vegit

A combination of exotic herbs, spices, and vegetables with papain from tropical papayas.

Whole-Wheat Pastry Flour

Made from "soft wheat," containing less fiber and gluten than whole-wheat flour. Commonly used in baked goods, such as muffins, piecrusts, cakes, or cookies.

Yves Products

Meat analogs free of preservatives and low in fat and sodium.

SODIUM ALERT!

To reduce sodium content of canned beans, always rinse them or buy them without salt added. This way, you save an average of some 800 mg of sodium per cup. Remember, we want to keep the sodium intake below 600 mg for the whole meal.

Focus on Beans

Beans are a nutritious, simple, and economical food. Use a variety of beans in salads, soups, Mexican dishes, or burgers, or just served as a topping over rice or baked potatoes. Beans are packed with carbohydrates, protein, fiber, amino acids, and other nutrients. To obtain the highest amount of nutrients, beans must be cooked thoroughly to improve digestion. The following is a chart containing approximate cooking times and water measurement for a variety of beans using the stove top method:

Crock-Pot Method

Sort and wash beans for cooking. Place in Crock-Pot with measured amount of water (according to the chart for the stove top method). Add vegetables, such as onions, celery, etc., if desired. Cook on high temperature setting overnight. (Some beans, such as garbanzos and soybeans, may take longer.) After cooking, add seasonings and salt according to taste and health requirements.

Helpful Hints

- Do not add salt to beans until they are cooked. Otherwise, beans may remain hard, as they will not cook well.

- To keep pot from boiling over, lightly grease the inside top edge of the pot.

- Want to save time? Then cook a large quantity of beans at one time and freeze them in convenient-sized portions. Of course, you can also use a pressure cooker.

Some people choose not to eat beans because they find them difficult to digest, often causing gas and bloating. Here are some easy steps to alleviate some of these symptoms.

Beans contain two unusual starches—stachyose and raffinose. These two starch molecules are not broken down by the starch-digesting enzymes found normally in the digestive tract. Therefore, they must remain in the digestive tract longer to come in contact with certain bacteria, which then break down these starches to carbon dioxide and hydrogen. These, however, are the two main components of gastrointestinal gas. To alleviate some of these annoying symptoms, these two starches need to be treated before ingesting them, so that they can be digested simply by the starch-digesting enzymes in our digestive tract.

While the following tips will help, please remember that when people move toward a plant-based diet, their digestive system and their intestinal bacteria begin to change as well. So introduce beans slowly into your Optimal Diet program. It will minimize those irritating symptoms, which usually disappear in less than four weeks.

Improve the Digestion of Beans

1. Wash beans thoroughly. Place beans in a bowl. Cover beans with water 2 inches above the beans. Let stand at room temperature for 8 hours, then drain off water.

2. Freeze soaked and drained beans, which will break up the troublesome starch molecules.

3. Place frozen beans in a large pot with plenty of water to double the volume of the beans. Bring water to a boil. Boil uncovered for about 10 minutes. Drain off water. Replace with fresh water. Cook beans until done.

4. While cooking, add a pinch of ginger or fennel. These will further aid in minimizing the potential gas and bloating.

5. Be sure beans are cooked well, or until soft.

6. Some have found it helpful to take papain, a papaya enzyme, before eating the beany meal.

Cooking Time and Measurements for Beans

Dried Legumes (1 cup)	Water	Cooking Time (stove top)
Black Beans	3 cups	1 to 1½ hrs
Garbanzos (Chickpeas)	4-5 cups	4 to 5 hrs
Great Northern Beans	3½ cups	1½ to 2 hrs
Kidney Beans	2½ cups	1½ to 2 hrs
Lentils (brown)	3 cups	35 to 45 min
Lentils (red)	3 cups	20 to 30 min
Lima Beans	3½ cups	1½ hrs
Navy and Pinto Beans	3 cups	1½ to 2 hrs
Soybeans	4 cups	3 to 4 hrs
Split Peas	3 cups	45 to 60 min

One cup dry beans yields about 2½ cups cooked beans.

Focus on Grains

Basically, all grains are cooked in the same manner. The difference is in the cooking time and the amount of water required. Place your measured grain in boiling water; cover the pot and reduce the heat to simmer for the suggested cooking time.

Your grains will be fluffier if you don't stir them while they simmer. After cooking time is up, remove from heat and leave the lid in place for a few more minutes (5 minutes). Before serving, fluff with a fork to separate the grain.

Amaranth

A very small but highly nutritious grain. Amaranth tastes great as a hot cereal.

Barley

Low in gluten and rich in soluble fiber, barley reduces blood cholesterol and stabilizes blood-sugar levels. Great in hearty soups and stews. An excellent option is pearl barley, which cooks very quickly.

Brown Rice

The staple of half the world's population, rice is available in short, medium, and long grain. While they are equal in nutrients, short-grain rice is the sweetest. Being gluten-free, rice is popular with people who have a gluten intolerance. Brown rice pasta is a good substitute for white pasta.

Brown Rice, Basmati

It is the most fragrant of all rice, and with its unique flavor it offers a nice change from basic brown rice. This rice is also available in short, medium, and long grain.

Buckwheat Groats

Known as kasha, it is a good contributor of B and E vitamins and minerals.

Bulgur Wheat

A hearty grain made from steamed, dried, and cracked wheat, it has a nutty flavor and a fluffy texture. Bulgur can substantially contribute to our daily fiber and B vitamin requirements. Commonly used in making tabbouleh, a Middle Eastern salad, and in pilafs, bulgur is also nice just cooked as a hot cereal.

Couscous

Pronounced kooz-kooz, it is a pasta made from durum wheat that is steamed, dried, and crushed. It has a mild flavor, cooks very quickly, and can be used in just about any recipe calling for a "bed of rice" or other grains. Choose the whole-wheat, unrefined couscous; it is nutritionally superior to the white couscous.

Kamut

Pronounced ka-moot, this ancient strain of wheat originated in Egypt. With its delicate, buttery flavor and chewy texture, kamut has several nutritional advantages over regular wheat. And those who are intolerant to wheat find kamut easier to digest. As a cooked grain, flour for baking, or made into pasta, kamut is gaining popularity.

Millet

A good contributor of various vitamins and minerals, millet cooks quickly and is quite versatile. It can be cooked as a porridge or made into burgers. Gluten-free and easy to digest, when used in breads it delivers a subtle crunch!

Grain (1 cup)	Water	Cooking Time
Amaranth	2½ cups	20 to 25 min
Barley	3 cups	1½ hrs
Barley, Pearl	2 cups	45 min
Brown Rice	2 cups	1 hr
Buckwheat (Kasha)	2 cups	17 min
Bulgur	2 cups	20 to 25 min
Cornmeal	4 cups	30 min
Couscous	2 cups	10 min
Kamut	3 cups	2 hrs
Millet	2 cups	30 min
Oats, large flakes	2 cups	30 min
Oats, quick	2 cups	5 min
Oats, whole	2½ cup	1½ hr
Quinoa	2 cups	15 min
Seven Grain	3 cups	1 hr
Spelt	3 cups	2 hrs
Wheat Berries	3 cups	2 hrs

Oat Groats

These whole-oat kernels (with their bran and germ layers intact) will cook in half the time if presoaked in cold water for an hour.

Oats

An excellent source of both insoluble and cholesterol-lowering soluble fiber, oats are also a good source of nutrients. Easily digested, oats have a delicate, slightly sweet flavor.

Oats, Rolled

These are groats that have been steamed, crushed, and dried. Steel-cut oats are hulled groats that are sliced but not rolled.

Quinoa

Pronounced keen-wah, quinoa is considered by some as one of the world's most perfect foods. Quinoa is often referred to as the "mother grain." High in nutrients and high in quality protein, quinoa is gluten-free, easily digested, and an excellent first food for infants. It's also quick and easy to prepare. Just be sure to wash quinoa well prior to cooking in order to remove the bitter coating on the grain. Use a fine-mesh colander.

Spelt

An ancient strain of wheat, spelt is easily digested and well tolerated by most wheat-sensitive individuals because of its unique gluten structure. Spelt makes an exceptional bread flour and can serve as a rice substitute.

As an intelligent shopper, you will want to be aware of the meaning of some commonly used nutrition terms.

Focus on Nutrition Terms

FAT FREE

Product has less than ½ (0.5) gram of fat per serving. This value will then be rounded to 0.

99 percent FAT FREE

Every 100 grams of food will have 1 gram or less of fat.

LOW FAT

Product has 3 grams of fat or less per serving.

REDUCED FAT

Fat has been reduced by at least 25 percent (compared to a similar food).

LIGHT (*Lite*)

Product has 33 percent fewer calories or 50 percent less fat per serving than a comparable product.

LEAN

For meat and poultry only. Per serving, product has less than 10 grams fat, less than 4 grams saturated fat, and less than 95 milligrams of cholesterol per serving.

LOW CALORIE

Product has 40 calories or less per serving.

SATURATED FAT FREE

Product has less than 0.5 grams of saturated fat per serving. This value will then be rounded to 0.

LOW IN SATURATED FAT

Product has no more than 1 gram of saturated fat per serving.

CHOLESTEROL FREE

Product has less than 2 milligrams of cholesterol per serving. This value will then be rounded to 0.

LOW CHOLESTEROL

Product has no more than 20 milligrams of cholesterol and 2 grams of saturated fat per serving.

SODIUM FREE

Product has less than 5 milligrams of sodium per serving. This value will then be rounded to 0.

VERY LOW SODIUM

Product has no more than 35 milligrams of sodium per serving.

LOW SODIUM

Product has no more than 140 milligrams of sodium per serving.

GOOD SOURCE

Used for fiber, protein, vitamins, or minerals. Product has at least 10 percent of the Daily Value for the particular nutrient.

HIGH IN (*Excellent Source*)

Used for fiber, protein, vitamins, or minerals. Product has at least 20 percent of the Daily Value for the particular nutrient.

SALT *versus* SODIUM

One teaspoon of salt (5 grams or 5,000 milligrams) contains 2 grams or 2,000 milligrams of sodium. To go from salt to sodium, multiply the number of grams or milligrams by .4. To go from sodium to salt, multiply by 2.5.

Focus on Fats and Oils

Good fats, bad fats . . . good cholesterol, bad cholesterol . . . It all gets very confusing very quickly. Here are some key words and definitions that help explain fats in foods and lipids in your blood.

Types of Fats in Foods

Monounsaturated fat is missing one (mono) hydrogen atom on its chemical chain and is liquid at room temperature. Monounsaturated fat is found in plant foods, such as vegetable oils, olive oil, canola oil, and avocados. There is no set Daily Reference Value (DRV) for monounsaturated fat. Monounsaturated fat may lower total and LDL cholesterol, while maintaining beneficial HDL cholesterol.

Polyunsaturated fat is missing more than one (poly) hydrogen atom on its chemical chain and is also liquid at room temperature. It is found mostly in plant foods, such as corn and soy oil. There is no set DRV for polyunsaturated fat. Polyunsaturated fats are a main contributor to excess calories, which fuel obesity and its related diseases.

Saturated fat has all of the hydrogen atoms that it can hold on its chemical chain (it is saturated) and is firm at room temperature. It is found mainly in animal products, such as butter, meat, milk, and cheese. Saturated fat is called the "bad" fat because it drives up the dangerous LDL cholesterol.

Trans fats result from adding hydrogen to unsaturated vegetable oils to increase their shelf life and to improve their texture. The hydrogen is added to the chemical chain, changing its shape and making the fat more solid at room temperature. Trans fats are found in such foods as cookies, crackers, some margarines, baked goods, and fried foods. They are also naturally occurring in very small amounts in meat and dairy products. Trans fats are probably just as likely as saturated fats to increase total and LDL cholesterol. In addition, they may decrease the beneficial HDL cholesterol levels.

Cholesterol is a compound found only in animal products, such as meats, fowl, fish, eggs, and full-fat dairy products.

Lipids in Your Blood

Total cholesterol is a powerful predictor for estimating cardiovascular risk. It is the sum of HDL plus LDL cholesterol plus one fifth of triglycerides in the blood.*

HDL (high-density lipoprotein) cholesterol is the good blood cholesterol, composed mostly of protein. HDL transports LDL cholesterol in your blood back to the liver to get rid of it. LDL (low-density lipoprotein) cholesterol is the bad cholesterol, composed mainly of fat. You want low levels of LDL circulating in your blood. More recently LDL cholesterol has emerged as the strongest predictor for coronary artery disease. Ideal levels are below 90mg% (2.3 mmol/L). Once LDL levels are ideal, then total cholesterol, triglyceride, and HDL levels become clinically less meaningful.

Triglycerides are a measure of the amount of circulating fat in the blood. Within the context of high LDL levels, triglycerides add to the coronary risk. Triglycerides are ideal up to about 150mg% (1.7 mmol/L). They become more significant over 200 (2.2). Any triglycerides above 500 (5.6) deserve medical attention.

This formula does not apply if triglycerides are above 400 mg% (4.4 mmol/L).

To Know About Oils

There are two basic ways that manufacturers extract oil from a seed or bran: the expeller (or pressure) method, and the solvent extraction process.

In the expeller method, ground or flaked seeds are fed into a large cylinder and driven against a backplate by a screw. Tremendous pressure squeezes out up to 95 percent of the oil in the seeds.

In solvent extraction, ground seeds are bathed in a solution of hexane or other petroleum solvent. The resulting oil-solvent solution is then heated to 160°F to evaporate the solvent. Most oil processors prefer this method because it extracts about 99 percent of the oil from the seed.

Hot- and Cold-pressed

The terms *hot-pressed* and *cold-pressed* refer to the expeller method of extraction and are essentially meaningless unless you know the exact temperature at which the oils were pressed. *Cold-pressed* is especially misleading, because it suggests that the oil is not exposed to heat in the extraction process.

In fact, all commercial oil-extracting processes involve a fair amount of heat—at least 130° F to 150° F. Furthermore, many cold-pressed oils are refined, bleached, and deodorized after extraction, and thus they are exposed to even greater temperatures.

The major steps in the refining process are these:

Degumming

The oil is mixed with water at a temperature of 90° F to 120° F and is centrifuged to separate out various substances, including phosphatides, which cause oil to darken at high temperatures. One of these phosphatides is lecithin, a substance added to commercially prepared baked goods and also sold as a dietary aid.

Alkali Refining

An alkali (a substance that can neutralize acid), such as lye or caustic soda, is added to oil, followed by one or two water washes. It is then agitated and heated to remove unwanted substances by chemical reaction and centrifuged to separate the oil. A by-product of this process is called soap stock. Almost all oils that have passed through the alkali refining stage are also bleached and deodorized.

Bleaching

The oil is mixed with specially treated clays, called activated earths, to which unwanted particles of pigment will cling. The oil is then heated, agitated, and finally filtered to remove the activated earths and any particles it has picked up.

Hydrogenating

For certain purposes, hydrogen gas is bubbled through oil to "stabilize" it—to change the liquid oil to a semisolid or solid fat. This process raises the melting point of the fat or oil, allows for air to be incorporated into baked goods, prevents oil separation, and extends shelf life. But it makes these changes at the expense of nutritional value. Hydrogenation chemically changes many of the oil's unsaturated fatty acids to saturated fatty acids. Margarine, shortening, imitation cheese products, and some commercial peanut butters contain hydrogenated fats.

Deodorizing

During this final stage the oil is processed by steam-stripping it at temperatures above 400° F. This removes all odors, objectionable flavors, some of the remaining pigment, and peroxides in the oil that contribute to rancidity. In this process, from 30 to 40 percent of the vitamin E that was present in the oil is removed.

Focus on Flax

- You've heard fish is good for you! A primary reason is that fish is high in omega-3 fatty acids. And yet flaxseed has the highest concentrations of omega-3 fatty acids in nature!

- Flaxseed meal (ground flaxseed) is digestible; whole flaxseed is *not*.

- The chemical compounds in flaxseed may block the body's synthesis of carcinogens and decrease bad cholesterol levels.

- Omega-3 fatty acids could be a potential weapon against asthma, arthritis, and psoriasis.

- Mounting evidence indicates that modest amounts of omega-3 fatty acids help ward off heart attacks, such autoimmune diseases as rheumatoid arthritis, and severe menstrual cramps.

- Omega-3 fatty acid deficiencies may be the cause of some major mental illnesses.

- Ground flaxseed is rich in lignan, which has been shown in lab tests to shrink existing breast and colon cancer tumors and stop new ones from forming.

- In summary, it's good for your head, your heart, your skin, your joints, and more.

To obtain the optimal fat/oil mix while following a very-low-fat diet, we recommend small amounts of nuts and 1-2 tablespoons of freshly ground flaxseed sprinkled on top of your hot breakfast cereal on a daily basis. Start with 1 teaspoon, then increase every week to avoid the laxative effect.

Focus on Protein

What are proteins?

Proteins are important for tissue growth and repair. They are made up of more than 20 building blocks called amino acids. Those building blocks that the body cannot make are called "essential" and must be present in our food every day.

How much protein do we need?

Less than you've probably heard we do! Women need about 40-45 grams a day; men need 50-55 grams, and children 25-35 grams. Yet most people in North America consume 100-130 grams (3.5- 4.5 ounces) of protein a day, and 70 percent comes from animal sources. In contrast, rural people in China consume 50-70 grams (2-2.5 ounces) of protein a day, and almost all of it comes from plant sources.

Don't you have to have more protein in order to have good endurance?

Tests have proved that athletes on meatless diets have more than twice the endurance of those on meat diets.

What foods are protein-rich?

Natural sources are: dried peas, beans, and whole grains. Animal sources are: milk and cheese, eggs, meat, fish, and poultry.

Isn't it hard to get enough protein without meat?

Figure it out! The rule of thumb is that every half cup of vegetables has 2-3 grams of protein, and every half cup of cooked cereal has 2-3 grams or more. A slice of bread has 3 grams. A potato has 3 grams. A half cup of beans has 7 grams. And a glass of soy milk has 8 grams. It's easy to get your 40-60 grams of protein a day. It's virtually impossible not to get adequate protein on a whole-food, plant-based diet!

Most main meals are planned around meat, the protein-rich entrée. Is that necessary?

Why not stop worrying so much about protein-rich entrées? Let the "main dish" be scalloped potatoes, rice, beans, or a vegetable casserole. When meals are planned with the natural food groups in mind, the protein will automatically be there. Our concern should not be "Do we get enough protein?" On the contrary, we should ask the question "How can I avoid the harm done by our current high-protein diet?" After all, the current protein intake is 100-130 grams per day, which provides two to three times more protein than is recommended!

Focus on Soy

What are soybeans?

Soybeans are creamy yellow-colored beans of medium size that grow on hip-high plants inside fuzzy green pods. For centuries they have been the primary source of protein in eastern Asia; now they are increasingly being used in North America for both human and animal consumption.

Also available are black soybeans, which are the same as cream-colored beans except for the outside skin. They are often imported from China.

How do I use them?

To cook whole soybeans, soak them for several hours or overnight in four times as much water as you have dry beans. Replace the water with fresh water or soup stock, then cook the beans for at least three hours. Cook them very thoroughly to improve digestibility.

Pressure-cooking soybeans saves time and generally cooks them more completely. After soaking and draining the water, add just enough fresh liquid to cover the swelled beans and cook for 30 minutes at full pressure. They have a tendency to foam, so add a tablespoon of cooking oil to the water to prevent a clogged vent.

To find out if a soybean is cooked thoroughly, press one against the roof of your mouth with your tongue. If the bean is still hard, continue cooking until tender.

TVP (textured vegetable protein)

TVP is made from either defatted or full-fat soy flour that is compressed until the protein fibers change in structure. This results in a fibrous-textured product that resembles meat. TVP can be used on its own or can be flavored and colored to simulate ham, beef, bacon, or any other meat product. The "bacon bits" often used in salads and omelets are a type of TVP.

Chunk-style TVP must be cooked with liquid before eating. Add it to stews, vegetable pies, or soup stock as it boils. Granulated TVP may be used dry as a meat extender by mixing it with hamburger or other raw meat to extend the protein value while decreasing the cost per serving. To hydrate the granules, add close to 1 cup (7/8, to be exact!) of boiling water to 1 cup of TVP. This will yield about 2 cups of hydrated TVP. Stir until all the water is absorbed, and let it soak for 10 minutes.

How nutritious are they?

Soybeans are high in B-complex vitamins, calcium, phosphorus, and potassium. Also present are vitamin A and iron. Soybeans are 40 percent fat (in terms of total calories).

Soybeans contain trypsin inhibitors, substances that interfere with the action of trypsin, an enzyme in the intestine that digests protein. Laboratory tests have shown that 70-80 percent of all trypsin inhibitors present in soybeans must be destroyed before the body can make use of all the bean's protein. Trypsin inhibitors are deactivated only by heat, and this is why cooking soybeans thoroughly is important. Soaking and grinding whole soybeans greatly reduces the cooking time needed to destroy the trypsin inhibitors. Thus, soy flour, soy grits, and soybean sprouts need less cooking time than do whole soybeans.

Soy milk

Soy milk is obtained by either finely grinding soaked soybeans, mixing them with water, straining off the "milk" and heating it, or blending soy flour with water and heating it.

Soy milk has been popular in Japan for many years, while in North America it has been consumed or known of mainly by vegetarians who chose to avoid dairy products. Since the mid-1980s, however, soy milk has become a popular beverage in natural food stores throughout North America, and as Silk milk it is now commonly found in supermarkets.

Soy milk can be used interchangeably with cow's milk in most recipes.

Cow's milk has more calcium, saturated fat, sodium, and contaminants than soy milk; cow's milk also contains cholesterol. Plain soy milk has less fat than cow's milk, although some brands of flavored soy milk may have more fat per ounce than cow's milk. The protein content of cow's milk and soy milk is about the same: about 1 gram per ounce. Soy milk may be fortified with vitamins and minerals to resemble the composition of cow's milk more closely.

Focus on Sugar

What is it?

Sugar is made up of sweet white crystals and found in a bowl on the kitchen table or in envelopes that show up on restaurant tables now and then. Sugar has been tagged with all sorts of names—from nature's quickest energy food to "killer white." Then there's brown sugar, molasses, and raw or turbinado sugar.

All these sweeteners come from the same plants: sugarcane or sugar beets. Sugarcane is a tall, tropical stalk, whereas sugar beets are large, bulbous roots related to the beets we eat as vegetables. Both sugarcane and sugar beets are grown specifically for sugar.

How are sugars made?

First, canes or beets are crushed and flushed with water to extract a syrup, which is 13-15 percent sucrose. The syrup is heated until some of the water evaporates and the sugar begins to crystallize; then it is spun in a centrifuge to separate the crystals from the liquid (molasses). This process of heating, crystallizing, and centrifuging is repeated two more times to get as much sugar as possible from the syrup. The sugar crystals are then cleaned, clarified, filtered, and dried.

Molasses

Molasses is a by-product of the sugar refining process. It varies in color and sweetness. Light molasses is what remains after the first extraction of sugar crystals, and it is quite sweet. Medium or dark molasses is obtained from the second extraction and is moderately sweet. Blackstrap molasses is the liquid left after the third extraction. It is slightly sweet and very aromatic.

In contrast to sugar, molasses contains some minerals and trace elements, such as iron, calcium, zinc, copper, and chromium. Since sugarcane and sugar beets leach minerals from the soil, the mineral content of molasses will de-pend on whether the soil was adequately fertilized.

Turbinado (raw) sugar

Technically, "raw" sugar is the light-brown crystalline substance that is separated from molasses in the first extraction. This sugar is banned from sale in the United states because it often contains insect parts, molds, bacteria, soil, or waxes. If it is sanitized by steaming, it can be sold as turbinado sugar.

Turbinado is marketed as a minimally processed, natural, and nutritious sweetener. Actually, this sweetener is hardly any different from its white cousin. It is a highly processed product in that it has gone through all but the final filtration of sugar refining. It contains 95 percent sucrose. The traces of a few minerals are nutritionally insignificant.

White (granulated) Sugar

This sweetener is produced by further refining turbinado sugar. After being washed and centrifuged, then clarified with lime or phosphoric acid, the sugar is filtered through charcoal to whiten it and to remove any calcium or magnesium salts. Finally, it is crystallized and dried into granules that are pure (99.9 percent) sucrose. Everything else in the original sugarcane or sugar beet has been removed. Only the sucrose remains.

Brown sugar

Where then does brown sugar fit in the processing? It's the last step: brown sugar is made by adding a small amount of molasses to refined white sugar. Sometimes caramel coloring—burnt white sugar—is added instead. Brown sugar is about 96 percent sucrose.

How nutritious is sugar?

Sugar is a highly refined simple carbohydrate. It contributes no vitamins, minerals, or micronutrients. It is nutritionally empty, a "naked" calorie.

Focus on Carob

What is it?

A chocolate substitute? That is what carob has come to be known for, although it rightly deserves credit on its own.

The carob plant is an evergreen tree with dark-green glossy leaves and small clustered red flowers. Long brown pods form on the tree, which hold five to 15 seeds within sweet pulp. These seeds are the source of locust bean gum (carob gum), an additive used in ice cream, cheeses, and confections to improve the texture by thickening and stabilizing the food.

After being sun-dried, the seeds are removed, and the pulp of the carob pods is ground into carob powder (also called carob flour). To make carob syrup, the powder is dissolved in water and boiled until it is the consistency of honey.

Carob confections are becoming quite popular in the natural foods industry. However, when manufacturers mix sweeteners, fat, and other ingredients to make carob chips to replace chocolate chips, these carob powders lose some of their health advantages. These same mixtures are also used for carob candies; as coatings for nuts, seeds, or raisins; and for blocks of carob for baking or cooking purposes.

How do I use it?

Carob is a naturally sweet addition to baked goods. Its taste is not as rich as chocolate or cocoa.

Carob powder can be used to supplement or replace sweeteners and chocolate in brownies and puddings. Use carob one for one as a cocoa substitute, but reduce the amount of sweeteners in the recipe by about half. For the called-for amount of cocoa or chocolate chips in a recipe, however, just replace it with an identical amount of carob powder or carob chips. Carob powder comes plain or roasted. Use the roasted kind for a darker, richer brown color. Pick your carob chips carefully, because most of them contain hydrogenated palm kernel oils and wax. Choose those carob chips that use nonhydrogenated oils and more natural ingredients. Try adding carob powder to the dough of dark breads (such as pumpernickel or Russian rye) for extra color and flavor.

One comment about carob powder: it is less soluble than cocoa, and it is gritty—that is, all the particles of carob powder do not dissolve, and sediments may remain in beverages or other foods. This problem can be minimized by making a smooth paste of carob powder and warm water before adding it to the other ingredients in a recipe.

How nutritious is it?

Carob is high in carbohydrates. It also contains calcium, phosphorus, and a trace of iron. In comparison to chocolate, carob has a very low fat content, no caffeine, and is less allergenic. It does, however, contain a notable level of tannin—as do cocoa, coffee, and teas. When used in large amounts, tannin can bind elements together to form indigestible compounds if it is combined with protein.

In contrast, chocolate is about 50 percent fat, most of which is saturated. The fat content of cocoa ranges from 8 to 25 percent fat, depending on how much cocoa butter was extracted. The stimulants caffeine and theobromine are present in chocolate and cocoa but not in carob.

Focus on Vitamin B_{12}

Vitamin B_{12} deficiency is uncommon among both lacto-ovovegetarians and vegans. Although unsupplemented vegan diets are devoid of vitamin B_{12}, a number of factors may help to reduce the risk for B_{12} deficiency in this population. Here are some guidelines from Vegetarian Nutrition, a dietetic practice group of the American Dietetic Association.

Vitamin B_{12} requirements and deficiency

The need for vitamin B_{12} is extremely small. The adult recommended daily allowance is 2 micrograms. The World Health Organization recommends a minimum intake of just 1 microgram of vitamin B_{12} per day. Although needs are extremely small, a lack of this nutrient can have severe effects. Vitamin B_{12} is necessary for cell division. One result of deficiency is the megaloblastic anemia that occurs when red blood cells fail to mature. Deficiency also results in demyelination of nerve cells. The symptoms, which can include numbness and tingling in arms and legs, poor balance, fatigue, and psychiatric disorders, may be irreversible. Vitamin B_{12}-deficient children often show signs of development delay and failure to thrive. Because subtle neurological symptoms can occur prior to the onset of anemia, the early stages of B_{12} deficiency may go undetected.

Absorption of vitamin B_{12} is complex. Intrinsic factor, a protein that is necessary for B_{12} absorption, tends to decrease with aging and with some diseases. Lack of intrinsic factor is by far the most common reason for B_{12} deficiency symptoms.

Vitamin B_{12} status in vegans

Although unsupplemented vegan diets essentially lack vitamin B_{12}, clinically overt deficiency of this vitamin is rare among vegans. There are a number of possible reasons for this.

- Large amounts of vitamin B_{12}—enough to last for as long as 10 years—are stored in the liver. Because of these stores, symptoms of vitamin B_{12} deficiency are unlikely to show up for several years even when the diet contains no B_{12}.
- Most of the B_{12} in the body (about 65 to 75 percent) is recycled via the enterohepatic circulation. This contributes to the ability of the body to conserve vitamin B_{12} even when it is absent or limited in the diet.
- Although bacteria in the lower intestine produce vitamin B_{12}, it is generally accepted that this vitamin B_{12} is unavailable for absorption, since it is produced well below the site of absorption. Vitamin B_{12} may also be produced in the small intestine, but the amount produced and its bioavailability is unknown at this time. There is some evidence to suggest that small amounts of vitamin B_{12} are produced in the mouth, although these amounts are believed to be inconsequential.
- Some vegans may get vitamin B_{12} from produce that is not adequately washed.
- Many vegans avoid deficiency because they use foods fortified with B_{12}.

It is likely that all or many of these factors combine to contribute to the adequate B_{12} status of most vegans. Despite this, vitamin B_{12} deficiency can occur in vegans, and *low* blood levels of vitamin B_{12} are common in vegans. A number of case studies have shown infants born to vegan mothers on unsupplemented diets to be at an especially high risk. Evidence is that stored vitamin B_{12} may be available to the fetus and infant. Therefore, vitamin B_{12} supplements or fortified foods are crucial for pregnant and breast-feeding vegan women.

Also, vegetarian diets are typically high in folic acid. Since folic acid can mask the symptoms of vitamin B_{12} deficiency, some cases of deficiency may go undetected in the early stages.

Vegan food sources of vitamin B_{12}

Although claims have been made for a high vitamin B_{12} content in fermented soyfoods (miso and tempeh) and for sea vegetables and spirulina, laboratory assays show that these foods contain primarily B_{12} analogs ("look-alikes"). Since vitamin B_{12} analogs may interfere with B_{12} absorption, vegans who depend on these foods for their B_{12} are at higher risk for deficiency. It should be assumed that, unless fortified, no plant food contains significant amounts of active vitamin B_{12} or cobalamin.

However, many products that are acceptable to vegans are fortified with vitamin B_{12}. These include some brands of soy milk, breakfast cereals, and meat analogs. Since fortification can change over time, it is a good idea to check labels periodically. For vegans who don't regularly use fortified foods, a vitamin B_{12} supplement is recommended. The amount of vitamin absorbed decreases dramatically with higher intakes so that people may absorb as little as 1 microgram of B_{12} from a pill containing 50 micrograms. A supplement of only 5 micrograms of vitamin B_{12} will ensure that 1 microgram is absorbed.

Recommendations for vegans

Although clinically overt vitamin B_{12} deficiency is fairly rare among vegans, it can be a serious deficiency disease. To be on the safe side, all vegans should use supplements or consume foods fortified with B_{12} on a regular basis. A regular source of vitamin B_{12} in the diet is crucial for pregnant and breast-feeding mothers—or for breast-fed infants if the mother's diet is not supplemented.

For more information, please contact the Vegetarian Resource Group at:

Vegetarian Resource Group
P.O. Box 1463
Baltimore, MD 21203
(410) 366-VEGE

Vitamin B_{12} Content of Fortified Plant Foods

Commercial Cereals   mcg
Post Grape-Nuts, ¼ cup 1.5
Kellogg's Nutri-Grain, ⅔ cup 1.5
Kellogg's Raisin Bran, ¾ cup 1.5

Meat Analogs *(use only sparingly)*
1 serving as listed by the package
Loma Linda "Chicken" Nuggets . .3.0
Morningstar Farm Grillers 6.7

Loma Linda Sizzle Franks 2.0
Worthington Stakelets 5.2
Green Giant Harvest Burgers 1.5

Fortified Soy Milk/Vegetable Milks (1 cup)
Better Than Milk (soy milk) 0.6
Edensoy Extra 3.0
Insta-Soy 1.5
Silk Milk 1.0
Soyagen .1.5
Take Care (soy milk) 0.9
Vegelicious (vegetable milk) 0.6
White Tofu Drink 0.9

Other
Nutritional Yeast
    Red Star Brand T6635, 1 tbsp . . .4.0

Focus on Yeast

What is it?

Yeast is a type of microscopic fungi that grows on plant sugars. The tiny, single-celled plant occurs naturally in honey, soil, and tree sap, and on rinds or peelings of fruits, such as grapes. It can grow by budding—one cell shooting a bud as do leaves on tree branches—or sexually by spore formation within a "mother" cell.

There are about 350 different species of yeast, but the main one used for baking, brewing, and nutrition is grown in factories under carefully controlled conditions to produce pure strains that will respond uniformly to temperature humidity—unlike "wild" natural yeast that might contain impurities or grow sporadically.

The two main functions of commercial yeast are fermentation and growing nutrients. Fermenting yeasts include those used in baking and in brewing wine or beer. Nutrient-growing yeasts produce vitamins, enzymes, amino acids, and other microbial nutrients used in scientific research studies as well as for human or animal consumption.

How is it made?

Baking and nutritional yeast are grown by introducing pure strain cultures of yeast to a sugar medium. Beet or cane molasses is typically used, although the medium can also be starch from potatoes or grains.

The yeasts grow in the medium and cause it to ferment. This converts the sugar to alcohol and carbon dioxide. When fermentation ceases, the liquid yeast is washed and concentrated by separators to become yeast cream. After refrigeration the yeast cream will become one of three types of yeast:

Compressed: Excess water is pressed out of the yeast cream, resulting in a spongy cake of yeast.

Active dry: After the removal of excess water, the yeast cake is pressed into thin threads and dried under controlled temperatures and humidity to a moisture content of 5 to 8 percent.

Compressed and active dry yeasts are refrigerated to prevent further yeast growth during storage. Some active dry yeast is packaged under nitrogen gas into laminated aluminum foil envelopes and does not require refrigeration.

Nutritional: The yeast cream is pasteurized to stop further yeast growth, dried in huge drums, and then ground into textures ranging from flakes to fine powder. It is a pale-yellow color and has a distinct but pleasant aroma. Nutritional yeast needs no refrigeration.

Two other types of yeast are available to consumers: brewer's yeast and food yeast. Brewer's yeast is left over from the beer-brewing process. The original yeast is grown on barley malt, rice, corn, or corn syrup, and hops. After brewing, the yeast is removed from the vats, debittered (to get out the hops flavor), and dried into a powder. The resulting product is "spent," or nonactive, yeast that is quite nutritious. Brewer's yeast is sold as a food supplement, usually in capsules or mixed with other vitamin and mineral supplements.

Food yeast comes largely from the torula strain—grown on food-grade ethyl alcohol, which is obtained as a by-product of petroleum refining and papermaking. Torula yeast is added to such processed foods as dessert toppings and pastries, and it is used as a meat substitute in imitation meat products or as a meat extender. Known in the industry as Torutein, torula yeast is more than 50 percent protein (high in the amino acid lysine) and relatively inexpensive to produce. This accounts for its popularity in the food industry.

How nutritious are they?

Nutritional and food yeasts are 40-55 percent protein and contain all of the essential amino acids. They are very high in B-complex vitamins and provide many trace minerals, including iron, phosphorus, and potassium.

Food Additives You Might Want to Subtract From Your Diet

Many food additives serve useful purposes. They keep bread from developing mold, slow the growth of bacteria in wine, and prevent oils from turning rancid, fruit from browning, and peanut butter from separating. Others just add color or flavor. For the vast majority of people, additives pose little or no health hazard. But for a few, some additives may be a big headache—literally.

According to the American Academy of Allergy, Asthma, and Immunology (AAAAI), food additives are not likely to trigger true allergic reactions. But a few people seem to be sensitive to certain additives and experience allergy-like symptoms, including rashes, itching, nausea, headaches, even difficulty in breathing.

At least five groups of additives have been identified by AAAAI as potentially troublesome.

Aspartame

AKA: NutraSweet, Equal. *What It Is:* noncaloric sweetener made from two amino acids; approved by the Food and Drug Administration (FDA). *Found In:* soft drinks, juices, cereals, ice cream, puddings, gelatin desserts, chewing gum, mints. *Health Concerns:* Though unconfirmed, adverse reactions (more than for any other additive) have been reported to the FDA, including headaches, dizziness, nausea, respiratory problems, itching, and hives. Anyone with the genetic disorder phenylketonuria (PKU) must avoid aspartame altogether.

BHA and BHT

AKA: butylated hyroxyanisole and butylated hydroxytoluene. *What They Are:* preservatives and antioxidants used to retard spoilage and prevent changes in flavor, color, and texture in both high-fat and dry foods; considered GRAS (generally recognized as safe) by the FDA. *Found In:* cereals, seasonings, frostings, dessert mixes, instant potatoes, packaged popcorn, baked goods, piecrusts, meat products, chewing gum. *Health Concerns:* There's conflicting information about whether they promote or prevent cancer and inconclusive evidence of side effects. Complaints have included rashes, hives, and a "tight" chest.

FD&C Yellow Dye No. 5

AKA: tartrazine. *What It Is:* certified artificial food coloring. *Found In:* beverages, dessert mixes, custards, seasonings, pickles, relish, baked goods (cookies, wafers), bread mixes, frosting, packaged potatoes and pastas, mints, candy, baked snacks, beverages, pie dough, ice cream. *Health Concerns:* May cause itching, hives, and runny nose in a small number of people, more so in aspirin-sensitive people who also have asthma.

MSG

AKA: monosodium glutamate. *What It Is:* flavor enhancer that imparts a supposed "fifth taste" sensation called "umami"; considered GRAS by FDA. *Found In:* condiments, soups (including broths and bouillon), sauces, canned beans and chili, seasoning mixes, dips, rice mixes, gravies, chips, Asian cuisine. *Health Concerns:* May trigger reactions in people with asthma and in people who eat large amounts of the additive, especially on an empty stomach. Reactions include facial and chest pressure, tingling, numbness, burning on back of neck, skin flushing, headache, nausea, dizziness, drowsiness, and difficulty breathing.

Sulfites

AKA: sulfur dioxide, sodium sulfite, sodium or potassium bisulfite, sodium or potassium metabisulfite. *What They Are:* preservatives used primarily to prevent discoloration of dried fruit and inhibit bacterial growth in wine. *Found In:* dried fruit, peeled and dried potatoes, marinades, sauces, rice mixes, mustard, molasses, candy, fruit juice, bottled lemon juice, shrimp, vinegar, wine (especially white), beer. *Health Concerns:* A small percentage of people are sensitive to sulfites. The most common reaction is difficulty breathing, though life-threatening anaphylactic-like events are rare. Stomach upset, nausea, and hives have also been reported. Anyone with asthma may want to avoid sulfites altogether (consult your physician). Read product labels and take extra precautions when dining out.

—*Andrea Klausner, M.S., R.D.*

Advice on Additives

In general, don't panic over the presence of additives. The small amounts ingested don't bother most healthy people. If you do suffer unexplained allergic-like responses, see a specialist to determine their true cause. Here are some additional pointers:

- Choose simple, fresh whole foods. Avoid processed foods with many ingredients.
- Read food labels carefully if you're sensitive. Compare brands and flavors; not all flavors contain the same additives. Some "natural flavorings" contain plant material that can provoke reactions in people with food or pollen allergies.
- If you have sensitivities (especially to sulfites), inquire about recipe ingredients when eating out.
- For a larger selection of additive-free foods, shop at a health food supermarket.

Calcium Content in Common Food Sources*

FOOD, typical edible portion	Quantity	Calcium (mg)	Magnesium (mg)	Sodium (mg)	Protein (g)
Vegetables, Legumes, Nuts, and Seeds					
Almonds	23 almonds	70	78	0	6
Broccoli	1 cup boiled	178	36	44	6
Brussels sprouts	1 cup boiled	40	28	23	6
Butternut squash, baked	1 cup mashed	46	22	5	3
Chickpeas (garbanzo beans)	1 cup cooked	80	80	12	14
Chinese cabbage	1 cup boiled	158	19	58	3
Collards	1 cup cooked	357	51	85	5
Green beans	1 cup cooked	65	30	12	2
Kale	1 cup cooked	179	23	20	4
Mustard greens	1 cup cooked	152	20	38	3
Navy beans	1 cup cooked	126	96	0	15
Okra	½ cup cooked	88	47	3	2
Parsley, raw	5 tbsp	26	10	11	1
Sesame tahini, roasted	1 tbsp	64	14	17	3
Soybeans	1 cup cooked	260	108	25	22
Soybean milk, calcium-fortified	1 cup	268	39	96	7
Spinach, raw	1 cup chopped	56	44	44	1
Sweet potato, boiled	1 cup mashed	68	32	42	3
Tofu, firm, w/calcium	½ cup	253	47	15	10
Turnip greens	1 cup boiled	250	43	25	5
White beans	1 cup boiled	161	113	11	17
Grains					
Cheerios	1 cup	80	64	280	3
Tortilla, corn	6-oz med	45	17	3	1
Fruit					
Blackberries, raw	1 cup	42	29	1	2
Figs, dried	5	90	50	5	2
Orange	1 med	52	13	0	1
Papaya	1 med	52	31	9	2
Dairy					
Milk, nonfat	1 cup	300	26	128	8
Yogurt, nonfat, plain	1 cup	488	46	128	14
Aquatic Food					
Kelp, dried	3.5 oz	168	121	233	2
Salmon, canned, pink, w/bones, no salt	3 oz	185	30	64	17
Sardines, w/bones	2 med	92	9	121	8
Trout	3 oz	37	19	44	18

*Whole unprocessed plant foods also have other minerals, such as boron, zinc, and manganese, and an abundance of phytochemicals and antioxidants. All of these help the body to make strong, healthy bones, and they also promote a strong, healthy immune system. Weight-bearing exercises, such as walking and using light weights for the arms and shoulders, make an essential contribution to building strong bones.

Sources: *Food Values of Portions Commonly Used*, 17th ed. (Bowes & Churches, 1998). USDA National Nutrient Database, August 2005.

Breakfasts and Brunches

Apples and Rice

Baked Barley With Apples

Baked Oatmeal

Breakfast Potatoes

Blueberry-Oat Pancakes

Brown Rice Porridge

Buckwheat-Oat Waffles

Dr. Diehl's Crock-Pot Breakfast

French Toast

Tofu Crepes

Granola

Fruit Topping

Fruity Maple Syrup

Millet Pudding

Cashew-Oat Waffles

Creamed Pears Topping

Multigrain Waffles

Wheat-Oat Crepes

Whole-Wheat Pancakes

Scrambled Tofu

Muesli

1. Tofu Crepes, *p. 31*
2. Creamed Pears Topping, *p. 35*

APPLES AND RICE

Preparation Time: 20 minutes
Complexity: Easy

2 cups	brown rice, cooked
1	apple, large, cored, peeled, and chopped
⅓ cup	apple juice, unsweetened
2 tbsp	maple syrup
1 tbsp	lemon juice
½ tsp	cinnamon (or substitute)

1. Combine all ingredients in casserole dish. Cover.
2. Bake at 350° F for 45 minutes.
3. Serve warm or cold.

CHEF'S TIP:

• Can also be served as a light supper.

Serves: 4

PER 1-CUP SERVING:	160 Calories	2 g Prot (5%)	36 g Carb (90%)	1 g Fat (5%)	9 g Sugar
	2 g Fiber	3 mg Sodium	0 mg Chol	23 mg Calcium	

BAKED BARLEY WITH APPLES

Preparation Time: 15 minutes
Complexity: Easy

2 cups	water
1 cup	barley
⅓ cup	maple syrup
1 tsp	cinnamon (or substitute)
1½	apples, diced fresh
¼ tsp	salt (optional)

1. Place all ingredients in a small Crock-Pot.
2. Cook on low temperature overnight, about 8 hours.

Will be ready and hot to serve in the morning!

Serves: 4

PER 1-CUP SERVING:	260 Calories	6 g Prot (8%)	57 g Carb (88%)	1 g Fat (4%)	20 g Sugar
	9 g Fiber	10 mg Sodium	0 mg Chol	44 mg Calcium	

BAKED OATMEAL

Preparation Time: 20 minutes
Complexity: Easy

3 cups	rolled oats
⅓ cup	shredded coconut, unsweetened
⅓ cup	dates, chopped
⅓ cup	raisins
1 tsp	vanilla or maple extract
2 cups	soy milk
2 cups	water

1. Lightly oil-spray a glass 9" x 9" baking dish.
2. Layer first four ingredients in dish in the order given.
3. Mix together soymilk, water, and vanilla or maple extract.
4. Pour soy milk mixture evenly over the dry mixture in baking dish.
5. Cover dish and place in refrigerator overnight.
6. Bake uncovered at 350° F for 45 minutes or until heated through. Serve hot with additional soy or nut milk.

CHEF'S TIP:

• As a delightful option, add some fresh or frozen blueberries as an additional layer prior to baking!

Serves: 6

PER 1-CUP SERVING:	255 Calories	10 g Prot (13%)	45 g Carb (70%)	5 g Fat (17%)	13 g Sugar
	5 g Fiber	37 mg Sodium	0 mg Chol	154 mg Calcium	

BREAKFAST POTATOES

Preparation Time: 20 minutes
Complexity: Easy

6	**potatoes, large**
2 tbsp	**olive oil**
½ tsp	**garlic powder**
1 tsp	**Spike, or your favorite seasoning**

1. Wash potatoes but do not peel them. Cut each potato into 1-inch cubes.

2. Toss potatoes with olive oil and seasoning.

3. Place in a large baking dish or on a baking sheet. Bake at 400°F for 20-30 minutes or until golden brown and tender.

4. Serve hot with homemade *Ketchup* (p. 64).

CHEF'S TIP:

- If available, you may wish to substitute the dried seasoning with fresh chopped herbs and some Mrs. Dash.

Serves: 6

Analysis done using 1 tsp Spike seasoning.				
PER 1½-CUP SERVING: 189 Calories	4 g Prot (6%)	32 g Carb (71%)	5 g Fat (23%)	1 g Sugar
4 g Fiber	205 mg Sodium	0 mg Chol	22 mg Calcium	

BLUEBERRY-OAT PANCAKES

Preparation Time: 30 minutes
Complexity: Easy

2 cups	**oat flour**
1 cup	**spelt or whole-wheat flour**
½ tsp	**salt**
2 tsp	**baking powder**
2½ cups	**soy milk**
1 pkg (12 oz, 349 g)	**tofu, silken, firm** (lite)
¾ cup	**blueberries, frozen or fresh**

1. Measure dry ingredients into a mixing bowl. Mix well.

2. In a blender, blend soy milk and tofu until smooth. Add to dry mixture in mixing bowl.

3. Gently fold in blueberries; be careful not to overmix.

4. On a preheated nonstick griddle, pour ½ cup batter to form each pancake.

5. Fry each pancake until golden brown, then flip and repeat for the other side.

6. Serve hot immediately.

CHEF'S TIPS:

- Blenderize dry rolled oats to make oat flour.
- Very good with *Creamed Pears Topping* (p. 35).

Serves: 6

PER SERVING: 289 Calories	16 g Prot (21%)	45 g Carb (61%)	6 g Fat (18%)	3 g Sugar
(1 pancake) 6 g Fiber	308 mg Sodium	0 mg Chol	159 mg Calcium	

BROWN RICE PORRIDGE

Preparation Time: 15 minutes
Complexity: Easy

4 cups	water
2½ cups	brown rice flakes
⅓ cup	dates, chopped
⅓ cup	raisins
¼-½ tsp	salt

1. Bring water to a boil in a medium-sized pot.
2. Add remaining ingredients. Stir well.
3. Simmer for 5 minutes or until desired texture is achieved.
4. Serve with nondairy milk.

CHEF'S TIPS:
- Excellent for people who are celiac or sensitive to wheat or oats.
- Variation: Substitute brown rice flakes with quick oats.

Serves: 4

PER 1-CUP SERVING:	326 Calories	5 g Prot (6%)	72 g Carb (88%)	2 g Fat (6%)	17 g Sugar
	5 g Fiber	152 mg Sodium	0 mg Chol	17 mg Calcium	

BUCKWHEAT-OAT WAFFLES

Preparation Time: 20 minutes
Complexity: Intermediate

2¼ cups	water
1½ cups	rolled oats
1 tbsp	olive oil
½ cup	buckwheat flour
¼ cup	soy flour
½ tsp	salt

1. Blenderize all ingredients in blender until smooth.
2. Let batter stand for 10 minutes to thicken.
3. Blenderize batter again before pouring onto a hot, lightly oil-sprayed nonstick waffle iron.
4. Bake 10 minutes or until light brown and steam is minimal. (Warning: do not lift lid too soon!)
5. Serve hot with your favorite waffle toppings (pp. 34, 35).

Serves: 3

PER 3" x 3" WAFFLE SQUARE:	72 Calories	3 g Prot (15%)	11 g Carb (62%)	2 g Fat (23%)	1 g Sugar
(without topping [5])	2 g Fiber	99 mg Sodium	0 mg Chol	13 mg Calcium	

DR. DIEHL'S CROCK-POT BREAKFAST

Preparation Time: 10 minutes
Complexity: Easy

1 cup	seven-grain cereal (Bob's Red Mill)*
3-4 cups	water
1 tbsp	flaxseed, ground

*Or make your own:
brown rice, oats, barley,
millet, wheat, corn, quinoa.

1. Spray the inside upper edge of a Crock-Pot with a nonstick spray.
2. Put cereal and water into the Crock-Pot.
3. Turn the Crock-Pot on low. Cover. Let cook overnight.
4. Serve with non-dairy milk. Use CHIP Tips.

CHEF'S TIP:
- Add your choice of the following items (before or after cooking): fresh fruit, dried fruit, raisins, walnuts, or cardamom. Top with freshly ground flaxseeds (1 tbsp).

Serves: 3

Analysis does not include toppings and is based on a mixture of grains.					
PER 1-CUP SERVING:	130 Calories	4 g Prot (12%)	25 g Carb (75%)	2 g Fat (13%)	0 g Sugar
	7 g Fiber	2 mg Sodium	0 mg Chol	30 mg Calcium	

FRENCH TOAST

Preparation Time: 30 minutes
Complexity: Intermediate

1 pkg (12 oz, 350 g)	tofu, silken, firm (lite)
¾ cup	water
1 tbsp	maple syrup
1 tsp	vanilla extract
1 loaf	whole-grain bread

1. Place in a blender: tofu, water, maple syrup, and vanilla. Blend until smooth. Pour mixture into a flat-bottom dish.

2. Preheat a nonstick griddle or frying pan.

3. Dip one slice of bread in blended tofu mixture, making sure slice of bread is thoroughly coated on both sides.

4. Place dipped bread on hot skillet. Cook until golden brown. Flip, and repeat until second side is golden brown.

5. Repeat with the remaining bread slices until all of the tofu batter is used up.

CHEF'S TIP:
• Serve fresh and hot with fruit as a topping such as applesauce, pears, berries, etc. (pp. 34, 35).

Serves: 6

Nutrients may vary according to bread used.				
PER 2-SLICE SERVING: 220 Calories	12 g Prot (22%)	36 g Carb (67%)	3 g Fat (11%)	3 g Sugar
6 g Fiber	162 mg Sodium	0 mg Chol	166 mg Calcium	

TOFU CREPES (see p. 26)

Preparation Time: 25 minutes
Complexity: Intermediate

1 pkg (10 oz, 300 g)	soft tofu
1½ cups	soy milk
1 tbsp	honey
1 tbsp	baking powder
1¼ cups	whole-wheat pastry flour

1. Preheat a 6-inch nonstick skillet or crepe pan.
2. Place all ingredients into a blender. Blend until very smooth.
3. Pour approximately ⅓ cup of batter into hot frying pan.*
4. Fry until lightly brown on both sides.
5. Serve rolled with thickened fruit or *fruit topping* in the middle (p. 34).

CHEF'S TIP:
• Pour batter into frying pan, then tip until batter thinly covers the bottom of pan evenly. Good served with *Creamed Pears Topping* (p. 35).

Makes 16 6-inch crepes   *Serves: 4-6*

PER 1-CREPE SERVING: 60 Calories	4 g Prot (20%)	11 g Carb (64%)	1 g Fat (16%)	1 g Sugar
(without filling) 2 g Fiber	16 mg Sodium	0 mg Chol	73 mg Calcium	

GRANOLA

Preparation Time: 20 minutes
Complexity: Easy

10 cups	whole rolled or quick oats
½ cup	unsweetened coconut, shredded (optional)
1 cup	sliced almonds
2 cups	wheat germ
1 cup	raw sunflower seeds
½ cup	brown sesame seeds
½ tsp	salt (optional)
1½ tbsp	maple extract
1 cup	water
⅔ cup	olive oil
¾ cup	maple syrup
	or
½ cup	brown sugar
1 cup	raisins
1 cup	dates, chopped

1. In a large bowl, mix together dry ingredients except raisins and dates.
2. Stir together: maple extract, water, olive oil, and syrup or sugar. Pour over dry mixture. Mix very well.
3. Divide granola between two baking sheets and spread out evenly.
4. Bake at 350° F for approximately 40 minutes, or until golden brown. Stir every 10 minutes.
5. Remove granola from oven and cool. Mix in raisins and dates.
6. Store in an airtight container to retain freshness.

CHEF'S TIP:
• Bake at 175° F overnight. For further browning: in the morning, turn temperature up to 300° F, stirring every 10 minutes, until desired color is achieved.

Makes: 16 cups

PER ½-CUP SERVING:	261 Calories	8 g Prot (11%)	31 g Carb (48%)	13 g Fat (41%)	7 g Sugar
	5 g Fiber	41 mg Sodium	0 mg Chol	55 mg Calcium	

1. Cashew-Oat Waffles, *p. 35*
2. Fruit Topping, *p. 34*
3. Creamed Pears Topping, *p. 35*
4. Muesli, *p. 37*
5. Scrambled Tofu, *p. 37*

FRUIT TOPPING (see p. 32)

Preparation Time: 20 minutes
Complexity: Easy

3 cups	frozen fruit (example: strawberries, blueberries, peaches, etc.)
2 cups	apple juice, unsweetened
3 tbsp	cornstarch

1. Place frozen fruit in a medium saucepan and thaw at room temperature.
2. Dissolve cornstarch in apple juice. Pour into saucepan with fruit.
3. Bring to a boil over medium heat. Simmer until juice becomes thick and clear.

CHEF'S TIPS:
- Use on waffles, pancakes, french toast, granola, or as a topping for "cheesecake."
- May substitute apple juice with water and some sweetener.

Serves: 8

Nutrient values will change according to fruit used. Strawberries were used in this analysis.

PER ½-CUP SERVING:	70 Calories	0 g Prot (2%)	18 g Carb (96%)	0 g Fat (2%)	4 g Sugar
	2 g Fiber	4 mg Sodium	0 mg Chol	18 mg Calcium	

FRUITY MAPLE SYRUP

Preparation Time: 10 minutes
Complexity: Easy

2 cups	white grape or apple juice, unsweetened
1½ tbsp	cornstarch
3 tbsp	maple syrup
2 tbsp	maple extract

1. Combine all ingredients in a small pot.
2. Bring to a simmer over medium heat. Continue to simmer until sauce has thickened.
3. Pour sauce into a small pitcher. Chill in refrigerator before serving, if desired.

CHEF'S TIP:
- Serve on pancakes, waffles, french toast, etc.

Makes: 2¼ cups

Analysis done using apple juice.

PER 2-TBSP SERVING:	28 Calories	0 g Prot (0%)	6 g Carb (99%)	0 g Fat (1%)	2 g Sugar
	0 g Fiber	1 mg Sodium	0 mg Chol	4 mg Calcium	

MILLET PUDDING

Preparation Time: 15 minutes
Complexity: Easy

¾ cup	millet, uncooked
¼ tsp	salt
2 cups	soy milk
2 cups	water
⅓ cup	raisins
⅓ cup	dates, chopped
2 tsp	vanilla extract

1. Preheat oven to 350° F.
2. In a medium-sized casserole dish, combine all ingredients. Mix well.
3. Cover dish. Place in oven and bake for 45 minutes or until golden brown on top, and millet is soft.
4. Garnish with mandarin orange segments.
5. Serve warm or cold, with or without nondairy milk.

Serves: 4

PER 1-CUP SERVING:	279 Calories	9 g Prot (12%)	54 g Carb (77%)	4 g Fat (11%)	18 g Sugar
	5 g Fiber	199 mg Sodium	0 mg Chol	108 mg Calcium	

CASHEW-OAT WAFFLES (see p. 32)

Preparation Time: 20 minutes
Complexity: Intermediate

⅓ cup	raw cashews
1 cup	water
1 cup	soy milk
2 tbsp	wheat germ
1 tsp	vanilla extract
1 tsp	olive oil
2 cups	quick oats
½ tsp	salt
1 tbsp	sugar or honey (optional)

1. Blenderize cashews in water and soy milk until smooth in blender.

2. Add remaining ingredients, then blend together.

3. Let mixture stand 5 minutes to thicken.

4. Cook approximately 7 minutes in hot waffle iron until golden brown.

5. Serve hot with your favorite toppings (pp. 34, 35).

CHEF'S TIP:
- Waffles freeze well and can be easily reheated in a toaster or microwave.

Serves: 2-3

ONE 3" x 3" WAFFLE SQUARE: 150 Calories	6 g Prot (15%)	21 g Carb (55%)	5 g Fat (30%)	1 g Sugar
(without topping) 3 g Fiber	110 mg Sodium	0 mg Chol	26 mg Calcium	

CREAMED PEARS TOPPING (see pp. 26 and 32)

Preparation Time: 10 minutes
Complexity: Easy

⅓ cup	raw cashews
1 tsp	vanilla extract
3½ cups (28 oz)	canned pears, unsweetened

1. Drain juice off canned pears and reserve.

2. Place all ingredients into blender.

3. Blend until very smooth. Slowly pour juice reserved from pears into blender as needed until the desired consistency is reached.

Variation:
- Substitute canned peaches or frozen thawed strawberries for canned pears.

CHEF'S TIP:
- Use as a topping for waffles, pancakes, fruit salad, apple crisp, granola, or strawberry shortcake.

Makes: 4 cups

PER ¼-CUP SERVING: 55 Calories	1 g Prot (7%)	8 g Carb (58%)	2 g Fat (35%)	5 g Sugar
1 g Fiber	3 mg Sodium	0 mg Chol	7 mg Calcium	

MULTIGRAIN WAFFLES

Preparation Time: 20 minutes
Complexity: Intermediate

½ cup	rolled oats
½ cup	rye flour
½ cup	whole-wheat flour
½ cup	soy flour
½ tsp	salt
2¼ cups	water
1 tbsp	olive oil

1. Blenderize all ingredients until smooth.
2. Let batter stand for 10 minutes to thicken.
3. Blenderize batter again before pouring onto a hot, lightly oil-sprayed nonstick waffle iron.
4. Bake 10 minutes. (Warning: do not lift lid too soon!)
5. Serve hot with your favorite waffle toppings (pp. 34, 35)

Serves: 2-3

ONE 3" x 3" SQUARE WAFFLE:	78 Calories	4 g Prot (21%)	11 g Carb (56%)	2 g Fat (23%)	1 g Sugar
(without topping)	3 g Fiber	99 mg Sodium	0 mg Chol	15 mg Calcium	

WHEAT-OAT CREPES

Preparation Time: 30 minutes
Complexity: Intermediate

1½ cups	whole-wheat pastry flour
1 tbsp	baking powder
1½ cups	rolled oats
4⅓ cups	soy milk
1 tbsp	dates

1. Blenderize all ingredients until smooth.
2. Let batter stand 5 minutes, then blend again until smooth.
3. Heat a small nonstick skillet or crepe pan; lightly oil-spray.
4. Spoon 3 tablespoons batter into crepe pan; spread evenly by tilting skillet.
5. Brown crepes lightly on both sides.
6. Serve rolled with thickened fruit in the middle.

Makes 24 six-inch crepes
Serves: 6

PER 4 SIX-INCH CREPES:	251 Calories	11 g Prot (17%)	42 g Carb (66%)	5 g Fat (17%)	2 g Sugar
(without filling)	6 g Fiber	66 mg Sodium	0 mg Chol	74 mg Calcium	

WHOLE-WHEAT PANCAKES

Preparation Time: 30 minutes
Complexity: Easy

3 cups	whole-wheat flour
2½ tsp	baking powder
½ tsp	salt
4 cups	soy milk
2 tbsp	olive oil
3 tsp.	Ener-G Egg Replacer powder (dissolved in 4 tbsp water)

1. Mix dry ingredients together.
2. Add remaining ingredients and stir gently until well mixed. Do not overmix.
3. Drop mixture by spoonfuls on a hot nonstick griddle. Fry until golden brown. Flip pancake and repeat process.
4. Serve with topping (pp. 34, 35).
5. Garnish with mandarin orange segments and kiwi slices.

CHEF'S TIP:
- For a thinner pancake, add water until desired consistency is achieved.

Serves: 6

PER PANCAKE:	155 Calories	7 g Prot (16%)	25 g Carb (61%)	4 g Fat (23%)	0 g Sugar
(without topping)	4 g Fiber	131 mg Sodium	0 mg Chol	178 mg Calcium	

SCRAMBLED TOFU (see p. 32)

Preparation Time: 20 minutes
Complexity: Easy

1 pkg (16 oz, 454g)	**medium/firm tofu**
½ tsp	**garlic powder**
½ tsp	**onion powder**
⅛-¼ tsp	**turmeric**
½ tbsp	**dried parsley flakes**
½ tbsp	**Bragg's All Purpose Seasoning**
1-3 tsp	**chickenlike seasoning of your choice, to taste**
½ tbsp	**nutritional yeast flakes**

1. Preheat a large nonstick frying pan.

2. Drain and rinse tofu. Chop and mash with spoon into frying pan.

3. Sprinkle all seasonings equally over tofu. Mix well.

4. Stir occasionally. Cook until most of the moisture has disappeared. Serve fresh and hot.

5. Garnish with fresh parsley and tomato wedges.

CHEF'S TIP:
• For added nutrition, color, and flavor, you may wish to sauté onion, mushrooms, peppers, etc., in a small amount of water before adding tofu.

Serves: 4

PER ½-CUP SERVING:	80 Calories	8 g Prot (39%)	3 g Carb (14%)	4 g Fat (47%)	0 g Sugar
	1 g Fiber	107 mg Sodium	0 mg Chol	204 mg Calcium	

MUESLI (see p. 32)

Preparation Time: 15 minutes
Complexity: Easy

3 cups	**whole rolled oats**
3 cups	**fruit juice** (unsweetened apple, orange, pineapple, etc.)
1 tsp	**lemon juice**
1½ cups	**apple, shredded**

1. Place all ingredients into a serving bowl and mix together.

2. Cover, then chill in refrigerator overnight.

3. Serve cold with your choice of toppings: soy milk, vanilla soy yogurt, fresh berries, sliced peaches and/or bananas, sliced almonds, applesauce, cinnamon, etc.

CHEF'S TIP:
• Replace shredded apple with banana by blending the banana and juice together in a blender prior to adding to the oats.

Serves: 6

Analysis done using orange juice.					
PER 1-CUP SERVING:	272 Calories	8 g Prot (12%)	51 g Carb (75%)	4 g Fat (13%)	14 g Sugar
(without topping)	5 g Fiber	3 mg Sodium	0 mg Chol	56 mg Calcium	

Breads and
Muffins

Bran Muffins

Banana-Nut Bread

Spelt Bread

Cornmeal Buns and Breadsticks

Blueberry-Spelt Muffins

Mom's Homemade Bread

Dark Rye Bread

Cranberry-Orange Bread

Corn Bread

Multigrain Bread

Oatmeal-Raisin Bread

Potato Focaccia

Ron's Sweet Rolls

Oat Crackers

Pocket Bread

Whole-Wheat Bagels

• Banana-Nut Bread, *p. 42*

Breadmaking

When making your homemade bread, be sure to use whole grains, such as wheat, spelt, rye, and barley. These are wonderful grains. They make delicious breads, and they are full of nutrients, especially B vitamins.

If you choose to purchase your bread, then choose brands that are not filled with preservatives, stabilizers, or conditioners, and select those that are made from whole grains. So-called enriched flour, used in most commercial breads, has most of is food value removed and only a small portion replaced. By using the word "enriched," we are tricked into believing we're getting a "bonus" of nutrients when in reality we're getting "robbed." When wheat is milled into bleached flour, we lose, among other nutrients:

- 30 percent of the protein
- 90.7 percent of the fiber
- 60 percent of the calcium
- 50 percent of the copper
- 90 percent of the manganese
- 85 percent of the B_1 vitamin
- 40 percent of the healthy fat
- 85 percent of the iron

When you realize how much nutrition is lost, how enriched do you feel now?

Tips for making bread:

1. To begin with, try a simple, basic recipe.

2. Salt and fat both slow the growth of the yeast and should not be added to the yeast mixture until it has grown strong and lively by feeding on sugar and starch.

3. Develop the gluten of the wheat flour in the batter by beating thoroughly with a spoon or whisk before adding other kinds of flour.

4. When using a quick-rising yeast, it is important to do a thorough job of kneading before the first rising or before placing the dough into the loaf pans.

5. When forming dough into the shape of a loaf, be sure to make a seam down the middle of the bottom of the loaf. This will make your loaf rise into a nice even shape. If your seam is off to one side, then your loaf of bread will hang over to that one side.

6. Never fill pans too full. Give the bread enough room to expand without having to rise out over the sides, causing cracked, overbrowned crusts.

7. Be careful not to "overraise" breads when in loaf pans. Bake the bread when the loaf has doubled in bulk.

8. Be imaginative! Make a wide variety of breads: use different ingredients, such as multigrains, dried fruits, nuts, seeds, and various combinations.

9. Add 1 tablespoon of lemon juice for every 4 cups of flour in a recipe. This will give you a lighter, high-rising bread.

10. Add 1 tablespoon of gluten flour for every 4 cups of flour in a recipe to make bread less crumbly and to help it rise nicely.

11. Add 1 tablespoon of liquid or granulated lecithin to your recipe to make bread less crumbly.

12. Bake several loaves of bread at one time, then freeze for future use. This will save you time and money!

13. It is important to bake each loaf thoroughly. When the bread slips easily out of the baking pan, it is thoroughly baked.

NOTE: *Bread just hot out of the oven is difficult to digest. It is probably better to wait at least 12 hours!*

Common Problems of Breadmaking and Possible Causes:

- Dry and crumbly:
    too much flour in dough
    overbaked

- Heavy
    insufficient kneading

- Cracks in crust
    cooling in a draft
    baking before sufficiently raised
    oven temperature too hot at first
    yeast water too hot

- Crust is too thick or dry
    oven temperature set too low
    bread baked too long
    too much salt used

- Sogginess
    too much liquid used
    insufficient baking

- Poor-shaped loaf
    not molded well originally when placed into pans
    too large a loaf for the pan used

BRAN MUFFINS (see p. 46)

Preparation Time: 20 minutes
Complexity: Easy

2 cups	**whole-wheat pastry flour**
2 cups	**wheat bran**
1½ tsp	**baking soda**
2 tsp	**baking powder**
2 cups	**apple, grated**
¾ cup	**raisins**
1 cup	**dates, chopped**
⅓ cup	**honey**
⅓ cup	**olive oil**
4 tsp	**Ener-G Egg Replacer powder** (dissolved in 6 tbsp water)
2 cups	**soy milk**

1. In mixing bowl, combine dry ingredients. Mix well.
2. Add grated apple, raisins, and dates. Mix well until evenly distributed throughout dry mixture.
3. Make a "well" in the center and add remaining four ingredients. Fold gently. Do not overmix. Stir just enough to mix ingredients together; otherwise muffins may be heavy.
4. Spray muffin tins with a nonstick spray, or line with muffin cups. Fill muffin tins two-thirds full.
5. Bake at 350° F for 20 minutes.

CHEF'S TIP:
- May substitute 2 cups of whole-wheat pastry flour with 1 cup whole-wheat flour and 1 cup unbleached white flour.

Makes: 18 muffins

PER 1 MUFFIN:	178 Calories	4 g Prot (7%)	36 g Carb (68%)	5 g Fat (25%)	17 g Sugar
	5 g Fiber	123 mg Sodium	0 mg Chol	88 mg Calcium	

BANANA-NUT BREAD (see p. 38)

Preparation Time: 20 minutes
Complexity: Easy

2 cups	whole-wheat pastry flour
½ tsp	salt
½ cup	walnut pieces
1½ tsp	baking powder
1 tsp	finely grated orange or lemon peel (optional)
¼ cup	olive oil
⅓ cup	raw cashews
⅓ cup	honey
	or
⅔ cup	sugar
1¼ cups	ripe banana, mashed
1 tbsp	Ener-G Egg Replacer powder
1 tsp	lemon juice

1. In a medium-sized bowl, mix together dry ingredients.
2. Add remaing ingredients. Mix well.
3. Pour batter into a lightly oil-sprayed bread/loaf pan.
4. Bake at 350° F for 50 minutes or until inserted toothpick comes out clean.
5. Allow loaf to cool before slicing.

Makes: 1 loaf

CHEF'S TIPS:

- You may substitute whole wheat flour in place of the whole wheat pastry flour. Just note that it will come out a little heavier.
- optional: add 2 tbsp. ground flaxseed.

PER ½-INCH-THICK SLICE:	142 Calories	3 g Prot (7%)	21g Carb (56%)	6 g Fat (37%)	8 g Sugar
	3 g Fiber	74 g Sodium	0 mg Chol	31 mg Calcium	

SPELT BREAD

Preparation Time: 25 minutes
Complexity: Intermediate

¼ cup	quick-cooking oats
1½ cups	spelt flour
1 tbsp	active dry yeast
½ tsp	salt
⅓ cup	date paste (prepared by blending dates with enough hot water to make a paste)
1 tbsp	applesauce, unsweetened
3 cups	warm water
6-7 cups	spelt flour (or as needed)

1. Stir together first seven ingredients. Mix well.
2. Add spelt flour, 1 cup at a time, while mixing until dough is no longer sticky.
3. Let dough sit for 5 minutes.
4. With hands, knead for about 10 minutes.
5. Shape dough into two loaves and place them in lightly oil-sprayed bread pans.
6. Cover with a towel and allow to rise for 20 minutes.
7. Bake at 350° F for 30 minutes or until crust is golden brown.

CHEF'S TIP:

- You may choose to substitute whole-wheat pastry flour in place of the spelt flour.

Makes: 2 loaves

PER ½-INCH SLICE:	200 Calories	7 g Prot (78%)	39 g Carb (78%)	2 g Fat (8%)	1 g Sugar
	6 g Fiber	58 mg Sodium	0 mg Chol	19 mg Calcium	

CORNMEAL BUNS AND BREADSTICKS

Preparation Time: 40 minutes
Complexity: Advanced

4 cups	**water**
2 tsp	**salt**
1 cup	**cornmeal**
½ cup	**olive oil**
⅓ cup	**honey**
1 tsp	**honey**
1 cup	**warm water**
2 tbsp	**active dry yeast**
5 cups	**whole-wheat flour**
7 cups	**spelt or whole-wheat flour, as needed** (you may use unbleached white if you desire)

1. Bring water to a boil; add salt and cornmeal. Simmer until a mush. Allow to cool at room temperature.

2. Add oil and ⅓ cup honey to cooked cornmeal.

3. In a separate bowl, dissolve 1 teaspoon honey in 1 cup warm water. Mix in yeast. Let sit until the yeast bubbles. Add to cooled cornmeal mixture.

4. Add flour, kneading in 1 cup at a time until dough is not sticky. Set dough in a warm place covered with a towel. Let rise until doubled in size.

5. Roll out dough to ½ inch thick. Cut with a round cutter or shape into buns or breadsticks.

6. Let rise on lightly oil-sprayed baking sheets until doubled in size.

7. Bake in a 400° F oven for 15 minutes or until golden brown.

CHEF'S TIPS:

- If preparing breadsticks: brush breadsticks while hot from oven with some olive oil mixed with garlic powder and Spike seasoning.
- This recipe may easily be cut in half.

Makes: 6 dozen buns

PER 1 BUN:	93 Calories	3 g Prot (12%)	17 g Carb (71%)	2 g Fat (17%)	1 g Sugar
	3 g Fiber	63 mg Sodium	0 mg Chol	8 mg Calcium	

BLUEBERRY-SPELT MUFFINS (see p. 46)

Preparation Time: 15 minutes
Complexity: Easy

2 cups	**spelt flour**
½ cup	**cane sugar**
½ tsp	**salt**
2 tsp	**baking powder**
1½ cup	**soy milk**
3 tbsp	**olive or grapeseed oil**
1½ tsp	**Ener-G Egg Replacer powder** (dissolved in 2 tbsp water)
1 cup	**frozen blueberries**

1. Mix together dry ingredients. Make a well in the center.

2. Pour soy milk, oil, and egg replacer into the center well. Mix thoroughly.

3. Fold in blueberries.

4. Spray muffin tins with a nonstick spray, or line tins with muffin cups. Fill muffin tins two-thirds full with batter.

5. Bake at 400° F for 20 minutes or until golden brown.

CHEF'S TIP:

- May substitute whole-wheat pastry flour for spelt flour.

Makes: 1 dozen

PER 1 MUFFIN:	132 Calories	3 g Prot (9%)	21 g Carb (64%)	4 g Fat (27%)	6 g Sugar
	2 g Fiber	110 mg Sodium	0 mg Chol	90 mg Calcium	

MOM'S HOMEMADE BREAD (see p. 46)

Preparation Time: 25 minutes
Complexity: Intermediate

4 cups	warm water
2 tbsp	active dry yeast
1 tbsp	honey
1 tbsp	salt
4 cups	whole-wheat flour
½ cup	olive oil
2 tbsp	lecithin
2 tbsp	honey
3 tbsp	gluten flour
3 tbsp	lemon juice
¾ cup	flaxseed, ground fine
1 cup	quick-cooking oats
4-5 cups	whole-wheat flour

1. Mix water, yeast, and honey together in mixing bowl and let sit for 10 minutes.

2. Add salt, 4 cups of whole-wheat flour, oil, and lecithin. Blend in mixer on medium speed for 3 minutes.

3. Add remaining ingredients. Blend in mixer for 6 minutes. (Add enough flour so the dough is not sticky.)

4. Form into loaves and place into lightly oil-sprayed bread pans. Let sit in a warm place for 1 hour or until double in size.

5. Bake at 375° F for 15 minutes, then 325° F for 20 minutes or until golden brown.

6. Remove from pans and cool on racks.

Makes: 4 loaves (16 slices per loaf)

PER ½-INCH SLICE:	111 Calories	7 g Prot (22%)	15 g Carb (53%)	3 g Fat (25%)	1 g Sugar
	3 g Fiber	112 mg Sodium	0 mg Chol	18 mg Calcium	

DARK RYE BREAD

Preparation Time: 25 minutes
Complexity: Intermediate

2½ cups	very warm water
2 tbsp	molasses
1 tbsp	quick-rise baking yeast
¼ cup	gluten flour
1 tbsp	lemon juice
2 tbsp	carob powder
½ tsp	salt
3 cups	rye flour
3 cups	whole-wheat flour

1. In mixing bowl, combine first four ingredients. Mix well.

2. Add lemon juice, carob powder, salt, and rye flour. Mix well.

3. Add enough whole-wheat flour so dough is not sticky.

4. Knead dough by hand for about 8 minutes.

5. Prepare two lightly oil-sprayed bread pans.

6. Divide dough and shape into two loaves and place into pans.

7. Cover pans with a towel and set in a warm place until doubled in size.

8. Bake in a preheated oven at 375° F for about 30 minutes or until done.

Makes: 2 loaves (16 slices each)

PER ½-INCH SLICE:	119 Calories	4 g Prot (13%)	24 g Carb (81%)	1 g Fat (6%)	1 g Sugar
	4 g Fiber	52 mg Sodium	0 mg Chol	24 mg Calcium	

CRANBERRY-ORANGE BREAD

Preparation Time: 25 minutes
Complexity: Intermediate

3 cups	orange juice, unsweetened
1 tbsp	active baking yeast
1 tbsp	lemon juice
1 tbsp	gluten flour
½ tsp	salt
1 cup	pecans, chopped
1 cup	dried cranberries
3 cups	whole-wheat flour
4 cups	spelt, whole-wheat pastry, or unbleached white flour, as needed

1. Warm orange juice to above room temperature, but not hot. Place in a mixing bowl.
2. Sprinkle yeast into orange juice. Wait 10 minutes, or until yeast bubbles up to the surface.
3. Add remaining ingredients. Add enough flour so dough is not sticky.
4. Cover mixing bowl with a towel and set in a warm area. Allow dough to rise for about 1 hour or until doubled in size.
5. Knead dough and divide in half. Form each half into a round loaf and place on a baking sheet that has been prepared using a nonstick spray.
6. Cover loaves again with a towel and let stand for 20 minutes or until doubled in size.
7. Bake at 350° F for 30 minutes or until golden brown on top.
8. Cool bread on racks.

NOTE: These freeze well.

Makes: 2 loaves (16 slices per loaf)

PER ½ SLICE:	150 Calories	3 g Prot (8%)	28 g Carb (75%)	3 g Fat (17%)	2 g Sugar
	4 g Fiber	31 mg Sodium	0 mg Chol	12 mg Calcium	

CORN BREAD (see p. 78)

Preparation Time: 15 minutes
Complexity: Intermediate

1½ cups (10 oz, 300 g)	soft tofu, drained
3 tbsp	olive oil
1 tbsp	Ener-G Egg Replacer powder
½ tsp	salt
1 cup	cornmeal (uncooked)
1 cup (10 oz, 280 g)	cream-style corn, low sodium

1. Blenderize tofu, oil, and egg replacer powder until smooth.
2. Add blenderized ingredients to cornmeal in a bowl along with cream-style corn. Mix well.
3. Pour batter into a lightly oil-sprayed 9" x 9" glass baking dish.
4. Bake at 400° F for 30 minutes or until golden brown and set.
5. Allow to cool 5 to 10 minutes before serving.

CHEF'S TIPS:

- This corn bread has a very moist cake texture.
- Serve with *Chili 2* (p. 72) on top of cornbread.
- Make a homemade "cream-style" corn using 1 cup frozen kernel corn, 2/3 cup water, and 2 tbsp. cornstarch. Thicken on stove.

Serves: 9

PER 3-INCH-SQUARE PIECE:	129 Calories	4 g Prot (9%)	16 g Carb (49%)	6 g Fat (42%)	1 g Sugar
	1 g Fiber	137 mg Sodium	0 mg Chol	39 mg Calcium	

MULTIGRAIN BREAD (see p. 46)

Preparation Time: 25 minutes
Complexity: Intermediate

2 tbsp	quick-rise baking yeast
2½ cups	warm water
⅓ cup	honey
¾ tsp	salt
3 tbsp	olive oil
1 cup	wheat germ
1 cup	raw sunflower seeds
1 cup	rolled oats
½ cup	sesame seeds
5-6 cups	whole-wheat flour

1. Except for flour, mix all ingredients in large bowl.
2. Add 1 cup of flour at a time while mixing until dough is no longer sticky.
3. Let sit 10 minutes in a warm place.
4. Knead 10 minutes by hand, or in a mixing machine for about 5 minutes.
5. Shape dough into two loaves. Place into lightly oil-sprayed bread pans. Let sit in a warm place for 1 hour or until doubled in size.
6. Bake 30-35 minutes at 350° F until crust is brown.

CHEF'S TIP:

• For variation, try using rolled barley, spelt, or rye flakes in place of rolled oats.

Makes: 2 loaves

PER ½-INCH SLICE:	243 Calories	6 g Prot (15%)
	26 g Carb (68%)	3 g Fat (17%)
	3 g Sugar	4 g Fiber
	57 mg Sodium	0 mg Chol
	36 mg Calcium	

1. Strawberry Jam, *p. 65*
2. Bran Muffins, *p. 41*
3. Blueberry-Spelt Muffins, *p. 43*
4. Multigrain Bread, *p. 47*
5. Mom's Homemade Bread, *p. 44*
6. Apricot Jam, *p. 55*
7. Ron's Sweet Rolls, *p. 49*

OATMEAL-RAISIN BREAD

Preparation Time: 20 minutes
Complexity: Intermediate

2 tbsp	active dry yeast
½ cup	warm water
2 cups	hot water
¼ cup	honey
½ tsp	salt
¼ cup	olive oil
2 cups	whole rolled oats
¾ cup	raisins
¾ cup	golden raisins
3 cups	whole-wheat flour
2 tbsp	gluten flour
2-3 cups	unbleached white flour
1 tbsp	cinnamon (or substitute) (optional)

1. Dissolve yeast in water and allow to activate. Set aside.
2. Combine hot water, honey, salt, and oil. Cool to lukewarm.
3. Stir in oats, raisins, whole-wheat flour, and gluten flour.
4. Stir in yeast mixture.
5. Add remaining flour to make moderately stiff dough.
6. Turn dough out onto floured surface and knead until smooth.
7. Shape dough into a ball and cover with towel. Let rise in a warm place for about 1 hour or until doubled in size.
8. Spray two loaf pans with a nonstick spray.
9. Cut dough into two portions and shape each portion into a loaf. Place loaves into loaf pans. Cover again with towel and set in a warm place. Let rise about 1 hour or until doubled in size.
10. Bake at 350° F for 30-35 minutes or until golden brown.

Makes: 2 loaves (16 slices per loaf)

PER ½-INCH SLICE:	131 Calories	3 g Prot (9%)	26 g Carb (76%)	2 g Fat (15%)	7 g Sugar
	2 g Fiber	40 mg Sodium	0 mg Chol	19 mg Calcium	

POTATO FOCACCIA

Preparation Time: 30 minutes
Complexity: Intermediate

1 tsp	honey
½ cup	warm water
1 tbsp	active dry yeast
4 cups	spelt flour
1½ cups	whole-wheat flour
½ tsp	salt
1 cup	potato, cooked and mashed (save the water)

Optional Toppings:

sliced black olives, sun-dried tomatoes or sliced cherry tomatoes, minced fresh garlic, minced fresh onion, fresh or dried oregano and/or basil, herbal seasoning salt, olive oil

1. Dissolve honey in warm water. Sprinkle in yeast. Let stand 10 minutes
2. Add flour, salt, and mashed potatoes.
3. Add the "saved" potato water slowly while mixing until mixture forms a slightly sticky ball of dough.
4. Place in a bowl and cover with a towel. Let rise 45 minutes to 1 hour, or until doubled in size.
5. Punch dough down and form into a round ball. Flatten dough and place on a lightly greased pizza pan to about 1 inch in thickness.
6. Press toppings of your choice gently over the top of the dough. Sprinkle with herbal salt and drizzle some olive oil over the top, if desired.
7. Let rise in a warm place for 20 minutes.
8. Bake at 375° F for 20 minutes or until golden brown.

CHEF'S TIP:

• Serve with soup or stew. Cut into triangles to serve.

Serves: 8

PER 1 TRIANGLE:	307 Calories	10 g Prot (13%)	62 g Carb (81%)	2 g Fat (6%)	1 g Sugar
(without toppings)	11 g Fiber	146 mg Sodium	0 mg Chol	30 mg Calcium	

RON'S SWEET ROLLS (see p. 46)

(see p. 46)

Preparation Time: 40 minutes
Complexity: Advanced

1. Preheat oven to 350°F. Lightly oil-spray two (9" x 13") baking dishes.

2. Place dough ingredients in large mixing bowl. Let sit 10 minutes.

   DOUGH:

2 cups	warm water
1 tbsp	active dry yeast
1 tbsp	honey

3. Add:

½ tbsp	salt
2 cups	spelt flour or whole-wheat flour
¼ cup	olive oil
1 tbsp	gluten flour (optional)

4. Knead in a bread mixer for 3 minutes, or hand beat using a whisk for 5 minutes.

5. Add:

1 tbsp	honey
2 tbsp	lecithin
1 tbsp	lemon juice
1½ cups	unbleached white flour
2½ cups	spelt or whole-wheat flour

6. Mix in a bread mixer for 5 minutes, or hand knead for 10 min. Add enough flour so dough is not sticky.

7. Roll dough out into a large rectangle approximately ½ inch thick.

8. Sprinkle with filling:

2¼ cups	dates, chopped (rinse with hot water to soften, if needed)
2½ cups	apple, fresh, peeled and shredded
½ cup	pecans, chopped
1 tbsp	cinnamon or substitute

9. Roll up dough into a "log" shape.

10. Slice into 1-inch slices. Lay each piece flat in prepared baking dish.

11. Cover with a towel and place in a warm area.

12. Let rise for about 1 hour, or until doubled in size.

13. Bake at 350° F for 20-25 minutes or until golden brown.

CHEF'S TIP:
- These freeze well when stored in tightly sealed containers or plastic bags.

Makes: 2 dozen

PER 1 ROLL:	205 Calories	5 g Prot (8%)	37 g Carb (69%)	6 g Fat (23%)	13 g Sugar
	5 g Fiber	147 mg Sodium	0 mg Chol	22 mg Calcium	

OAT CRACKERS

Preparation Time: 20 minutes
Complexity: Intermediate

3 cups	quick-cooking oats
2 cups	whole-wheat pastry flour
1 cup	wheat germ
½ cup	olive oil
2 tbsp	honey (optional)
1¼ cups	water
½ tsp	salt

1. Place all ingredients in a mixing bowl and mix well.
2. Roll dough out on a baking sheet with rolling pin, keeping equal thickness throughout pan. (For thinner crackers, divide dough between two baking sheets.)
3. Cut dough into desired shape with a sharp knife, pizza cutter, or cookie cutter.
4. Sprinkle with herbs if desired.
5. Bake at 325° F for about 30 minutes or until golden brown.

CHEF'S TIP:
- You may wish to remove the outer crackers as they brown, allowing the middle crackers to bake longer.

Makes: 80 crackers (1¼" x 1½") each

PER 1 CRACKER:	32 Calories	1 g Prot (10%)	4 g Carb (46%)	2 g Fat (44%)	0 g Sugar
	1 g Fiber	19 mg Sodium	0 mg Chol	7 mg Calcium	

POCKET BREAD

Preparation Time: 30 minutes
Complexity: Intermediate

3 cups	warm water
2 tbsp	quick-rising yeast
2 tbsp	honey
½ cup	applesauce, unsweetened
½ tsp	salt
6 cups	whole-wheat flour
2 cups	unbleached white flour

1. Preheat oven to 550° F (or as high as your oven will go without broiling).
2. In a large mixing bowl, add water, yeast, honey, applesauce, and salt. Stir well.
3. Mix in whole wheat flour, then add 1 cup of unbleached flour at a time while kneading the dough until dough is no longer sticky.
4. Form dough into golf ball size or larger.
5. Roll each ball with a rolling pin until approximately ¼-inch thick.
6. Place on a lightly oil-sprayed cookie sheet. Raise for 10 minutes, then place in hot oven. Bake 3-5 minutes until they "puff up" and become golden brown. Let bread cool.
7. Cut with a sharp knife halfway around the side of each pocket bread.
8. Stuff each pocket with your favorite fillings, such as *Chili* (p. 72), fresh vegetables, *Mock Tuna* (p. 59), *Tofu Eggless Salad* (p. 67), or serve with hummus for dipping.

Serves: 12 (depending on size)

PER 1 LARGE 8-INCH POCKET:	289 Calories	5 g Prot (7%)	65 g Carb (90%)	1 g Fat (3%)	4 g Sugar
	8 g Fiber	100 mg Sodium	0 mg Chol	23 mg Calcium	

WHOLE-WHEAT BAGELS

Preparation Time: 50 minutes
Complexity: Advanced

3 tbsp	honey
2 cups	warm water
2 tbsp	active dry yeast
½ tsp	salt
5½ cups	whole-wheat flour

1. Dissolve honey in warm water. Sprinkle in yeast. Let stand for 5 minutes or until yeast bubbles up.

2. Add 2 cups of whole wheat flour. Beat well (1 minute in a bread mixer).

3. Add salt and enough flour to form a moderately stiff dough. Knead for 3 minutes in mixer.

4. Place in a lightly greased bowl. Cover and let rise for 15 minutes.

5. Fill a large pot with water. Heat until it boils.

6. Divide dough into 12 pieces and form each piece into a smooth ball. Punch your thumb into the middle of each ball and work dough into a smooth doughnut-shaped ring. Place on squares of lightly greased wax paper. Let rise 20 minutes.

7. Gently drop three of the rings into the boiling water. Cook for 3 minutes on each side. Remove from boiling water with a slotted spoon. Repeat the process with remaining bagels.

8. Transfer bagels to a lightly oil-sprayed baking sheet. Bake at 350° F for 25-30 minutes or until golden brown.

Variation: **Raisin Bagels**

Use *Whole Wheat Bagels* recipe and add 2 teaspoons cinnamon and ½ cup of raisins to batter when adding the first cup of flour. Follow procedure exactly as directed for whole wheat bagels.

CHEF'S TIP:

• When placing the bagel rings into the water, pick up the wax paper and allow the bagel to gently slide off to prevent handling it and causing the air to escape.

Makes: 1 dozen

Based on plain whole-wheat bagels.				
PER 1 BAGEL:	220 Calories	8 g Prot (14%)	45 g Carb (82%)	1 g Fat (4%)	5 g Sugar
	7 g Fiber	99 mg Sodium	0 mg Chol	21 mg Calcium	

Spreads, Sauces, and Condiments

Alfredo Sauce

Almond Cheese

Apricot Jam

Sweet-and-Sour Sauce

Bruschetta

Tofu Mayonnaise

Cheese Sauce

Chik-style Salad

Corn Butter

Gravy

Cranberry Sauce

Mock Tuna

Cream Cheese

Flaxseed Gel

Mushroom Gravy

Hummus 1, 2

Salsa

Ketchup

Strawberry Jam 1, 2

Bean Spread

Guacamole

Tofu Sour Cream

Tofu Eggless Salad

• Salsa, *p. 64*

53

ALFREDO SAUCE

Preparation Time: 15 minutes
Complexity: Easy

½ cup	cashew pieces
1¾ cups	water
1 tbsp	flour, unbleached white
1-3 tsp	chickenlike seasoning of your choice, to taste
½ tsp	oregano or basil
½ tsp	salt, to taste

1. Place all ingredients into a blender. Blend until smooth.
2. Pour mixture into a medium-sized pot. Simmer until thick and creamy. Add salt to taste if needed.
3. Toss over prepared fettuccine noodles. Serve immediately.

CHEF'S TIPS:

• This is such a quick and yet elegant dish that you'll be proud to serve it to company. Serve with steamed broccoli.

• Brown rice pasta is a nice choice. It is not as heavy and starchy as whole-wheat pasta can be.

Serves: 4

PER ¼-CUP SERVING:	79 Calories	3 g Prot (16%)	5 g Carb (26%)	5 g Fat (58%)	1 g Sugar
	1 g Fiber	293 mg Sodium	0 mg Chol	10 mg Calcium	

ALMOND CHEESE

Preparation Time: 15 minutes
Complexity: Intermediate

1 cup	hot water
2 tbsp	granulated agar (use more for a firmer cheese and less for a softer cheese if desired)
1 cup	almonds, slivered, blanched
1 tsp	salt
½ tsp	garlic powder
2 tbsp	nutritional yeast flakes
1 tsp	onion powder
1½ Tbsp	lemon juice
¼ cup	bell pepper, red, chopped

1. Blend together the hot water and granulated agar for a few seconds.
2. Add remaining ingredients. Blend until smooth.
3. Pour into a container or mold. Cover and refrigerate until firm.

CHEF'S TIPS:

• Lightly oil-spray the inside of the container or mold before pouring mixture into the container. This will make it simple to turn the cheese out onto a serving platter.

• When firm, cheese slices nicely for use in sandwiches or on crackers. It will melt when spread onto hot toast or bagels.

• Cheese freezes well.

• Freeze cheese prior to shredding.

Makes: 2½ cups

PER 1-TBSP SERVING:	28 Calories	1 g Prot (13%)	2 g Carb (32%)	2 g Fat (55%)	0 g Sugar
	1 g Fiber	57 mg Sodium	0 mg Chol	10 mg Calcium	

APRICOT JAM (see p. 46)

Preparation Time: 10 minutes
Complexity: Easy

1 cup	**apricots, dried**
1 cup	**pineapple juice**

1. Place dried apricots in a small bowl. Pour enough pineapple juice over the apricots just to cover them.

2. Allow apricots to soak in juice 2-3 hours or until they become soft and plump.

3. Drain apricots, reserving the juice, and place in a food processor. Process until smooth, adding reserved liquid until it reaches a thick yet spreadable jam consistency.

4. Chill jam before serving.

CHEF'S TIP:

• Freezes well.

Makes: 2 cups

PER 1-TBSP SERVING:	13 Calories	0 g Prot (5%)	3 g Carb (94%)	0 g Fat (1%)	3 g Sugar
	0 g Fiber	1 mg Sodium	0 mg Chol	2 mg Calcium	

SWEET-AND-SOUR SAUCE

Preparation Time: 15 minutes
Complexity: Easy

2 cups	**pineapple juice**
½ cup	***Ketchup*** (see p. 64)
2 tbsp	**tomato paste**
1 tbsp	**soy sauce, low-sodium** (or Bragg's All Purpose Seasoning)
1 tbsp	**honey**
1 tbsp	**lemon juice**
2 tbsp	**cornstarch**
¼ cup	**cold water**

1. Place all ingredients except cornstarch and cold water in a small saucepan.

2. Bring mixture to a boil.

3. Mix cornstarch in cold water. Add to saucepan mixture.

4. Stir constantly over medium heat until mixture has thickened.

5. Chill before serving.

CHEF'S TIPS:

• For ketchup, use a health food store brand or the homemade *Ketchup* (p. 64).
• Freezes well.
• Serve as a dipping sauce for spring rolls, or pour over veggies and tofu on rice.

Makes: 4 cups

Analysis is based on the use of homemade *Ketchup*.

PER ½-CUP SERVING:	59 Calories	0 g Prot (3%)	14 g Carb (97%)	0 g Fat (0%)	10 g Sugar
	0 g Fiber	83 mg Sodium	0 mg Chol	7 mg Calcium	

BRUSCHETTA (see p. 60)

Preparation Time: 15 minutes
Complexity: Easy

2	tomatoes, large, finely diced small
2 tbsp	basil, fresh minced
1-2	garlic cloves, minced
¼ tsp	salt
1 tbsp	olive oil (optional)

1. Combine all ingredients into a bowl. Mix well.
2. Cover; chill in refrigerator for 1 hour.
3. Drain excess liquid off if desired.
4. Spoon mixture onto lightly toasted slices of *Multigrain Bread* (p. 47), French bread, or buns just prior to serving.

CHEF'S TIP:

- This will keep for only approximately 1-2 days in the refrigerator, and tastes the nicest fresh.

Serves: 8

PER ¼-CUP SERVING:	8 Calories	0 g Prot (12%)	2 g Carb (79%)	0 g Fat (9%)	1 g Sugar
	1 g Fiber	67 mg Sodium	0 mg Chol	5 mg Calcium	

TOFU MAYONNAISE

Preparation Time: 15 minutes
Complexity: Easy

1 pkg (12 oz, 349 g)	tofu, silken, firm
½ cup	cashews, pieces
¼ cup	water
1 tbsp	lemon juice
¾ tsp	onion powder
½ tsp	garlic powder
½ tsp	salt

1. Blenderize all ingredients, except dill, until very smooth.
2. Pour mixture into a bowl, add dill, stir, and cover bowl.
3. Refrigerate to chill for a couple of hours to allow flavors to marinate before serving.
4. Use on sandwiches, buns, veggie burgers, or salads, or as a veggie dip.

CHEF'S TIP:

- Add 1 tbsp dried dill to mayonnaise for a nice variation.

Makes: 1½ cups

PER 1-TBSP SERVING:	37 Calories	2 g Prot (22%)	2 g Carb (22%)	2 g Fat (56%)	0 g Sugar
	0 g Fiber	54 mg Sodium	0 mg Chol	70 mg Calcium	

CHEESE SAUCE

Preparation Time: 20 minutes
Complexity: Easy

2 cups	water
¼ cup	pimento, chopped and unpickled, or roasted red peppers
2 tbsp	nutritional yeast flakes
½ tsp	salt
½ tsp	onion powder
¼ tsp	garlic powder
3 tbsp	cornstarch
1 cup	raw cashew pieces
1½ tbsp	lemon juice

1. Place all ingredients in a blender. Blend until smooth.

2. Pour mixture into a saucepan.

3. Cook over medium heat, stirring constantly until mixture becomes thick.

CHEF'S TIPS:
- Serve warm over pasta, steamed broccoli, or baked potatoes. Can also be served over baked corn chips for nachos topped with fresh diced tomatoes, chopped green onions, and sliced black olives.

- Refrigerate until firm to use as a "cheese spread."

Makes: 3 cups

PER ¼-CUP SERVING:	75 Calories	2 g Prot (10%)	6 g Carb (31%)	5 g Fat (59%)	1 g Sugar
	1 g Fiber	102 mg Sodium	0 mg Chol	6 mg Calcium	

CHIK-STYLE SALAD (see p. 60)

Preparation Time: 20 minutes
Complexity: Intermediate

2 cups	dry soy curls
½ cup	celery, finely chopped
½ cup	onions, finely chopped
¼ cup	parsley, fresh, or 2 tbsp parsley flakes
¼ cup	bell pepper, green, finely chopped
¼ cup	bell pepper, red, finely chopped
1 tsp	garlic powder
2 tsp	chickenlike seasoning of your choice, to taste
½ cup	Nasoya Nayonaise or *Tofu Mayonnaise* (p. 56)

1. Place soy curls in a bowl, cover with hot water, and soak for 10 minutes.

2. Drain soy curls and dice finely, or chop in a food processor. Place back in bowl.

3. Add remainder of ingredients and mix thoroughly.

4. Refrigerate. Serve as a sandwich filling or as a spread for crackers.

Serves: 8-12

PER ¼-CUP SERVING:	71 Calories	5 g Prot (28%)	6 g Carb (34%)	3 g Fat (38%)	1 g Sugar
	1 g Fiber	145 mg Sodium	0 mg Chol	20 mg Calcium	

CORN BUTTER

Preparation Time: 15 minutes
Complexity: Easy

¼ cup	cornmeal, dry
1 cup	water
2 tbsp	coconut, shredded, unsweetened
½ tsp	salt
½ cup	water
1 tbsp	nutritional yeast flakes

1. Simmer cornmeal in 1 cup water in a small pot on stove until soft and water is absorbed.

2. Blenderize hot cornmeal with remaining ingredients until very smooth.

3. Pour blended mixture into a container. Cover and chill until firm.

Variation: **Garlic Butter**

Add to the recipe and blend well—

1 tsp	garlic powder
	or
1-2	fresh garlic cloves

Stir in:

1 tbsp	parsley flakes

Pour mixture into container and chill, or use immediately by spreading onto bread slices, then toasting in the oven to make garlic toast.

Makes: 1½ cups

PER 2-TSP SERVING:	8 Calories	1 g Prot (10%)	1 g Carb (41%)	1 g Fat (49%)	0 g Sugar
	0 g Fiber	32 mg Sodium	0 mg Chol	0 mg Calcium	

GRAVY (see p. 126)

(see p. 126)

Preparation Time: 20 minutes
Complexity: Easy

4 cups	water
2 tbsp	olive oil (optional)
½ cup	whole-wheat flour
1-3 tbsp	chickenlike or beeflike seasoning of your choice, to taste
2 tbsp	Bragg's All Purpose Seasoning
	salt, to taste

1. Place all ingredients together in a saucepan. Whisk smooth to remove all lumps.

2. Bring to a boil, then simmer until thickened. Whisk occasionally to prevent lumping or burning.

3. Taste and adjust seasonings.

CHEF'S TIPS:

• Gravy, once made, freezes very well.

• Whole-wheat flour can be substituted with unbleached white flour.

Makes: 4 cups

PER ½-CUP SERVING:	32 Calories	3 g Prot (38%)	5 g Carb (68%)	0 g Fat (0%)	0 g Sugar
	1 g Fiber	120 mg Sodium	0 mg Chol	3 mg Calcium	

CRANBERRY SAUCE (see p. 126)

Preparation Time: 20 minutes
Complexity: Easy

1 cup	cranberries, frozen or fresh
½ cup	apple, shredded
1 cup	apple juice
1 tsp	cornstarch
3 tbsp	apple juice

1. Combine cranberries, shredded apple, and 1 cup apple juice in a medium-sized pot. Cook over medium temperature while stirring occasionally until mixture comes to a boil and berries have softened.

2. Dissolve cornstarch in 3 tablespoons apple juice. Add to the hot cranberry mixture.

3. Stir constantly and cook over medium heat until mixture returns to a boil. Simmer for about 1 minute or until cranberry mixture has thickened and turned to a clear red color.

4. Place cranberry sauce in a bowl and chill.

Makes: 2½ cups

PER ¼-CUP SERVING:	25 Calories	0 g Prot (1%)	6 g Carb (97%)	0 g Fat (2%)	4 g Sugar
	1 g Fiber	1 mg Sodium	0 mg Chol	3 mg Calcium	

MOCK TUNA

Preparation Time: 20 minutes
Complexity: Easy

1½ cups	garbanzo beans, cooked
1 tbsp	Bragg's All Purpose Seasoning
½ cup	parsley, chopped fine
½ cup	green onions, chopped fine
¼ cup	nutritional yeast flakes
½ cup	bell pepper, green, chopped fine
½ cup	bell pepper, red, chopped fine
1 cup	celery, chopped fine
½ cup	Nasoya Nayonaise or *Tofu Mayonnaise* (see p. 56)
½ tsp	kelp powder (optional)

1. In a bowl using a potato masher, or in a food processor, mash garbanzo beans. (Do not over-mash; should resemble a "flaked" texture.)

2. Add remaining ingredients to mashed garbanzo beans and mix well.

3. Chill in refrigerator. Serve on sandwiches or use on crackers or rice cakes.

CHEF'S TIP:

• Adding the kelp powder will give it a more distinctive "fishy" flavor. Kelp powder can be found at a natural food store.

Serves: 9 (may vary depending on how it is served)

Analysis based on the use of *Tofu Mayonnaise*.				
PER ½-CUP SERVING:	103 Calories	6 g Prot (23%)	13 g Carb (50%)	3 g Fat (27%)	1 g Sugar
	4 g Fiber	96 mg Sodium	0 mg Chol	29 mg Calcium	

CREAM CHEESE

Preparation Time: 15 minutes
Complexity: Easy

1 tbsp	agar powder
½ cup	hot water
½ cup	cashew pieces
¾ tsp	salt
1½ tbsp	lemon juice
½ pkg	tofu, medium/firm
(16 oz, 454 g)	

1. Place all ingredients into a blender and blend until smooth.

2. Pour mixture into a mold or container that has been sprayed with a nonstick spray for easy removal. Refrigerate until set.

3. Use as a spread for crackers, bagels, or use in recipes that call for "cream cheese."

Variation:

- Add ½ teaspoon onion powder and chopped green onions to blended mixture. Stir gently, then pour into mold or container.

Makes: 2 cups

PER 1-TBSP SERVING:	42 Calories	3 g Prot (29%)	1 g Carb (10%)	3 g Fat (61%)	0 g Sugar
	0 g Fiber	56 mg Sodium	0 mg Chol	49 mg Calcium	

1. Creamy Cucumber Dressing, *p. 96*
2. Bruschetta, *p. 56*
3. Chik-style Salad, *p. 57*
4. Tofu Eggless Salad, *p. 67*

61

FLAXSEED GEL

Preparation Time: 15 minutes
Complexity: Easy

2 cups	water
6 tbsp	flaxseeds, whole

1. Bring water to a boil in a medium saucepan.
2. Add flaxseeds. Boil for 5 minutes.
3. Remove from heat and immediately pour through a fine-mesh strainer into a bowl.
4. The gel in the bowl is to be used as an egg substitute in recipes for binding, such as "meatloafs" or patties. Use ¼ cup for each egg called for in a recipe. This gel will keep for approximately 1 week in your refrigerator. You may either discard the flaxseeds or use in your bread recipes.

Makes: 1½ cups (equivalent to approximately 6-8 eggs)

PER ¼-CUP SERVING:	48 Calories	2 g Prot (15%)	3 g Carb (26%)	3 g Fat (59%)	0 g Sugar
	0 g Fiber	6 mg Sodium	0 mg Chol	21 mg Calcium	

MUSHROOM GRAVY

Preparation Time: 25 minutes
Complexity: Easy

1	garlic clove, minced
½ cup	onions, chopped
2 cups	mushrooms, fresh sliced
4 cups	soy milk, plain
1 tbsp	Bragg's All Purpose Seasoning
3 tbsp	whole-wheat flour
½ tsp	salt, to taste

1. In a medium-sized pot, sauté garlic, onions, and mushrooms in a little water until soft.
2. Add remaining ingredients. Whisk in flour to prevent lumping.
3. Simmer 5-10 minutes until thickened.

Makes: 5 cups

PER ¼-CUP SERVING:	34 Calories	3 g Prot (24%)	4 g Carb (52%)	1 g Fat (24%)	1 g Sugar
	1 g Fiber	143 mg Sodium	0 mg Chol	100 mg Calcium	

HUMMUS 1

Preparation Time: 15 minutes
Complexity: Easy

2 cups	**garbanzo beans, cooked**
1 tsp	**tahini** (sesame butter)
1 tsp	**sesame oil**
1½ tbsp	**lemon juice**
¼ cup	**parsley, chopped**
¼ tsp	**garlic powder**
¼ cup	**green onions, chopped**
½ cup	**bell peppers, green, chopped** (optional)
	garbanzo liquid as needed

1. Place all ingredients into a blender and blend until smooth. Add enough liquid to make a thick spread.
2. Serve on toast.

Makes: 2 cups

PER ¼-CUP SERVING:	80 Calories	4 g Prot (19%)	13 g Carb (59%)	2 g Fat (22%)	1 g Sugar
	4 g Fiber	5 mg Sodium	0 mg Chol	27 mg Calcium	

HUMMUS 2

Preparation Time: 15 minutes
Complexity: Easy

2 cups	**garbanzo beans, cooked or canned**
	garbanzo liquid (as needed)
3-4 tbsp	**lemon juice**
2	**garlic cloves**
⅓ cup	**tahini** (sesame butter)
1 tsp	**onion powder**
¼-½ tsp	**salt, to taste**

1. Combine all ingredients in food processor or blender, and blend until very smooth. Add liquid as needed.
2. Taste. Add additional lemon juice, onion powder, garlic, or salt if desired.
3. Serve as dip for pita bread and veggies, or serve on bread or with *Falafels* (p. 122).

Makes: 3 cups

PER ¼-CUP SERVING:	82 Calories	4 g Prot (18%)	8 g Carb (40%)	4 g Fat (42%)	1 g Sugar
	3 g Fiber	115 mg Sodium	0 mg Chol	29 mg Calcium	

SALSA (see p. 52)

Preparation Time: 10 minutes
Complexity: Easy

1 can (16 oz)	**tomatoes, undrained and chopped**
1-2 tbsp	**green chilies, canned, diced**
½ cup	**bell pepper, green, finely chopped**
½ cup	**onions, finely chopped**
1	**tomato, ripe, large, peeled and chopped**
1-2 tbsp	**lemon juice**
½ tsp	**salt**
½ tsp	**oregano**
¼ tsp	**basil flakes**

1. Combine all ingredients in a bowl.
2. Stir well.

CHEF'S TIP:

• Use salsa as a dip, relish, salad dressing, or baked potato topping.

Makes: 3 cups

PER ¼-CUP SERVING:	20 Calories	1 g Prot (20%)	4 g Carb (80%)	0 g Fat (0%)	3 g Sugar
	1 g Fiber	172 mg Sodium	0 mg Chol	26 mg Calcium	

KETCHUP

Preparation Time: 10 minutes
Complexity: Easy

1 cup	**tomato sauce**
1 can (5.5 oz, 154g)	**tomato paste**
2 tbsp	**lemon juice**
2 tbsp	**honey**
½ tsp	**basil, crushed**
½ tsp	**garlic powder**
1 tsp	**onion powder**
½ tsp	**salt**

1. Combine all ingredients in a small bowl. Stir well.
2. Chill.

CHEF'S TIPS:

• Ketchup keeps for 1 week in the refrigerator; it freezes well.

• Purchase low-sodium or no-salt-added tomato sauce.

• Aside from its food coloring and preservatives, commercial ketchup is higher in sugar, ounce for ounce, than ice cream!

Makes: 2 cups

PER 1-TBSP SERVING:	11 Calories	0 g Prot (8%)	3 g Carb (89%)	0 g Fat (3%)	2 g Sugar
	0 g Fiber	118 mg Sodium	0 mg Chol	4 mg Calcium	

STRAWBERRY JAM 1 (see p. 46)

Preparation Time: 10 minutes
Complexity: Easy

2 cups	**strawberries, frozen**
1 cup	**pineapple, dried pieces**

1. Place dried pineapple into a medium-sized bowl.
2. Place strawberries over the top of the pineapple and allow to thaw at room temperature for a few hours. (Allow enough time for the juice of the fruit to soften the pineapple.)
3. Place mixture in a food processor and process until smooth.
4. Allow jam to set in refrigerator, or use immediately as a topping for waffles or pancakes.

Variation:

• Substitute raspberries, blueberries, or your choice of frozen fruit in place of the strawberries.

CHEF'S TIP:

• This jam will keep 1-2 weeks in the refrigerator, but also it freezes very well.

Makes: 2 ½ cups

PER 1-TBSP SERVING:	13 Calories	0 g Prot (4%)	3 g Carb (90%)	0 g Fat (6%)	3 g Sugar
	0 g Fiber	0 mg Sodium	0 mg Chol	0 mg Calcium	

STRAWBERRY JAM 2

Preparation Time: 20 minutes
Complexity: Easy

1 cup	**dates**
1 can (20 oz)	**pineapple, chunks**
4 cups	**strawberries, frozen, unsweetened**
3 tbsp	**cornstarch**
½ cup	**cold water**

1. Blenderize dates, pineapple, and one third of the strawberries.
2. Pour mixture into a medium-sized pot.
3. Mix 3 tablespoons cornstarch in water.
4. Add cornstarch mixture to blended fruit in pot.
5. Cook over medium heat while stirring constantly until mixture comes to a boil, thickens, and turns clear in color.
6. Slice remaining strawberries and place in a bowl.
7. Remove sauce from stove and pour over remaining strawberries. Stir gently.
8. Chill in refrigerator.

CHEF'S TIPS:

• Use as jam, or as a topping on waffles and pancakes.
• This jam freezes well.

Makes: 7 cups

PER 1-TBSP SERVING:	9 Calories	0 g Prot (2%)	2 g Carb (94%)	0 g Fat (4%)	2 g Sugar
	0 g Fiber	1 mg Sodium	0mg Chol	0 mg Calcium	

BEAN SPREAD

Preparation Time: 15 minutes
Complexity: Easy

2 cups	**kidney beans, cooked**
¾ cup	**celery, chopped fine**
1 tsp	**onion powder**
1 tsp	**garlic powder**
¼ cup	**onions, chopped fine**
½ cup	**Nasoya Nayonaise or *Tofu Mayonnaise*** (p. 56)

1. Mash beans using a potato masher or food processor.
2. Stir in remaining ingredients and mix well.
3. Cover bowl, and place in refrigerator to chill. Use as a spread on sandwiches, crackers, or rice cakes.

CHEF'S TIP:

- Substitute different varieties of beans, such as pinto, white navy, or black beans.

Serves: 6

PER ¼-CUP SERVING:	130 Calories	8 g Prot (24%)	18 g Carb (56%)	3 g Fat (20%)	1 g Sugar
	6 g Fiber	88 mg Sodium	0 mg Chol	48 mg Calcium	

GUACAMOLE

Preparation Time: 15 minutes
Complexity: Easy

1	**avocado, large ripe**
1-2 tbsp	**lemon juice**
1 tsp	**garlic powder**
	or
1	**fresh, small clove garlic**
½ tsp	**onion powder**
	salt to taste
1 tbsp	**salsa** (optional)

1. Cut the avocado in half and remove the pit. Then, using a spoon, remove avocado from skin.
2. Blend avocado in food processor until smooth.
3. Stir in remaining ingredients.
4. Serve immediately.

CHEF'S TIPS:

- Guacamole tends to turn brown when exposed to the air. To prevent this, store with the pit. Serve as a dip for baked nachos or use on tacos, burritos, or *Rice Stacks* (p. 125).
- For a more "chunky" guacamole, mash avocado using a fork instead of the food processor.

Serves: 4

PER ¼-CUP SERVING:	86 Calories	1 g Prot (5%)	5 g Carb (21%)	7 g Fat (74%)	1 g Sugar
	3 g Fiber	4 mg Sodium	0 mg Chol	8 mg Calcium	

Spreads, Sauces, and Condiments

TOFU SOUR CREAM

Preparation Time: 15 minutes
Complexity: Easy

1 pkg	**tofu, silken, firm**
(12 oz, 349 g)	
½ cup	**cashews, pieces, raw**
½ cup	**water**
½ tsp	**salt**
¼–½ tsp	**garlic powder**
¾ tsp	**onion powder**
1–2 tbsp	**lemon juice**

1. Place all ingredients into a blender.
2. Blend until very smooth. Pour into a bowl, cover, then chill in the refrigerator for a few hours before serving to allow flavors to marinate.

CHEF'S TIP:
• Replace salt with a favorite seasoning salt for a different flavor.

Makes: 1½ cups

PER 1-TBSP SERVING:	31 Calories	2 g Prot (18%)	2 g Carb (21%)	2 g Fat (61%)	0 g Sugar
	0 g Fiber	54 mg Sodium	0 mg Chol	70 mg Calcium	

TOFU EGGLESS SALAD (see p. 60)

Preparation Time: 10 minutes
Complexity: Easy

1 pkg	**tofu, firm water-packed package**
(12 oz, 349 g)	
1 tbsp	**lemon juice**
1 tsp	**Spike seasoning** (with salt)
¼ tsp	**garlic powder**
¼ tsp	**onion powder**
¼ tsp	**paprika**
2 tsp	**mustard, yellow, prepared** (optional)
2 tbsp	**Nasoya Nayonaise or Tofu Mayonnaise** (p. 56)

1. Drain and rinse tofu.
2. Place tofu in a bowl, then mash really well with a fork until you achieve the look of mashed egg.
3. Add remaining ingredients and mix well. Add additional Nayonaise or mayonnaise if you desire.
4. Chill mixture 1 hour prior to serving. Serve on buns or bread.

CHEF'S TIPS:
• Serve with lettuce, dill pickles, and black olives.
• May substitute yellow prepared mustard with 3/4 teaspoon ground mustard seed powder.

Serves: 6

PER ½-CUP SERVING:	68 Calories	5 g Prot (30%)	3 g Carb (18%)	4 g Fat (52%)	0 g Sugar
	1 g Fiber	53 mg Sodium	0 mg Chol	201 mg Calcium	

Soups and Stews

Potato Soup

Butternut Squash Soup

Condensed Celery Soup

Condensed Mushroom Soup

Chili

Pasta Chili

Cream of Broccoli Soup

Creamy Carrot Soup

Quinoa Soup

Borscht

Easy Lentil Soup

Hearty Mediterranean Soup

Squash Stew

Barley-Tomato Vegetable Soup

Minestrone Soup

Spanish Gazpacho Soup

Split Pea Soup 1, 2

Zucchini Soup 1, 2

Tuscan Bean Soup

Vegetable Stew

Corn Chowder

Pumpkin Soup

• Butternut Squash Soup, *p. 70*

POTATO SOUP

Preparation Time: 30 minutes
Complexity: Intermediate

2 cups	onions, chopped
5	garlic cloves, minced
10 cups	water
8 cups	potatoes, cubed (5-6 medium)
½ tsp	Spike seasoning, salt-free
½ tsp	thyme
2-6 tbsp	chickenlike season- ing of your choice, to taste
1 tsp	basil
½ tsp	salt, to taste

1. Sauté onions and garlic in a little water in a large pot, until softened.

2. Add measured amount of water to pot along with cubed potatoes.

3. Add seasonings and simmer until potatoes are soft.

4. Blend soup mixture until smooth in a blender. Add salt to taste.

5. Heat soup thoroughly before serving.

CHEF'S TIP:

• Garnish with a sprinkle of finely minced fresh basil.

Serves: 10

PER 1-CUP SERVING:	148 Calories	4 g Prot (10%)	35 g Carb (90%)	0 g Fat (0%)	1 g Sugar
	3 g Fiber	195 mg Sodium	0 mg Chol	16 mg Calcium	

BUTTERNUT SQUASH SOUP (see p. 68)

Preparation Time: 25 minutes
Complexity: Intermediate

2 cups	butternut squash, cooked and mashed
1 cup	onions, chopped
1-2 tbsp	chickenlike season- ing of your choice, to taste
2 cups	water
2 cups	potato, diced
⅛ tsp	thyme
½ cup	cashew pieces
2 cups	water
½ tsp	salt, to taste

1. Cook and mash butternut squash, then set aside.

2. In a large pot, sauté onions in a little water until soft.

3. Add to pot chickenlike seasoning, 2 cups water, potato, and thyme. Cook until potato is soft.

4. Place hot mixture into a blender, and blend until smooth. Return mixture to pot.

5. Place cashews and 2 cups water into the blender. Blend until it becomes a very smooth milk.

6. Add cashew milk and squash to pot. Add salt to taste.

7. Heat over low temperature, stirring occasionally, until desired temperature is achieved. Serve immediately.

CHEF'S TIPS:

• To cook squash: wash squash and cut in half lengthwise. Scrape out seeds and pulp. Lay cut sides down in baking dish side by side. Add water until it covers ½ inch in the bottom of dish. Cover dish. Bake at 350° F or microwave until squash is soft. Scoop squash out using a spoon.

• Garnish with a dash of nutmeg or cardamom.

Serves: 6

PER 1-CUP SERVING:	150 Calories	4 g Prot (9%)	25 g Carb (67%)	4 g Fat (24%)	3 g Sugar
	3 g Fiber	228 mg Sodium	0 mg Chol	48 mg Calcium	

CONDENSED CELERY SOUP

Preparation Time: 25 minutes
Complexity: Intermediate

3 cups	celery, chopped
½ cup	onions, chopped
2 cups	water
1½ cups	nondairy milk
3 tbsp	cornstarch
2 tbsp	whole-wheat flour
2 tbsp	unbleached white flour
¾-2 tsp	chickenlike seasoning of your choice, to taste
½ tsp	salt, to taste

1. Cook celery and onions in 2 cups of water.
2. Place two thirds of cooked celery and onions in blender with remaining ingredients.
3. Blend until smooth. Add remaining cooked celery and onions. Blend only 2 seconds, just to break pieces up.
4. Pour mixture into a medium saucepan. Bring to a boil over medium heat, stirring constantly. Boil 2 minutes.
5. Divide into three containers (1¼ cups each) and freeze. Use in recipes in place of commercial condensed celery soup.

CHEF'S TIP:
- Add soy milk or water to desired consistency when making into soup. Add salt to taste.

Makes: 3 1¼-cup portions
Serves: 6 if eaten as a soup

PER ½-CUP SERVING: (condensed)	62 Calories	3 g Prot (15%)	11 g Carb (70%)	1 g Fat (15%)	2 g Sugar
	1 g Fiber	233 mg Sodium	0 mg Chol	104 mg Calcium	

CONDENSED MUSHROOM SOUP

Preparation Time: 25 minutes
Complexity: Intermediate

1½ cups	mushrooms, chopped fresh
½ cup	onions, finely chopped
1½ cups	nondairy milk
1 cup	water
¾-2 tsp	chickenlike seasoning of your choice, to taste
½ tsp	salt, to taste
1 tsp	basil flakes
4 tbsp	spelt or whole-wheat flour
3 tbsp	cornstarch

1. In a small pot, saute mushrooms and onions in a little water until soft.
2. Reserve one third of sauteed mixture.
3. Put all ingredients in blender, using only two thirds of mushroom-and-onion mixture. Blend until smooth.
4. Add the reserved mushrooms and onions, and blend for a couple of seconds.
5. Pour mixture into a medium-sized pot and cook over medium heat until thickened, stirring frequently to keep from burning.
6. Divide into three containers (1¼ cups each) and freeze. Use in recipes in place of commercial condensed mushroom soup.

CHEF'S TIP:
- Add soy milk to desired consistency when making into soup. Add salt to taste.

Makes: 3 1¼-cup portions
Serves: 6 if eaten as a soup

PER ½-CUP SERVING: (condensed)	58 Calories	3 g Prot (16%)	10 g Carb (69%)	1 g Fat (15%)	1 g Sugar
	1 g Fiber	212 mg Sodium	0 mg Chol	98 mg Calcium	

CHILI (see p. 78)

Preparation Time: 25 minutes
Complexity: Easy

2 cups	onion, diced
4	garlic cloves, minced
1 cup	bell pepper, green, diced
1 cup	corn, whole-kernel
2 cups	ground gluten or vegetarian "ground burger" substitute
2 cups	black beans, home-cooked or 1 can (19 oz), rinsed
2 cups	beans, mixed variety, home-cooked or 1 can (19 oz), rinsed
1 can (28 oz, 748 g)	tomatoes, diced, plain or seasoned
2 cups	tomato sauce, low sodiium
½ tsp	chili powder, to taste
	salt, to taste

1. In a large pot, sauté onions, garlic, and green pepper in a little water until soft.

2. Add remaining ingredients. Simmer until flavors are well blended. Add salt to taste.

CHEF'S TIPS:

• Serve in a bowl with some whole-grain bread, or use as a topping for rice or baked potatoes.

• Garnish with a sprig of fresh parsley.

Serves: 12 cups

Analysis based on the use of ground gluten.

PER 1-CUP SERVING:	183 Calories	14 g Prot (27%)	27 g Carb (58%)	3 g Fat (15%)	4 g Sugar
	8 g Fiber	460 mg Sodium	0 mg Chol	46 mg Calcium	

PASTA CHILI

Preparation Time: 25 minutes
Complexity: Easy

2 cups	onions, chopped
3	garlic cloves, minced
1 cup	ground gluten or TVP granules (rehydrated using hot water)
3 cups	kidney beans, cooked, unsalted
1 can (28 oz)	tomatoes, pureed
1 can (28 oz)	tomatoes, diced
3 cups	water
2 cups	pasta, whole-grain elbow
½ tbsp	chili powder
½ tsp	salt, to taste

1. In a large pot, sauté onions and garlic in a little water until soft.

2. Add remaining ingredients. Simmer until pasta is done.

CHEF'S TIPS:

• Serves well with *Corn Bread* (p. 45).

• Garnish with a sprig of fresh parsley.

Serves: 16 cups

PER 1-CUP SERVING:	161 Calories	9 g Prot (24%)	29 g Carb (74%)	1 g Fat (2%)	4 g Sugar
	6 g Fiber	366 mg Sodium	0 mg Chol	62 mg Calcium	

CREAM OF BROCCOLI SOUP (see p. 78)

Preparation Time: 30 minutes
Complexity: Intermediate

4 cups	broccoli, washed and cut into bite-sized pieces
1-2 tbsp	chickenlike season-ing of your choice, to taste
½ tsp	salt, to taste
4 cups	water
2 cups	soy milk (or cashew milk) (see p. 158)
4 tbsp	unbleached white flour (or 3 tbsp whole-wheat flour)

1. Place broccoli, chickenlike seasoning, salt and water into a medium-sized pot. Cover pot and simmer over medium heat until tender.
2. Remove two thirds of the broccoli from broth using a slotted spoon, and place in a blender.
3. Add soy milk and flour to broccoli in blender. Blenderize until smooth.
4. Using a potato masher, mash the broccoli left in the pot with broth.
5. Pour the blended mixture back into the pot.
6. Stir soup constantly while soup thickens and heats through.
7. Add salt to taste if desired.

CHEF'S TIP:
  • Garnish with croutons.

Serves: 9 cups

PER 1-CUP SERVING:	43 Calories	3 g Prot (24%)	6 g Carb (56%)	1 g Fat (20%)	0 g Sugar
	0 g Fiber	226 mg Sodium	0 mg Chol	99 mg Calcium	

CREAMY CARROT SOUP

Preparation Time: 30 minutes
Complexity: Intermediate

4 cups	carrots, peeled (or well scrubbed) and sliced
1-2 tbsp	chickenlike season-ing of your choice, to taste
½ tsp	salt, to taste
3 cups	water
1½ cups	onions, chopped
3 tbsp	unbleached white flour (or 2 tbsp whole-wheat flour)
3 cups	nondairy milk

1. Combine carrots, chickenlike seasoning, salt, water, and onions in a large pot. Cook until vegetables are tender.
2. Place hot vegetables and broth into a blender. Add flour.
3. Blend until very smooth. Return mixture to pot.
4. Bring to a boil over medium-high heat. Simmer until thick-ened. Stir constantly.
5. Add soy milk.
6. Heat through, but do not boil. Serve immediately.

CHEF'S TIP:
  • Garnish with a thin slice of curled carrot on a small sprig of fresh dill.

Serves: 9 cups

PER 1-CUP SERVING:	86 Calories	5 g Prot (20%)	14 g Carb (63%)	2 g Fat (17%)	4 g Sugar
	3 g Fiber	271 mg Sodium	0 mg Chol	58 mg Calcium	

QUINOA SOUP

Preparation Time: 25 minutes
Complexity: Easy

10 cups	water
3 cups	carrots, sliced
2 cups	zucchini, sliced
2 cups	onions, chopped
2 cups	celery, chopped
3 cups	cabbage, green, shredded
1 cup	string beans, green, cut
1 cup	quinoa, washed in a fine-mesh strainer
3	garlic cloves, minced
1 tsp	crushed basil
2-5 tbsp	chickenlike seasoning of your choice, to taste
½ tsp	salt, to taste

1. Place all ingredients into a large soup pot. Stir well.

2. Simmer for approximately 30 minutes, or until vegetables are tender and quinoa has swelled.

3. Serve hot.

CHEF'S TIPS:
- Stir in fresh chopped basil just prior to serving.
- Garnish with a fresh basil leaf.

Serves: 16 cups

PER 1-CUP SERVING:	90 Calories	5 g Prot (22%)	16 g Carb (70%)	0 g Fat (8%)	3 g Sugar
	3 g Fiber	115 mg Sodium	0 mg Chol	41 mg Calcium	

BORSCHT

Preparation Time: 30 minutes
Complexity: Intermediate

10 cups	water
1-3 tbsp	beeflike seasoning of your choice, to taste
2 cups	onions, chopped
2	garlic cloves, minced
4 cups	beets, coarsely grated or diced small
1½ cups	carrots, coarsely grated or diced small
1 cup	celery, diced
3 cups	potatoes, diced small
4 cups	cabbage, green, shredded
2 cups	tomatoes, diced
1 tbsp	lemon juice
1 tbsp	Bragg's All Purpose Seasoning

1. Bring water to a boil in a large pot.

2. Add seasoning, onions, garlic, beets, carrots, and celery. Simmer 15 minutes.

3. Add potatoes. Cook for another 10 minutes.

4. Add cabbage, tomatoes, lemon juice, and Bragg's seasoning. Simmer until vegetables are tender. Add salt to taste.

CHEF'S TIPS:
- To make a cream soup, blenderize ½ cup of raw cashews and 1 cup water until smooth. Add to soup. Heat to serve.
- Garnish with a dollop of *Tofu Sour Cream* (p. 67).
- Add 2 tbsp of fresh, minced dill just prior to serving.

Serves: 20 cups

PER 1-CUP SERVING:	60 Calories	10 g Prot (31%)	10 g Carb (66%)	0 g Fat (3%)	5 g Sugar
	3 g Fiber	75 mg Sodium	0 mg Chol	36 mg Calcium	

EASY LENTIL SOUP

Preparation Time: 15 minutes
Complexity: Easy

2½ cups	lentils, brown/green
4	green onions, chopped
1 cup	celery, chopped fine
1	bay leaf
10 cups	water
1 cup	carrots, diced
1½ cups	potatoes, diced
½ tsp	Mrs. Dash seasoning
1-3 tbsp	chickenlike seasoning of your choice, to taste
1 tsp	salt, to taste
1 tbsp	lemon juice

1. Sort and rinse lentils.

2. Combine all ingredients except lemon juice in a 5- to 6-quart slow cooker. Cover and cook on low 12 to 14 hours, or on high for 8 to 10 hours.

3. Remove bay leaf. Just before serving, stir in lemon juice. Taste and adjust seasoning.

CHEF'S TIP:
- Garnish with fresh chives, diced tomato, and a leaf of fresh basil.

Serves: 18 cups

PER 1-CUP SERVING:	101 Calories	8 g Prot (31%)	18 g Carb (67%)	0 g Fat (2%)	2 g Sugar
	9 g Fiber	210 mg Sodium	0 mg Chol	26 mg Calcium	

HEARTY MEDITERRANEAN SOUP

Preparation Time: 20 minutes
Complexity: Easy

1 cup	lentils, red, washed
2 cups	onions, chopped
2	garlic cloves, minced
½ tsp	ginger powder
½ tsp	paprika
3 cups	water
1-3 tbsp	beeflike seasoning of your choice, to taste
1 can (28 oz)	tomatoes, diced
2 cups	garbanzo beans, cooked (or 1 can [19 oz], drained)
½ tsp	oregano
1 tsp	crushed basil

1. In a colander, rinse and drain dry lentils.

2. Place all ingredients into a large pot. Bring to a boil, then reduce heat to a simmer. Simmer covered 30-40 minutes or until lentils are done.

3. Season with salt to taste if desired. Simmer uncovered for 5-10 minutes.

4. Serve hot.

CHEF'S TIP:
- Garnish with a sprig of fresh oregano or a couple small leaves of fresh basil.

Serves: 8 cups

PER 1-CUP SERVING:	193 Calories	10 g Prot (21%)	36 g Carb (75%)	1 g Fat (4%)	5 g Sugar
	8 g Fiber	30 mg Sodium	0 mg Chol	76 mg Calcium	

SQUASH STEW

Preparation Time: 30 minutes
Complexity: Easy

1 (8 cups)	**winter squash, large** (remove seeds and stringy pulp; peel and cube)
4 cups	**water**
5 cups	**water**
1 cup	**onions, chopped**
1½ cups	**potato, peeled and diced**
1	**garlic clove, minced**
1½ cups	**lentils, brown**
½ cup	**peas, frozen**
½ tsp	**thyme**
1 tsp	**basil**
½ tsp	**salt**
½ tsp	**garlic powder**
1 tbsp	**Bragg's All Purpose Seasoning**

1. Cook squash in 4 cups water in a partially covered pot.

2. Mash cooked squash with a potato masher, then set aside.

3. In another pot, bring 5 cups water to a boil. Add onions, potato, garlic, and lentils. Cook until soft.

4. Add cooked and mashed squash to the pot of cooked lentils and veggies.

5. Stir in peas and seasonings. Simmer until heated through.

CHEF'S TIPS:

• Serves well with whole-wheat pita bread.

• You may use your favorite squash in this recipe. Changing the type of squash will change the color and the flavor of the stew.

• Garnish with fresh sprig of parsley.

Serves: 16 cups

PER 1-CUP SERVING:	107 Calories	7 g Prot (26%)	19 g Carb (71%)	0 g Fat (3%)	3 g Sugar
	7 g Fiber	107 mg Sodium	0 mg Chol	39 mg Calcium	

BARLEY-TOMATO VEGETABLE SOUP

Preparation Time: 20 minutes
Complexity: Easy

2	**garlic cloves, minced**
1 cup	**onions, red, diced small**
1 cup	**celery, finely diced**
6 cups	**water**
2 cups	**potatoes, finely diced**
½ cup	**barley, pearl**
2 cups	**carrots, coarsely grated**
½ tsp	**basil, crushed**
½ tsp	**garlic powder**
1 tbsp	**parsley flakes**
2 tsp-2 tbsp	**chickenlike seasoning of your choice, to taste**
½ tsp	**salt, to taste**
1 can (15-24 oz)	**tomato sauce**

1. In a large pot, saute garlic, onions, and celery in a little water until soft.

2. Add water, potatoes, and barley. Simmer for 20 minutes.

3. Add remaining ingredients. Simmer for 10 more minutes.

4. Serve hot.

CHEF'S TIPS:

• Garnish with ¼ cup of fresh minced parsley just prior to serving.

• Works well in a slow cooker on high, 5 to 6 hours (low, 10 to 12 hours). Add herbs and tomato sauce after soup is cooked, to preserve the fresh herb flavors.

Serves: 15 cups

PER 1-CUP SERVING:	54 Calories	2 g Prot (9%)	12 g Carb (88%)	0 g Fat (3%)	3 g Sugar
	2 g Fiber	286 mg Sodium	0 mg Chol	22 mg Calcium	

MINESTRONE SOUP

Preparation Time: 30 minutes
Complexity: Easy

10 cups	water
1 cup	onions, chopped
1	garlic clove, minced
¾ cup	celery, diced
2 cups	carrots, diced
1 cup	potatoes, diced
1 cup	cabbage, shredded
1 cup	string beans, french-cut
1 cup	elbow noodles, rice, brown or whole-wheat
1 cup	peas
2 cups	navy or kidney beans, cooked or canned
1 can (28 oz)	tomatoes, diced
1½ tsp	basil
1 tsp	parsley flakes
1	bay leaf
½ tsp	salt, to taste
2-6 tbsp	beeflike seasoning of your choice, to taste

1. Bring water to a boil in a large pot.
2. Add onions, garlic, celery, carrots, and potatoes. Simmer for 10 minutes.
3. Add remaining ingredients and simmer, partially covered, for 30 minutes or until vegetables are tender. (Add more liquid if needed.)
4. Serve hot.

CHEF'S TIP:

• Garnish with a sprig of fresh curly parsley.

Serves: 20 cups

PER 1-CUP SERVING:	83 Calories	4 g Prot (14%)	16 g Carb (75%)	1 g Fat (11%)	3 g Sugar
	4 g Fiber	171 mg Sodium	0 mg Chol	39 mg Calcium	

SPANISH GAZPACHO SOUP

This is a refreshing cold soup!
Preparation Time: 25 minutes
Complexity: Intermediate

2 cups	tomatoes, chopped
1 cup	zucchini, chopped
½ cup	celery, chopped
4 cups	tomato juice (no salt added)
1 cup	cucumber, peeled and chopped
1	garlic, clove, minced
½ cup	green onions, chopped
¼ cup	bell pepper, green, chopped
1 cup	green chili salsa, canned
	lime juice, to taste
	salt, to taste

Garnish:
lime slices and fresh parsley

1. Combine chopped tomatoes, zucchini, and celery in a bowl. Mix well.

2. Transfer one third of this mixture to a blender, add a little tomato juice, and puree.

3. Pour the pureed vegetables back into the bowl and mix in remaining ingredients.

4. Chill soup in the refrigerator.

5. Serve garnished with lime slices and fresh parsley.

CHEF'S TIP:

• To reduce sodium content, use a low-sodium tomato juice.

Serves: 8 cups

PER 1-CUP SERVING:	46 Calories	2 g Prot (17%)	9 g Carb (73%)	0 g Fat (10%)	6 g Sugar
	3 g Fiber	23 mg Sodium	0 mg Chol	29 mg Calcium	

1. Corn Chowder, *p. 83*
2. Chili, *p. 72*
3. Cream of Broccoli Soup, *p. 73*
4. Corn Bread, *p. 45*

SPLIT PEA SOUP 1

Preparation Time: 30 minutes
Complexity: Easy

1 cup	peas, green, split, dry
6 cups	water
1½ cups	onions, diced
2 cups	celery, diced
2 cups	carrots, diced
2 tsp-2 tbsp	chickenlike seasoning of your choice, to taste
¾ tsp	basil, crushed
½ tsp	salt, to taste

1. Wash split peas using a colander.
2. In a medium-large pot, bring water to a boil. Add all ingredients.
3. Bring to a boil, then simmer until split peas and vegetables are tender.
4. Pour hot soup into a blender and blend until very smooth. Return to pot.
5. Add salt to taste. Heat through.
6. Serve with whole-grain crackers.

CHEF'S TIPS:
- This is a very filling and satisfying soup when served with a slice of bread.
- Garnish with a fresh leaf of basil and a thin slice of carrot curled.

Serves: 6 cups

PER 1-CUP SERVING:	181 Calories	12 g Prot (27%)	31 g Carb (69%)	1 g Fat (4%)	7 g Sugar
	11 g Fiber	218 mg Sodium	0 mg Chol	62 mg Calcium	

SPLIT PEA SOUP 2

Preparation Time: 30 minutes
Complexity: Easy

6 cups	water
1 cups	peas, green, split, dry
¼ cup	barley, whole-grain
1 cup	onions, sauteed
1	bay leaf
1½ cups	potato, chopped
1½ cups	carrot, chopped
1 cup	celery, chopped
1 tsp	thyme
⅓ cup	parsley, chopped
1 tsp	basil
½ tsp	salt, to taste

1. Place water, split peas, barley, onions, and bay leaf into a Crock-Pot. Cook until almost done.
2. Add remaining ingredients and cook another 45-60 minutes. Add water if necessary, and salt.

CHEF'S TIPS:
- Leftovers become firm when cold. Can be used for sandwich spread or as a potato topping.
- Garnish with a fresh leaf of basil and a thin slice of carrot curled.

Serves: 6 cups

PER 1-CUP SERVING:	205 Calories	12 g Prot (23%)	37 g Carb (72%)	1 g Fat (5%)	8 g Sugar
	14 g Fiber	166 mg Sodium	0 mg Chol	78 mg Calcium	

ZUCCHINI SOUP 1

Preparation Time: 25 minutes
Complexity: Intermediate

4 cups	zucchini, sliced
½ cup	onions, chopped
3 cups	water
1-2½ tbsp	chickenlike seasoning of your choice, to taste
½ tsp	basil, crushed
1 cup	water
¾ cup	cashew pieces
½ tsp	salt, to taste

1. Sauté zucchini and onions in a little water in a large pot until tender.
2. Add 3 cups water, chickenlike seasoning, and basil. Cook 15 minutes over medium heat.
3. Place soup into a blender and blend smooth. Return blended mixture to pot.
4. Place 1 cup water and cashews into a blender. Blend until very smooth. Add to soup in pot.
5. Season with salt. Heat through, but do not boil.

CHEF'S TIPS:
- Do not skin the zucchini, unless it is very ripe and the skin is tough. The skin will add extra color and nutrients.
- Garnish with a thin slice of fresh zucchini and a small leaf of fresh basil.

Serves: 9 cups

PER 1-CUP SERVING:	120 Calories	4 g Prot (14%)	8 g Carb (27%)	9 g Fat (59%)	2 g Sugar
	1 g Fiber	199 mg Sodium	0 mg Chol	21 mg Calcium	

ZUCCHINI SOUP 2

Preparation Time: 25 minutes
Complexity: Intermediate

6 cups	zucchini, cubed
2 cups	potatoes, unpeeled, chunked
1 cup	onions, chopped
1	large garlic clove, quartered
2-4 tbsp	chickenlike seasoning of your choice, to taste
2 cups	water
1 tsp	salt, to taste
½ tsp	basil, crushed
½ tsp	Mrs. Dash seasoning
½ cup	tofu/soy milk powder
½ tsp	dill
¼ tsp	paprika
¼ cup	fresh chives

1. Place zucchini, potatoes, onions, and garlic in a large soup kettle.
2. Dissolve chickenlike seasoning in 2 cups of water and pour over vegetables in pot.
3. Cover pot and cook for 8-10 minutes or until the vegetables are tender.
4. Puree the cooked vegetables in a blender along with liquid stock, tofu/soy milk powder, and herbs (except chives) until smooth.
5. Return mixture to soup kettle and heat until hot enough to serve.
6. Pour soup into bowls and garnish with fresh chives.

Serves: 9 cups

PER 1-CUP SERVING:	57 Calories	3 g Prot (19%)	10 g Carb (65%)	1 g Fat (16%)	3 g Sugar
	2 g Fiber	354 mg Sodium	0 mg Chol	105 mg Calcium	

TUSCAN BEAN SOUP

Preparation Time: 25 minutes
Complexity: Easy

1½ cups	onions, chopped
2-3	garlic cloves, minced
2 cups	carrots, thinly sliced
4 cups	rutabaga or turnip, peeled and sliced into strips (¼ inch thick, 1 inch long)
4 cups	cabbage, green shredded
2 cans (16 oz)	lima beans, drained
1 can (28 oz)	tomatoes, diced with juice
6 cups	water
2-6 tbsp	beeflike seasoning of your choice, to taste
1 tbsp	parsley flakes

1. In a large pot, saute onions and garlic in a little water over medium heat until translucent.

2. Add carrots and turnips. Cook for 3 minutes.

3. Stir in remaining ingredients and bring to a boil.

4. Cover and simmer for about 25 minutes or until vegetables are tender.

5. Add salt to taste if desired.

CHEF'S TIP:

- Garnish with a sprig of fresh parsley.

Serves: 24 cups

PER 1-CUP SERVING:	65 Calories	3 g Prot (19%)	12 g Carb (75%)	0 g Fat (6%)	3 g Sugar
	4 g Fiber	80 mg Sodium	0 mg Chol	47 mg Calcium	

VEGETABLE STEW

Preparation Time: 25 minutes
Complexity: Easy

5 cups	water
1 cup	TVP granules or chunks
3 cups	potatoes, diced
3 cups	carrots, diced
1½ cups	onions, diced
2 cups	celery, diced
½ cup	flour, unbleached white or whole-wheat
1 cup	water
1½ cups	peas, frozen
2-4 tbsp	beeflike seasoning of your choice, to taste
2 tsp	basil, crushed

1. Bring 5 cups water to a boil in a large pot.

2. Add TVP, potatoes, carrots, onions, and celery. Simmer partially covered until vegetables are tender.

3. Whisk together flour and 1 cup water. Slowly pour into vegetable soup mixture while stirring.

4. Add peas, seasonings, and salt to taste if desired.

5. Simmer stew until thickened and heated through.

CHEF'S TIPS:

- Serves well with whole-grain biscuits.
- Substitute kidney beans for the TVP granules or chunks.

Serves: 16 cups

PER 1-CUP SERVING:	125 Calories	10 g Prot (32%)	20 g Carb (66%)	0 g Fat (2%)	3 g Sugar
	6 g Fiber	60 mg Sodium	0 mg Chol	37 mg Calcium	

CORN CHOWDER (see p. 78)

Preparation Time: 40 minutes
Complexity: Intermediate

4	corn, large ears (or 3 cups canned "salt free" or frozen whole-kernel corn)
6 cups	water, or reserved "corn water"
3 cups	potatoes, peeled and cut into 1-inch cubes
1 cup	potatoes, finely chopped
1¼ cups	carrots, finely diced
1½ cups	onions, diced
2	bay leaves
½ tsp	garlic powder
¼ cup	fresh parsley, minced
2-4 tbsp	chickenlike seasoning of your choice, to taste
½ tsp	salt, to taste

1. Boil corn on the cob in a large pot until done. Reserve water from corn. Scrape corn off of the cob.
2. Measure out 6 cups of reserved water, and place in a pot. Add 3 cups of the diced potatoes. Simmer until potatoes are cooked.
3. Scoop potatoes out of the pot with a little of the broth and place in a blender. Blend until smooth. Pour back into pot.
4. Add finely diced potatoes, carrots, onions, and seasonings.
5. Simmer over low heat until vegetables are tender.
6. Add corn and salt. Heat through. Remove bay leaves. Serve.

CHEF'S TIPS:
• For a "creamier" soup, add 1 cup soy milk or cashew milk to soup when adding the corn. Heat soup through, but ***do not boil.***
• Garnish with a sprig of fresh parsley.

Serves: 16 cups

PER 1-CUP SERVING:	82 Calories	2 g Prot (9%)	19 g Carb (86%)	0 g Fat (5%)	2 g Sugar
	2 g Fiber	100 mg Sodium	0 mg Chol	11 mg Calcium	

PUMPKIN SOUP

Preparation Time: 25 minutes
Complexity: Intermediate

1½ cups	onions, chopped
3 cups	potatoes (3 medium-sized), **peeled and diced**
4 cups	water
1½-4 tbsp	chickenlike seasoning of your choice, to taste
½ tsp	thyme
1 tsp	basil
2 cups	pumpkin, cooked and mashed, unsalted
1 cup	nondairy milk
½ tsp	salt, to taste

1. In a large pot, add onions, potatoes, water, and seasonings. Bring to a boil, then simmer, partially covered until potatoes and onions are soft.
2. Blenderize hot potato mixture until smooth. Return mixture to pot.
3. Add cooked pumpkin, soy milk, and salt.
4. Heat through, but do not boil. Serve.

CHEF'S TIP:
• Serve hot soup in a cleaned-out pumpkin shell as a soup tureen. Make a lid using the cut-off circular portion of the pumpkin (including the stem as a handle) to cover the tureen and keep the soup warm. Cut a small square out of the edge of the lid to allow the soup ladle handle to remain in the pumpkin tureen for serving.

Serves: 8½ cups

PER 1-CUP SERVING:	59 Calories	2 g Prot (12%)	12 g Carb (82%)	1 g Fat (6%)	2 g Sugar
	2 g Fiber	223 mg Sodium	0 mg Chol	73 mg Calcium	

Salads and Dressings

SALADS
Bean Salad

Tabouli Salad

Black Bean Mexican Salad

Bok Choy Salad

California Lettuce Salad

Squash Slaw

Cauliflower Salad

Coleslaw

Greek Salad 1, 2

Mandarin Orange Salad

Pasta Veggie Salad

Quinoa Salad

Potato Salad

Quinoa and Bean Sprout Salad

Vegetable Pasta Salad

Spinach Salad

DRESSINGS
Creamy Cucumber Dressing

French Dressing

Greek Salad Dressing

Garlic Omega Dressing

Gourmet Salad Dressing

Italian Dressing

Onion Veggie Dip

Thousand Island Dressing

Zestful Lemon-Dill Dressing

• Quinoa Salad, *p. 93*

BEAN SALAD (see p. 92)

Preparation Time: 15 minutes
Complexity: Easy

1 can (16 oz)	cut beans, yellow
1 can (16 oz)	cut beans, green
1 can (16 oz)	kidney beans
1 can (16 oz)	garbanzo beans
½ cup	bell pepper, green, finely diced
½ cup	bell pepper, red, finely diced
½ cup	celery, finely diced
¼ cup	parsley, minced (optional)
½ cup	onions, finely diced
⅓ cup	lemon juice
3 tbsp	olive oil
½ tsp	salt

1. Drain and rinse beans.
2. Mix beans, peppers, celery, parsley, and onions together in a salad bowl.
3. In a separate small bowl, mix together lemon juice, olive oil, and salt.
4. Pour dressing over bean mixture and mix thoroughly.
5. Marinate in refrigerator a couple of hours before serving.

CHEF'S TIP:
• You may choose to use 1½-cup measurements of home-cooked beans in place of the canned beans.

Serves: 8

PER ¾-CUP SERVING:	128 Calories	5 g Prot (15%)	16 g Carb (50%)	5 g Fat (35%)	2 g Sugar
	6 g Fiber	104 mg Sodium	0 mg Chol	51 mg Calcium	

TABOULI SALAD
A Middle Eastern Favorite

Preparation Time: 20 minutes
Complexity: Easy

1 cup	bulgur wheat, uncooked
2 cups	boiling water
4	tomatoes, finely diced
1	cucumber, finely diced
1 cup	parsley, finely chopped
3 tbsp	mint, fresh, chopped (or 2 tsp dry mint)
¼ tsp	garlic powder
½ cup	lemon juice
½ cup	green onions, chopped
1 cup	cooked garbanzos

1. Three hours before mealtime, place uncooked bulgur wheat in a bowl and pour boiling water over it.
2. Cover bulgur with clean towel and soak for 1 hour. Drain well.
3. Stir in the remaining ingredients, mix well, add salt to taste if desired. Chill for 1-2 hours.
4. Serve as a grain dish or salad. Leftovers can be added to soups or stuffed into pita (pocket) bread.

CHEF'S TIPS:
• For those who find it hard to digest uncooked wheat, sprout it! In this recipe, just skip the soaking of bulgur wheat and begin with the cup of sprouted wheat.
• Served chilled, this nutritious dish is ideal for hot days. Can be prepared ahead of time.

Serves: 6

PER 1-CUP SERVING:	93 Calories	4 g Prot (18%)	17 g Carb (73%)	1 g Fat (9%)	4 g Sugar
	3 g Fiber	14 mg Sodium	0 mg Chol	45 mg Calcium	

BLACK BEAN MEXICAN SALAD

Preparation Time: 20 minutes
Complexity: Easy

1½ cups	black beans, drained and rinsed
8 cups	spinach, fresh baby
1 cup	tomato, yellow or red, diced
½ cup	onions, white, finely chopped
1 cup	bell pepper, orange diced
1½ cups	jicama, peeled and diced
½ cup	TVP granules
1 cup	avocado, diced

1. Rehydrate TVP using enough hot water to just cover the dry granules.

2. Toss all ingredients together in a salad bowl.

3. Serve fresh with homemade *Thousand Island Salad Dressing* (p. 99), *Garlic Omega Dressing* (p. 97), *French Dressing* (p. 96), or one of your favorite dressing.

CHEF'S TIPS:

- For a tasty option, add some taco seasoning to the rehydrated TVP before mixing into salad.
- Delightful served with multigrain garlic toast.

Serves: 8

PER 2-CUP SERVING:	135 Calories	8 g Prot (22%)	17 g Carb (51%)	4 g Fat (27%)	1 g Sugar
	8 g Fiber	35 mg Sodium	0 mg Chol	50 mg Calcium	

BOK CHOY SALAD

Preparation Time: 20 minutes
Complexity: Easy

1	bok choy, large (8 cups)
2 cups	mung bean sprouts
½ cup	sunflower seeds
1 cup	pea pods, fresh
Dressing:	
¼ cup	olive oil
2 tbsp	water
2 tbsp	lemon juice
1 tbsp	maple syrup
½ tsp	garlic powder, or 1 clove fresh garlic minced

1. Wash and finely chop bok choy, including the green leaves and the white stock. Place chopped bok choy in a large salad bowl.

2. Wash mung beans using a colander. Place in salad bowl.

3. Add sunflower seeds.

4. Wash pea pods, and cut into halves or thirds. Add to salad.

5. Mix together ingredients for dressing in a separate small bowl. Mix well.

6. Pour dressing over salad and toss well just prior to serving.

CHEF'S TIP:

- Salad is nicest when chopped fine or shredded.

Serves: 12

PER 1-CUP SERVING:	73 Calories	2 g Prot (7%)	5 g Carb (26%)	6 g Fat (67%)	3 g Sugar
	1 g Fiber	6 mg Sodium	0 mg Chol	49 mg Calcium	

CALIFORNIA LETTUCE SALAD

Preparation Time: 15 minutes

Complexity: Easy

1	butter lettuce, large head, torn into bite-sized pieces
2	tomatoes, large chopped
½ cup	avocado, cubed
½ cup	watercress sprouts
1	cucumber, peeled and thinly sliced
½ cup	onions, purple, finely chopped
4 tbsp	parsley, finely chopped

1. Toss all ingredients together in a large salad bowl.
2. Drizzle salad with a dressing of your choice.

Serves: 6

PER 1-CUP SERVING:	47 Calories	2 g Prot 11%	6 g Carb (50%)	2 g Fat (39%)	2 g Sugar
	3 g Fiber	9 mg Sodium	0 mg Chol	33 mg Calcium	

SQUASH SLAW

Preparation Time: 25 minutes

Complexity: Intermediate

4 cups	spaghetti squash, coarsely grated
½ cup	carrots, coarsely grated
¼ cup	bell pepper, red, finely diced

Dressing:

1 tbsp	olive oil
2 tbsp	water
1 tsp	lemon juice
1 tsp	maple syrup
¼ tsp	Spike seasoning (with salt)
¼ tsp	ginger powder

1. In a salad bowl, toss squash, carrot, and red pepper. Chill in refrigerator until ready to serve.
2. In a small bowl, whisk together dressing ingredients well.
3. Mix dressing into salad prior to serving.

Serves: 6

PER ¾-CUP SERVING:	60 Calories	1 g Prot (6%)	7 g Carb (47%)	3 g Fat (47%)	1 g Sugar
	2 g Fiber	42 mg Sodium	0 mg Chol	20 mg Calcium	

CAULIFLOWER SALAD

Preparation Time: 20 minutes
Complexity: Easy

1	**bell pepper, green, finely chopped**
1	**cauliflower, medium head, cut into bite-sized pieces**
1 can (2 oz)	**black olives, sliced**
pinch	**Mrs. Dash**
1	**garlic clove, minced**
¼ tsp	**salt, to taste**
2 tbsp	**lemon juice**
1 tbsp	**olive oil** (optional)
1 cup	**tofu, silken, soft** (lite)

1. Toss together green pepper, cauliflowerets, and olives in a bowl.

2. Blend together Mrs. Dash, garlic, salt, lemon juice, oil (if desired), and tofu in a blender until smooth.

3. Pour blended dressing over cauliflower mixture and toss.

Serves: 8

PER 1-CUP SERVING:	44 Calories	3 g Prot (25%)	6 g Carb (50%)	1 g Fat (25%)	3 g Sugar
	3 g Fiber	149 mg Sodium	0 mg Chol	32 mg Calcium	

COLESLAW

Preparation Time: 20 minutes
Complexity: Intermediate

4 cups	**cabbage, green, shredded**
4 cups	**cabbage, red, shredded**
2 cups	**carrots, coarsely grated**
2 tbsp	**sesame seeds**
1 tbsp	**dill, dry**
⅔ cup	*Tofu Mayonnaise* (p. 56) **or Nasoya Nayonaise** (commercial)
¼ cup	**nondairy milk**

1. Place cabbage, carrots, sesame seeds, and dill in a salad bowl. Toss well.

2. Mix mayonnaise with nondairy milk. Pour over salad. Mix well. (Add additional tofu/soy milk to dressing if needed so salad is not dry.)

CHEF'S TIP:

• For a more tangy flavor, add 1 tbsp lemon juice.

Serves: 10

PER 1-CUP SERVING	88 Calories	4 g Prot (18%)	9 g Carb (41%)	4 g Fat (41%)	4 g Sugar
	3 g Fiber	58 mg Sodium	0 mg Chol	47 mg Calcium	

GREEK SALAD 1 (see p. 92)

Preparation Time: 20 minutes
Complexity: Easy

3 cups	tomatoes, chopped into ½-inch pieces
3 cups	cucumber, English, chopped into ½-inch pieces
2 cups	bell peppers, red, yellow, or orange, diced into ½-inch pieces
1 cup	black olives, large, pitted
1½ cups	onions, red, thinly sliced rings
1 pkg (16 oz, 454 g)	tofu, extra-firm, cubed into ½-inch pieces

Dressing:

3 tbsp	olive oil
2 tbsp	water
¼ cup	lemon juice
½ tsp	oregano
¼ tsp	thyme
½ tsp	garlic powder
¼ tsp	salt

1. Mix together dressing ingredients. Pour dressing over cubed tofu in a bowl, and marinate 2-3 hours.

2. Place prepared tomato, cucumber, peppers, olives, and onions, into a salad bowl. Toss gently.

3. Pour dressing with tofu onto salad and mix gently. Chill in refrigerator ½ hour prior to serving.

Serves: 10

PER 1-CUP SERVING:	149 Calories	8 g Prot (19%)	10 g Carb (25%)	10 g Fat (56%)	3 g Sugar
	3 g Fiber	186 mg Sodium	0 mg Chol	338 mg Calcium	

GREEK SALAD 2

Preparation Time: 20 minutes
Complexity: Easy

½	onion, red
3	tomatoes, roma
½	romaine lettuce, medium head
½	bell pepper, green, large
½	long cucumber
½	garlic clove, minced
½ cup	garbanzos
12	olives, Greek
1 cup	*Greek Salad Dressing* (p. 96)

1. Chop all ingredients except garbanzos and olives.

2. Place all ingredients into a salad bowl.

3. Add dressing and mix well.

Serves: 6

PER 1-CUP SERVING:	84 Calories	2 g Prot (10%)	13 g Carb (56%)	3 g Fat (34%)	5 g Sugar
	5 g Fiber	79 mg Sodium	0 mg Chol	31 mg Calcium	

MANDARIN ORANGE SALAD

Preparation Time: 20 minutes
Complexity: Easy

8 cups	romaine lettuce, large head, chopped
1 cup	green onions, sliced
1 can (8 oz)	mandarin oranges, drained
¼ cup	almonds, sliced, lightly toasted

Dressing:

3 tbsp	olive oil
3 tbsp	lemon juice
2 tsp	honey
1 tsp	parsley flakes

1. Mix dressing ingredients together well. Set aside in refrigerator.
2. Toss together lettuce, green onions, mandarin oranges, and almonds.
3. Toss salad with dressing. Serve immediately.

CHEF'S TIP:
- To add a festive touch, add some pomegranate seeds.

Serves: 8

PER 1-CUP SERVING:	128 Calories	2 g Prot (6%)	12 g (37%) Carb	8 g Fat (57%)	6 g Sugar
	3 g Fiber	8 mg Sodium	0 mg Chol	44 mg Calcium	

PASTA VEGGIE SALAD (see p. 92)

Preparation Time: 25 minutes
Complexity: Easy

3 cups	radiatore or shell pasta
2 cups	cauliflower, cut into small pieces
2 cups	broccoli, cut into small pieces
1 cup	carrots, grated
1½ cups	bell pepper, red, chopped
1½ cups	bell pepper, yellow, chopped
¼ cup	green onions, chopped
3 tbsp	almonds, sliced, lightly roasted

Dressing:

2 tbsp	olive oil
2 tbsp	water
¼ cup	lemon juice
¾ tsp	dill, dry
½ tsp	garlic powder
1 tsp	Spike seasoning (with salt)
1 tsp	maple syrup (optional)

1. Cook pasta in boiling water for about 10 minutes or until tender but firm. Drain. Rinse in cold water. Drain well. Place into a large bowl.
2. Place cauliflower, broccoli, carrots, and peppers in a pot with a small amount of water. Bring water to a boil, then drain quickly. Rinse vegetables in cold water. Drain well. Add to bowl with pasta.
3. Add chopped green onions and sliced almonds to pasta and vegetables. Toss together.
4. Mix dressing ingredients in a small bowl. Whisk well with fork.
5. Pour dressing over pasta salad and mix well.

Serves: 10

PER 1-CUP SERVING:	143 Calories	6 g Prot (15%)	20 g Carb (55%)	5 g Fat (30%)	2 g Sugar
	4 g Fiber	116 mg Sodium	0 mg Chol	36 mg Calcium	

QUINOA SALAD (see p. 84)

Preparation Time: 25 minutes
Complexity: Intermediate

1½ cups	**quinoa**
2½ cups	**water**

Add to cooled quinoa:

½ cup	**green onions, sliced**
2 oz	**black olives, sliced**
1½ cups	**tomato, diced small**
1½ cups	**cucumber, English, diced small**
1½ cups	**bell peppers, red, green, yellow**

Dressing:

2-3 tbsp	**olive oil**
3 tbsp	**lemon juice, to taste**
½ tsp	**garlic powder**
1 tsp	**salt, to taste**

1. Rinse quinoa under faucet using a fine-mesh colander.

2. In a medium-sized pot, bring water to a boil. Add quinoa.

3. Cover and simmer approximately 15 minutes until water is absorbed.

4. Remove from heat; allow to cool. Add remaining ingredients to cooled quinoa. Chill.

5. Mix together dressing ingredients thoroughly.

6. Toss over salad.

7 Allow salad to marinate 30 minutes in refrigerator before serving.

CHEF'S TIP:

• Serve with whole-grain pita bread and hummus for a great meal!

Serves: 8

PER 1-CUP SERVING:	166 Calories	5 g Prot (9%)	24 g Carb (59%)	6 g Fat (32%)	1 g Sugar
	3 g Fiber	374 mg Sodium	0 mg Chol	36 mg Calcium	

1. Pasta Veggie Salad, *p. 91*
2. Greek Salad 1, *p. 90*
3. Bean Salad, *p. 86*

POTATO SALAD

Preparation Time: 25 minutes
Complexity: Intermediate

6 cups	**potatoes, peeled and diced**
2 cups	**sweet potatoes, diced**
1 cup	**green onions, sliced**
1 cup	**radishes, sliced**
1 cup	**carrots, coarsely grated**
1 tsp	**dill, dry**
½ tsp	**salt, to taste**
¾ cup	***Tofu Mayonnaise*** (p. 56)

1. Prepare potatoes by washing, peeling, and dicing.
2. Boil potatoes until tender but not mushy. Chill potatoes in a salad bowl in the refrigerator.
3. To the chilled potatoes, add onions, radishes, carrots, dill, and salt to taste if desired.
4. Mix in enough salad dressing to make salad moist.
5. Chill salad thoroughly before serving.

CHEF'S TIPS:
- You may substitute a commercial mayonnaise in place of the tofu mayonnaise. Nayonaise and Vegenaise are good choices.
- For extra fiber, leave skins on the potatoes. Red potatoes are a nice choice for extra color.

Makes: 12 cups

PER 1-CUP SERVING:	159 Calories	3 g (8%) Prot	30 g Carb (75%)	3 g Fat (17%)	4 g Sugar
	5 g Fiber	142 mg Sodium	0 mg Chol	33 mg Calcium	

QUINOA AND BEAN SPROUT SALAD

Preparation Time: 25 minutes
Complexity: Intermediate

1 cup	**quinoa**
2 cups	**water**
4 cups	**mung bean sprouts**
⅓ cup	**green onions, sliced**
¼ cup	**pine nuts, lightly toasted**

Dressing:

3 tbsp	**Bragg's All Purpose Seasoning**
1 tbsp	**sesame oil**
1 tbsp	**lemon juice**
1 tsp	**maple syrup**
½ tsp	**garlic powder**

1. Wash quinoa very well under faucet using a fine-mesh colander or sieve.
2. In a medium-sized pot, bring water to a boil. Add quinoa.
3. Cover and simmer for 15 minutes until water is absorbed.
4. Remove from heat. Chill in refrigerator.
5. Add mung bean sprouts, green onions, and pine nuts to chilled quinoa.
6. In a small bowl, whisk together dressing ingredients.
7. Pour dressing over salad and toss gently.
8. Serve immediately.

Serves: 8

PER 1-CUP SERVING:	143 Calories	6 g Prot (15%)	20 g Carb (53%)	5 g Fat (32%)	2 g Sugar
	3 g Fiber	175 mg Sodium	0 mg Chol	24 mg Calcium	

VEGETABLE PASTA SALAD

Preparation Time: 30 minutes
Complexity: Intermediate

3 cups	spiral or shell pasta (whole-grain)
2 cups	carrots, sliced thin diagonally
1 cup	celery, sliced thin diagonally
1 cup	onions, red, sliced into thin rings
2 cups	broccoli, cut into bite-sized pieces
2 cups	cauliflower, cut into bite-sized pieces
½ cup	peas, cooked
1 cup	kidney beans, cooked
1 cup	*French Dressing* (p. 96)

1. Cook pasta until tender, then drain and rinse. Chill in refrigerator.
2. Steam raw carrots, broccoli, and cauliflower in a little water until tender yet crisp, approximately 3-4 minutes. Drain and rinse vegetables immediately with cold water.
3. In a salad bowl, mix together pasta, steamed vegetables, and remaining ingredients. Mix well. Chill in refrigerator.
4. Mix 1 cup or desired amount of *French Dressing* on pasta salad prior to serving.

Serves: 12

Analysis includes the use of *French Dressing*.

PER 1-CUP SERVING	118 Calories	5 g Prot (17%)	20 g Carb (68%)	2 g Fat (15%)	1 g Sugar
	5 g Fiber	65 mg Sodium	0 mg Chol	36 mg Calcium	

SPINACH SALAD

Preparation Time: 20 minutes
Complexity: Easy

8 cups	spinach, fresh baby
2 cups	mung bean sprouts
1 cup	bell pepper, orange, thinly sliced
1 cup	bell pepper, yellow, thinly sliced
2 cups	jicama, peeled and diced into ¼-inch cubes
3 tbsp	pine nuts

1. Prepare vegetables by washing and cutting them.
2. In a salad bowl or on individual salad plates, layer ingredients in the order listed.
3. Serve with your favorite dressing if desired.

Variation:
• May substitute sunflower seeds for pine nuts.

Serves: 7

PER 2-CUP SERVING:	79 Calories	3 g Prot (15%)	10 g Carb (50%)	3 g Fat (35%)	3 g Sugar
	4 g Fiber	31 mg Sodium	0 mg Chol	47 mg Calcium	

CREAMY CUCUMBER DRESSING (see p. 60)

Preparation Time: 10 minutes
Complexity: Easy

1 cup	tofu, silken, firm (lite)
1	garlic clove, small, chopped
½ cup	cucumber, peeled and cubed
2 tsp	lemon juice
1 tbsp	dill weed
¼ tsp	salt, or to taste

1. Place all ingredients into a blender or food processor and blend until very smooth.

2. Pour dressing into a serving container and chill in refrigerator at least 1 hour before serving.

Makes: 1½ cups

PER 1 TBSP:	3 Calories	0 g Prot (47%)	0 g Carb (37%)	0 g Fat (16%)	0 g Sugar
	0 g Fiber	27 mg Sodium	0 mg Chol	6 mg Calcium	

FRENCH DRESSING

Preparation Time: 10 minutes
Complexity: Easy

1 can (10½ oz)	tomato soup, reduced sodium, condensed
3 tbsp	olive oil
⅓ cup	lemon juice
1 tsp	onion powder
½ tsp	paprika
¼ tsp	garlic powder
¼ tsp	celery seeds

1. Place all ingredients into a blender.

2. Blend until smooth. Add salt to taste if desired. Chill.

Makes: 2 cups

PER 1 TBSP:	16 Calories	0 g Prot (3%)	1 g Carb (32%)	1 g Fat (65%)	0 g Sugar
	0 g Fiber	28 mg Sodium	0 mg Chol	3 mg Calcium	

GREEK SALAD DRESSING

Preparation Time: 10 minutes
Complexity: Easy

¼ cup	garbanzo juice
⅓ cup	lemon juice
1 tbsp	olive oil
2 tbsp	honey
½ tsp	oregano

1. Place ingredients in a small bowl.

2. Whisk dressing with a fork until smooth.

3. Chill well.

Makes: 1 cup

PER 1 TBSP:	17 Calories	0 g Prot (1%)	2 g Carb (40%)	1 g Fat (59%)	2 g Sugar
	0 g Fiber	2 mg Sodium	0 mg Chol	2 mg Calcium	

GARLIC OMEGA DRESSING

Preparation Time: 10 minutes
Complexity: Easy

2	garlic cloves, large
¾ cup	flaxseed oil
1½ tbsp	lemon juice
¼ cup	water
½ tsp	salt
3 tbsp	nutritional yeast flakes
½ tbsp	parsley flakes

1. Slice garlic into blender. Add flaxseed oil, lemon juice, water, salt, and nutritional yeast flakes.

2. Blend until smooth.

3. Stir in parsley.

4. Chill in refrigerator.

CHEF'S TIPS:
- Try it on baked potatoes!
- For a lower fat variation: use ¼ cup flaxseed oil, 3 tbsp. lemon juice, and 6 tbsp. water. Add garlic and seasonings. Blend well.

Makes: 1 cup

PER 1 TBSP:	77 Calories	1 g Prot (3%)	1 g Carb (4%)	8 g Fat (93%)	0 g Sugar
	0 g Fiber	57 mg Sodium	0 mg Chol	2 mg Calcium	

GOURMET SALAD DRESSING

Preparation Time: 10 minutes
Complexity: Easy

1 cup	tofu, silken, firm (lite)
1 tbsp	olive oil (optional)
1 tbsp	dill weed, fresh or flakes
½ tsp	salt
1	garlic clove, minced
2 tbsp	lemon juice
¼ cup	onions, chopped

1. Place all ingredients in a blender. Blend until smooth.

2. Chill for 1 hour in the refrigerator for flavors to mature.

Makes: 1½ cups

PER 1 TBSP:	9 Calories	1 g Prot (57%)	1 g Carb (27%)	0 g Fat (16%)	0 g Sugar
	0 g Fiber	57 mg Sodium	0 mg Chol	8 mg Calcium	

ITALIAN DRESSING

Preparation Time: 5 minutes
Complexity: Easy

½ cup	lemon juice
¼ cup	apple juice, unsweetened
¼ tsp	mustard, dry
½ tsp	garlic powder
¼ tsp	rosemary
½ tsp	oregano
½ tsp	onion powder
½ tsp	paprika
¼ tsp	thyme

1. Blend all ingredients together well.

2. Chill in refrigerator for at least 2 days for enhanced flavor.

3. Serve over salad of your choice.

Makes: ¾ cup

PER 1 TBSP:	8 Calories	0 g Prot (5%)	2 g Carb (90%)	0 g Fat (5%)	1 g Sugar
	0 g Fiber	1 mg Sodium	0 mg Chol	5 mg Calcium	

ONION VEGGIE DIP

Preparation Time: 10 minutes
Complexity: Easy

1 pkg (12 oz, 349 g)	tofu, silken, firm (lite)
1½ tbsp	lemon juice
⅓ cup	onion flakes
½ tsp	garlic salt
1 tsp	onion powder
2 tbsp	nutritional yeast flakes
½ cup	cashew pieces
½ cup	water

1. Place all ingredients in a blender or food processor. Blenderize until very smooth.

2. Place mixture in a bowl and chill in refrigerator for a minimum of 1 hour before serving.

Makes: 2¼ cups

PER 1 TBSP:	18 Calories	1 g Prot (25%)	2 g Carb (29%)	1 g Fat (46%)	0 g Sugar
	0 g Fiber	23 mg Sodium	0 mg Chol	6 mg Calcium	

THOUSAND ISLAND DRESSING

Preparation Time: 20 minutes
Complexity: Easy

½ cup	cashew pieces
½ cup	water
¼ cup	lemon juice
1 pkg	tofu, medium/firm
(16 oz, 454 g)	
½ tsp	salt
1 tsp	onion powder
2 tsp	honey
1 cup	tomato sauce
1 tsp	garlic powder
2 tbsp	bell pepper, green, finely chopped
2 tbsp	bell pepper, red, finely chopped

1. Blenderize all ingredients except peppers until smooth.

2. Stir in peppers.

3. Chill dressing in the refrigerator for a minimum of 1 hour before serving.

CHEF'S TIP:
- This recipe can be easily cut in half

Makes: 4 cups

PER 1 TBSP:	15 Calories	1 g Prot (22%)	1 g Carb (30%)	1 g Fat (48%)	0 g Sugar
	0 g Fiber	45 mg Sodium	0 mg Chol	4 mg Calcium	

ZESTFUL LEMON-DILL DRESSING

Preparation Time: 10 minutes
Complexity: Easy

2 cups	tofu, silken, firm (lite)
2 tbsp	lemon juice
½ tsp	lemon peel, grated
2 tsp	dill weed, fresh
½ tsp	salt, to taste
¼ tsp	celery seeds
4 tbsp	soy milk

1. Place all ingredients together in a blender. Blend until smooth.

2. Chill in refrigerator to meld flavors.

CHEF'S TIP:
- Excellent on salad greens or cooked vegetables, such as zucchini or broccoli.

Makes: 2 cups

PER 1 TBSP:	5 Calories	1 g Prot (49%)	0 g Carb (29%)	0 g Fat (22%)	0 g Sugar
	0 g Fiber	42 mg Sodium	0 mg Chol	6 mg Calcium	

Sprouting

Sprouts are delicious, economical, and nutritious!

Enjoy them raw in salads or sandwiches, or even sprinkle them on your bowl of soup! Serve them cooked in baked goods, gourmet entrees, casseroles, soups, or stews.

Sprouts are nutrient-manufacturing plants. They are rich in vitamins, minerals, and enzymes that multiply during the sprouting process as much as 10 times! They are a natural source of fiber and low in calories, making them a dieter's delight!

Pound for pound, penny for penny, sprouts are the most nutritious and economical food you can eat! Most varieties of seeds will yield six to eight times their volume in sprouts.

Try sprouting a variety of seeds, including alfalfa, radish, broccoli, and even sunflower seeds! Use your imagination, then have some fun and enjoy the tasty results!

Three Easy Steps to Make Your Own Sprouts:

1. Pour a measured amount of seeds and water into any standard widemouthed jar. (This will usually be a ratio of one part seeds to four parts water.) Place the proper screen top on the jar and soak seeds overnight.

2. The following morning, drain the water off the seeds in the jar through the screen top. Rinse sprouts by holding the jar under a running faucet until jar is filled with water. Swirl gently and then drain. Repeat this step, rinsing the sprouts every morning and evening. Rinse more often if desired for slightly faster growth. Stand jar on screen top feet for ventilation during draining, then prop jar on an angle with screen top facing down. This will ensure proper ventilation during sprouting.

3. As sprouts grow and throw off seed hulls,

SPROUT TABLE:

Seed Variety:	Dry Seed:	Yield:	Growing Time:
alfalfa seeds	2 tbsp	1 quart	4-5 days
garbanzos	¾ cup	1 quart	3-5 days
kidney beans	1⅓ cups	1 quart	3-4 days
lentils	¾ cup	1 quart	3-4 days
mung beans	⅓ cup	1 quart	3-4 days
radish seeds	¼ cup	1 quart	3-5 days
soybeans	1⅓ cups	1 quart	3-5 days
sunflower seeds	½ cup	1 quart	2-3 days
wheat berries	1 cup	1 quart	3-6 days

change to a large screen on top, if possible. As you rinse the sprouts, allow the water to overflow and flush out the hulls. Continue to swirl the jar under the running water until most of the hulls are rinsed away. Drain well and continue with cycle until sprouts reach about ¼ to ½ inch in length (depending on the seed chosen to be sprouted).

Suggested Screen Tops to Be Used:

Fine Screen: use for seeds such as alfalfa, radish, and other small seeds.

Medium Screen: use for lentils, mung beans, wheat, and other larger seeds. Also, use for rinsing hulls away from alfalfa, cabbage, radish, and other sprouts of a similar size.

Coarse Screen: use for black-eyed peas, garbanzos, and other large seeds. Also, use for rinsing hulls away from mung beans, radish, and other sprouts of similar size.

Additional Sprouting Tips:

- For all seeds, the water for soaking should be warm. The water for rinsing should be tepid. The water for the final rinse should be cold. Ideal sprouting temperature is 65°-75° F.

- The "soak water" from most seeds is full of valuable nutrients. You can use it for making soups or teas, or even for watering your plants. But do not drink or use the soak water of beans. (It may have an undesirable effect on your digestive system!)

- Avoid growing sprouts in direct sunlight. Having them exposed to some sunlight, however (especially after the first 48 hours), will help them develop a nice green color and produce chlorophyll.

- Seed hulls are not harmful and contain nutritional value, but most people prefer removing them to minimize mold problems and ensure the freshest tasting sprouts.

- Stored sprouts must be kept cold. Store jar covered with fine screen top in refrigerator. To freshen stored sprouts, use screen top and rinse with cold water, then drain well.

- You can prop your jar of sprouts almost anywhere for ventilation during sprouting. Prop jar with screen top facing down in a dish drain, in a deep bowl, or just propped up on a counter.

- You may choose to purchase the appropriate screens and lids at a health food store. These commercial sprouting lids come in the different sizes you will need. However, if you do not have these commercial lids, you may use a piece of cheesecloth or a piece of nylon stocking held on the jar with a sealer jar ring or an elastic band.

Vegetables

Baked Acorn Squash

Baked Brussels Sprouts

Baked Carrots

Baked Yams

Stir-fried Cabbage

Baked Zucchini

Sweet Potato Sticks

Chinese Stir-fried Vegetables

Cooked Beets

Ratatouille

Green Bean Almondine

Stuffed Green and Red Peppers

Oven-baked French Fries

Stuffed Bell Peppers

Rutabaga Puff

Scalloped Potatoes

Stuffed Squash

Zucchini Saute

• Stuffed Green and Red Peppers, *p. 110*

BAKED ACORN SQUASH

Preparation Time: 20 minutes
Complexity: Easy

3	**acorn squash**
1 can (12 oz)	**pineapple, crushed, drained**
¼ tsp	**ginger, ground**
3	**carrots, grated**
3 tbsp	**raisins**

1. Cut squash in half; remove seeds.
2. Place squash in a baking dish. Add a little water to cover the bottom of dish.
3. Mix together remaining ingredients and spoon into squash shells.
4. Cover dish and bake at 350° F for 40 minutes, or until squash is tender.

Serves: 6

PER SERVING (½ squash):	148 Calories	2 g Prot (5%)	35 g Carb (93%)	0 g Fat (2%)	11 g Sugar
	5 g Fiber	32 mg Sodium	0 mg Chol	92 mg Calcium	

BAKED BRUSSELS SPROUTS

Preparation Time: 20 minutes
Complexity: Intermediate

6 cups	**fresh brussels sprouts**
1¼ cup	*Condensed Mushroom Soup* (p. 71)
½ cup	**soy milk**
¼ tsp	**salt**
½ tsp	**dill, dry**

1. Trim and wash brussels sprouts. Cut the larger ones in half.
2. Steam brussels sprouts in a little water until tender yet crisp.
3. Drain off water and place brussels sprouts in a casserole dish.
4. Mix together *Condensed Mushroom Soup,* soy milk, salt, and dill. Pour over brussels sprouts in casserole dish.
5. Cover dish. Bake at 350° F for 20 minutes or until heated through.

Serves: 8

PER ¾-CUP SERVING:	53 Calories	3 g Prot (23%)	8 g Carb (60%)	1 g Fat (17%)	2 g Sugar
	3 g Fiber	101 mg Sodium	0 mg Chol	29 mg Calcium	

BAKED CARROTS

Preparation Time: 20 minutes
Complexity: Easy

6 cups (¼-inch thick)	**carrots, peeled and diagonally sliced**
½ cup	**onions, thinly sliced**
¼ cup	**water**
3 tbsp	**parsley, minced, fresh**

1. Place carrots in a glass casserole dish.
2. Add onions and water to dish and mix well. Add more water if necessary to cover the bottom of the casserole dish.
3. Cover dish. Bake in oven at 350° F for about 30 minutes or until carrots are tender.
4. Mix in minced parsley prior to serving.

Serves: 8

PER ¾-CUP SERVING:	44 Calories	1 g Prot (9%)	11 g Carb (87%)	0 g Fat (4%)	5 g Sugar
	3 g Fiber	35 mg Sodium	0 mg Chol	30 mg Calcium	

BAKED YAMS (see p. 108)

Preparation Time: 25 minutes
Complexity: Intermediate

2	**yams, medium-sized**
2 tbsp	**cornstarch**
2 cups	**pineapple juice**
1 can (14 oz)	**pineapple rings, drained**
10	**cranberries, fresh or frozen**

1. Wash and microwave raw unpeeled yams for 10 minutes.
2. Then peel and slice yams and arrange them in glass baking dish. Set aside.
3. In a small saucepan, dissolve cornstarch in pineapple juice. Bring to a boil over medium heat, stirring constantly. Simmer until mixture becomes thick and turns clear in color.
4. Lay pineapple rings neatly over the top of the cooked yams.
5. Pour thickened mixture evenly over yams and pineapple rings.
6. Place a cranberry in the center of each pineapple ring.
7. Bake in oven at 350° F for about 30 minutes.

CHEF'S TIPS:
- Use the pineapple juice that is drained off from the pineapple rings to make up the required 2 cups of pineapple juice.
- Replace yams with sweet potatoes as a variation.

Serves: 8

PER 1-CUP SERVING:	106 Calories	1 g Prot (4%)	26 g Carb (95%)	0 g Fat (1%)	11 g Sugar
	2 g Fiber	5 mg Sodium	0 mg Chol	22 mg Calcium	

STIR-FRIED CABBAGE

Preparation Time: 20 minutes
Complexity: Easy

6 cups	**Chinese cabbage, shredded**
1 tsp	**sesame oil**
1-3 tbsp	**chickenlike seasoning of your choice, to taste**
2 cups	**carrots, shredded**

1. In a large nonstick frying pan, saute cabbage in a little water and sesame oil until soft.
2. Add chickenlike seasoning. Saute a few minutes.
3. Add grated carrots and continue to saute until tender yet crisp.
4. Add salt to taste if desired
5. Serve immediately.

CHEF'S TIP:
- Garnish with lightly toasted cashews.

Serves: 6

PER 1-CUP SERVING:	61 Calories	4 g Prot (30%)	8 g Carb (60%)	1 g Fat (10%)	3 g Sugar
	4 g Fiber	37 mg Sodium	0 mg Chol	70 mg Calcium	

BAKED ZUCCHINI

Preparation Time: 10 minutes
Complexity: Easy

2   **zucchinis, large**

**Herbamare, Spike,
or Mrs. Dash
seasoning**

garlic powder

oregano

1. Wash zucchini well. Slice each zucchini lengthwise, then again in half widthwise.

2. Place zucchini skin side down in a lightly oil-sprayed baking dish.

3. Sprinkle desired amount of seasoning, garlic powder, and oregano over each zucchini.

4. Cover dish and bake at 350° F for about 20 minutes or until tender.

5. Slice to serve.

Serves: 8

PER 1-CUP SERVING:	14 Calories	1 g Prot (17%)	3 g Carb (73%)	0 g Fat (10%)	1 g Sugar
	1 g Fiber	4 mg Sodium	0 mg Chol	14 mg Calcium	

SWEET POTATO STICKS

Preparation Time: 15 minutes
Complexity: Easy

1   **sweet potato, large**

**Spike or Mrs. Dash
seasoning**

1. Peel the sweet potato, then cut into ½-inch-thick strips about 3 inches long.

2. Place the potato sticks evenly on a lightly oil-sprayed baking sheet. Lightly spray the potato sticks using the nonstick spray if desired.

3. Sprinkle with Spike or Mrs. Dash seasoning, and salt if desired.

4. Bake in oven at 400° F for 20 minutes or until crispy brown.

CHEF'S TIP:
• If eaten as french fries, dip in *Ketchup* (p. 64).

Serves: 4

PER 2-CUP SERVING:	34 Calories	1 g Prot (6%)	8 g Carb (94%)	0 g Fat (0%)	1 g Sugar
	1 g Fiber	14 mg Sodium	0 mg Chol	10 mg Calcium	

CHINESE STIR-FRY VEGETABLES

Preparation Time: 30 minutes
Complexity: Intermediate

1 lb (18 oz)	**tofu, firm, cut into bite-sized cubes**
2 tbsp	**chickenlike seasoning of your choice, to taste**
⅔ cup	**carrots**
1 cup	**cauliflower**
⅔ cup	**celery**
1 cup	**broccoli**
1 tbsp	**sesame or olive oil**
½ cup	**bean sprouts**
⅔ cup	**snow pea pods**
1 can (10 oz)	**water chestnuts**
1 can (10 oz)	**baby corn cobs**
⅔ cup	**bok choy, chopped**
¼ cup	**water**

1. Sprinkle tofu with chickenlike seasoning and brown evenly in a Pam-sprayed or nonstick skillet. Set aside.
2. Cut carrots, cauliflower, celery, and broccoli into bite-sized pieces.
3. Heat sesame oil in wok and add vegetables in the order listed. Allow each ingredient to partially cook before adding the next one. Stir several times between each addition.
4. Add browned tofu cubes and stir quickly to reheat the tofu.
5. Serve immediately over cooked brown rice.
6. Serve with sweet-and-sour sauce on the side.

CHEF'S TIPS:

- To reduce fat, avoid using any oil. Instead, saute veggies using only water, adding it a little at a time.
- Add a little Bragg's All Purpose Seasoning for a soy sauce flavor.

Serves: 4-5

PER 2-CUP SERVING:	148 Calories	11 g Prot (30%)	17 g Carb (46%)	4 g Fat (24%)	4 g Sugar
	4 g Fiber	89 mg Sodium	0 mg Chol	67 mg Calcium	

COOKED BEETS

Preparation Time: 15 minutes
Complexity: Easy

1 cup	**onions, diced**
4 cup	**beets, cooked, sliced or diced**

1. In a nonstick frying pan, sauté onions in a little water until soft.
2. Add beets to pan. Cook until heated through.

CHEF'S TIP:

- Add a little dill weed for a different flavor.

Serves: 6

PER ¾-CUP SERVING:	49 Calories	2 g Prot (13%)	11 g Carb (84%)	0 g Fat (3%)	7 g Sugar
	3 g Fiber	72 mg Sodium	0 mg Chol	20 mg Calcium	

RATATOUILLE

Preparation Time: 15 minutes
Complexity: Easy

1	eggplant, medium
1	zucchini, large
½	bell pepper, red, large
1	onion, red, medium
1 can	tomatoes, diced
(12 oz, 784 g)	
½ tsp	oregano
½ tsp	basil
½ tsp	salt, to taste
¾ tsp	garlic powder
	or
1	clove, minced

1. Wash, but do not peel, eggplant and zucchini. Dice into ¾-inch cubes. Place in a baking dish.

2. Cut red pepper into ½-inch cubes. Add to baking dish.

3. Cut red onion in half, then slice ¼-inch thick. Add to baking dish.

4. Add tomatoes and seasonings to baking dish and mix well.

5. Cover casserole and bake in oven at 350° F for 30 minutes.

6. Remove lid and continue to bake for another 10 minutes.

Serves: 6

PER 1-CUP SERVING:	85 Calories	3 g Prot (15%)	16 g Carb (75%)	1 g Fat (10%)	8 g Sugar
	6 g Fiber	319 mg Sodium	0 mg Chol	65 mg Calcium	

1. Baked Yams, *p. 105*
2. Green Bean Almondine, *p. 110*
3. Zucchini Saute, *p. 113*

GREEN BEAN ALMONDINE (see p. 108)

Preparation Time: 20 minutes
Complexity: Easy

2 cups	green beans, fresh or frozen
½ tsp	thyme
½ cup	bell pepper, red, finely diced
1 tbsp	almonds, slivered, lightly toasted

1. Simmer green beans in a bit of water until crisp-tender.

2. Drain water.

3. Add thyme and red pepper to green beans. Cover and allow to steam for a couple of minutes.

4. Place steamed beans in a bowl.

5. Mix in almonds and salt to taste. Serve immediately.

Serves: 4

PER ½-CUP SERVING:	33 Calories	2 g Prot (17%)	5 g Carb (55%)	1 g Fat (28%)	2 g Sugar
	3 g Fiber	4 mg Sodium	0 mg Chol	30 mg Calcium	

STUFFED GREEN AND RED PEPPERS (see p. 102)

Preparation Time: 40 minutes
Complexity: Intermediate

½ cup	tomatoes, canned
1 tbsp	tomato paste
1½	celery stalks, chopped
1½	onions, large, chopped
1 tsp	salt
½ tsp	basil
1 tsp	sage
½ tsp	thyme
½ tsp	garlic powder
¼ cup	walnuts, coarsely chopped
3 cups	brown rice, cooked
10	bell peppers, medium-sized, green, red, orange, or yellow
as needed	dry whole-wheat bread crumbs

1. In a medium-sized pot, simmer first four ingredients together until fairly dry and slightly tender.

2. Add remaining ingredients (except peppers and bread crumbs) to pot. Simmer mixture.

3. Add enough bread crumbs to mixture to make mixture fairly dry.

4. Cut off the bottom of each pepper about ½ inch above the surface, leaving stem intact. Reserve each "pepper lid."

5. Cut the core out of each.

6. Loosely pack each pepper with the rice mixture and place the "pepper lids" on top.

7. Place a couple tablespoons of water in the bottom of a large baking dish. Stand peppers in baking dish.

8. Bake at 350° F for 50 minutes, covered, then 10 minutes uncovered. (If using uncovered pan, cover dish with aluminum foil and bake 60 minutes.)

CHEF'S TIP:
- If you use different-colored peppers, exchange different-colored "pepper lids," i.e., cap green pepper with red pepper lid, etc.

Serves: 10

PER 1 PEPPER:	151 Calories	4 g Prot (12%)	28 g Carb (78%)	3 g Fat (20%)	2 g Sugar
	3 g Fiber	288 mg Sodium	0 mg Chol	38 mg Calcium	

OVEN-BAKED FRENCH FRIES

Preparation Time: 20 minutes
Complexity: Easy

4	medium/large potatoes
	Pam olive oil cooking spray
	garlic powder
	Mrs. Dash or Spike seasoning
	salt (optional)

1. Preheat oven to 450° F.
2. Wash and prepare potatoes. (Leave skins on.)
3. Cut potatoes into long strips about ½-inch wide.
4. Lightly oil-spray a baking sheet.
5. Place potato strips in a single layer on the baking sheet.
6. Lightly spray with cooking spray.
7. Sprinkle seasonings, and salt if desired, evenly over the potatoes.
8. Bake for approximately 30 minutes, or until nicely browned. Be sure to turn them once or twice during this time period.
9. Serve with *Ketchup* (p. 64).

Serves: 4

| PER 1½-CUP SERVING: | 148 Calories | 4 g Prot (10%) | 33 g Carb (89%) | 0 g Fat (1%) | 2 g Sugar |
| (1 potato) | 7 g Fiber | 26 mg Sodium | 0 mg Chol | 23 mg Calcium | |

STUFFED BELL PEPPERS

Preparation Time: 40 minutes
Complexity: Intermediate

6	bell peppers, green, medium-sized
4 cups	water
4 cups	couscous, whole-wheat
½ tsp	salt
⅓ cup	green onions, sliced
1½ cup	bell pepper, red, finely diced
1½ cup	onions, finely diced
3	garlic cloves, minced
1 tsp	dill weed
1 cup	carrots, grated
2 cups	zucchini, diced small
6 cups	spaghetti or tomato sauce, reduced sodium

1. Use some of the tomato sauce to cover the bottom of a 9" x 12" baking dish.
2. Cut green peppers in half lengthwise, remove stems, and clean out seeds. Place in baking dish with open side up.
3. Bring water to a boil in a medium-sized pot. Stir in couscous and salt. Remove from heat and cover. Let stand 5 minutes.
4. In a little water, saute remaining ingredients except tomato sauce. Add to cooked couscous, cover, and steam for another 5 minutes.
5. Fill each pepper with the couscous filling. Divide the filling evenly into each pepper.
6. Drizzle peppers with remaining tomato sauce. Cover and bake in a preheated oven at 375° F for 10 minutes.
7. Remove the cover and bake another 5 minutes or until desired texture is achieved.

Serves: 12

| PER ½ PEPPER: | 297 Calories | 9 g Prot (12%) | 63 g Carb (84%) | 1 g Fat (4%) | 4 g Sugar |
| | 6 g Fiber | 212 mg Sodium | 0 mg Chol | 48 mg Calcium | |

111

RUTABAGA PUFF

Preparation Time: 25 minutes
Complexity: Easy

1	**rutabaga, large**
1½ tsp	**Ener-G Egg Replacer powder** (dissolved in 2 tbsp water)
½ cup	**applesauce, unsweetened**
½ tsp	**salt**
1 cup	**bread crumbs, whole-wheat, dry**
1 tbsp	**olive oil**

1. Peel, cube, and cook rutabaga until tender. Drain and mash.

2. Add egg replacer, applesauce, salt and ½ cup of bread crumbs. Mix well. Pour into a lightly oil-sprayed casserole dish.

3. Combine remaining bread crumbs with oil. Sprinkle over the top of the rutabaga mixture.

4. Bake uncovered at 350° F for 35 minutes or until golden brown on top.

Serves: 8

PER ¾-CUP SERVING:	99 Calories	3 g Prot (12%)	18 g Carb (73%)	2 g Fat (15%)	7 g Sugar
	4 g Fiber	200 mg Sodium	0 mg Chol	70 mg Calcium 9	

SCALLOPED POTATOES

Preparation Time: 25 minutes
Complexity: Intermediate

12 cups	**potatoes, red** (6 large), **washed, peeled, and sliced into ¼-inch-thick rounds**
1½ cups	**onions, sliced**

Sauce:

3 cups	**water**
1 cups	**cashew pieces or almonds, blanched, slivered**
2	**garlic cloves**
½ cup	**onions**
½	**bell pepper, red**
3 tbsp	**nutritional yeast flakes**
1 tbsp	**lemon juice**
½ tsp	**salt**

1. Place sliced potatoes alternating with sliced onions in a lightly greased large (3-quart) baking dish.

2. In a blender, combine sauce ingredients and blenderize until very smooth.

3. Pour sauce over potatoes and onions in baking dish.

4. Cover dish and bake at 425° F for about 50-60 minutes or until potatoes are tender.

Serves: 10

PER 1¼ CUPS:	213 Calories	11 g Prot (20%)	28 g Carb (53%)	7 g Fats (27%)	3 g Sugar
	11 g Fiber	132 mg Sodium	0 mg Chol	58 mg Calcium	

STUFFED SQUASH

Preparation Time: 30 minutes
Complexity: Intermediate

| 1 | acorn squash, large |
| | (or 2-3 small ones) |

Stuffing:

4 cups	bread crumbs, whole-wheat, fresh (not dry)
2 cups	spelt grain, cooked
¼ cup	olive oil
¾ cup	water
½ tsp	salt
1½ tsp	poultry seasoning
	or
1 tsp	sage
1½ cups	onions, chopped fine
¼ cup	cranberries, dried
¼ cup	celery, diced
½ cup	carrots, grated

1. Cut the squash in half; remove the seeds and stringy portions.
2. Place the squash cut sides down in a large pan with 1 inch of water. Cover dish.
3. Bake in microwave on high 8 minutes or until tender, or approximately 20 minutes in oven at 400° F.

Stuffing:

1. Mix all ingredients together well.
2. Place in a glass dish and cover. Microwave on high 5 minutes. Stir and then place back in microwave on high for another 5 minutes. (Or bake in oven, covered, for about 20 minutes or until onion is soft.)
3. Spoon the dressing into squash halves and bake in oven at 400° F for about 10 minutes.
4. Serve immediately.

CHEF'S TIPS:
- Substitute spelt with another grain, such as brown rice, barley, or bulgar.
- Good served with a brown gravy and cranberries!
- Use as a side or main dish!
- Fits well into Thanksgiving dinner!

Serves: 10

| PER 1-CUP SERVING: | 237 Calories | 6 g Prot (10%) | 41 g Carb (70%) | 5 g Fat (20%) | 2 g Sugar |
| | 5 g Fiber | 123 mg Sodium | 0 mg Chol | 90 mg Calcium | |

ZUCCHINI SAUTÉ (see p. 108)

Preparation Time: 20 minutes
Complexity: Easy

4 cups	zucchini, sliced ¼ inch thick
4	garlic cloves, minced
2 tsp	basil, crushed
1 can	tomatoes, peeled, whole sliced in thirds
(28 oz)	

1. Saute sliced zucchini, minced garlic, and basil in a little water or Pam spray using a nonstick frying pan. Saute until zucchini begins to soften.
2. Add sliced, peeled tomatoes.
3. Saute 5 more minutes or until zucchini is crisp-tender. Add salt to taste, if desired.

CHEF'S TIP:
- Serve as a side dish or as a topping for rice, pasta, or couscous.

Serves: 6

| PER 1-CUP SERVING: | 40 Calories | 2 g Prot (19%) | 9 g Carb (75%) | 0 g Fat (6%) | 5 g Sugar |
| | 2 g Fiber | 339 mg Sodium | 0 mg Chol | 64 mg Calcium | |

Main Dishes

Baked Beans With Soy Curls
Baked Brown Rice
Black Bean Enchiladas
Black-eyed Bean Topping
Burrito Beans
Cabbage Rolls
Tofu-Millet Burgers
Cooked Lentils
Cashew Rice Roast
"Chicken" Cacciatore
Falafels
Meatless Patties
Curried Chickpeas
Curried Stir-fry
Dr. Diehl's Lasagna
Pasta Stir-fry
Lentil Roast
Rice Stacks
Shepherd's Pie
Gluten
Gluten Patties
Meatless Meatballs
Mexican Tortilla Lasagna
Mock Chicken-Asparagus Risotto
Savory Dressing/Stuffing
Nut Loaf
Vegetarian Lasagna
Potato Pie
Pecan-Rice Patties
Spaghetti Sauce
Savory Tofu Roast
Sweet-and-Sour Tofu
Veggie Fajitas
Whole-Wheat Pierogies
Pierogi Fillings

• Pasta Stir-fry, *p. 124*

BAKED BEANS WITH SOY CURLS

Preparation Time: 20 minutes
Complexity: Easy

2 cups	navy beans
6 cups	water
1 cup	soy curls, broken into bite-sized pieces, dry
½ cup	tomato paste
⅓ cup	onion flakes
1 tbsp	Bragg's All Purpose Seasoning
1½ tbsp	molasses
2 tsp	garlic powder
½ tsp	salt

1. Wash beans thoroughly and place in a Crock-Pot with measured amount of water. Cook on high overnight.

2. Add remaining ingredients to Crock-Pot. Continue to cook until heated through and soy curls are tender.

CHEF'S TIP:

- Substitute sliced "veggie hot dogs" for soy curls as a nice change.

Serves: 8

PER ¾-CUP SERVING:	231 Calories	14 g Prot (25%)	42 g Carb (70%)	2 g Fat (5%)	7 g Sugar
	14 g Fiber	257 mg Sodium	0 mg Chol	107 mg Calcium	

BAKED BROWN RICE

Preparation Time: 10 minutes
Complexity: Easy

1 cup	brown rice
2 cups	water
½ tsp	salt

1. Preheat oven to 350° F.

2. Place rice, water, and salt in a lightly oil-sprayed 2-quart baking dish.

3. Cover and bake in oven for 1 hour.

CHEF'S TIP:

- Substitute ¼ cup wild rice for ¼ cup brown rice, or try some unique types of rice, such as "red rice" (which is very high in potassium) or black rice. Be creative with the rice grain. Mixing a few types together can make a very attractive, elegant dish.

Serves: 6

PER ½-CUP SERVING:	113 Calories	2 g Prot (7%)	27 g Carb (88%)	1 g Fat (5%)	0 g Sugar
	2 g Fiber	195 mg Sodium	0 mg Chol	2 mg Calcium	

BLACK BEAN ENCHILADAS

Preparation Time: 30 minutes
Complexity: Advanced

1 cup	onions, chopped small
1½ cups	zucchini, cubed small
1 cup	bell pepper, green, diced small
2 cups	black beans, cooked, unsalted
1½ cups	corn, whole kernel
1 cup	tomato sauce
1 can (28 oz)	tomatoes, diced
1 tsp	basil, crushed
1 tsp	garlic powder
2 cans (28 oz)	tomato sauce, Italian seasoned
16	tortillas, large, whole-wheat

"Cheese" Sauce:

¾ cup	cashew pieces
¼ cup	nutritional yeast flakes
1½ tbsp	lemon juice
1	garlic clove
¼ cup	onions
⅔ cup	water
¼ cup	bell pepper, red
1 tbsp	Bragg's All Purpose Seasoning

1. Place all ingredients for the "cheese" sauce in a blender. Blend until smooth. Set aside.

2. Pour a ¼-inch layer of Italian tomato sauce in the bottom of a large baking dish. Set aside.

3. In a large nonstick frying pan, saute, in a little water, onions, zucchini, and green pepper until soft.

4. Add black beans, corn, plain tomato sauce, diced tomatoes, basil, and garlic powder. Remove from heat.

5. Place a generous amount of mixture, about 1 cup, in center of tortilla. Roll, then place seam side down in baking dish. Repeat, using up the entire filling.

6. Pour remaining Italian tomato sauce evenly over enchiladas.

7. Drizzle "cheese" sauce over enchiladas.

8. Bake in oven at 400°F for 10-15 minutes, or until heated through.

Makes 16 tortillas

PER 1 ENCHILADA:	326 Calories	11 g Prot (11%)	60 g Carb (72%)	6 g Fat (17%)	4 g Sugar
	7 g Fiber	175 mg Sodium	0 mg Chol	139 mg Calcium	

BLACK-EYED BEAN TOPPING

Preparation Time: 30 minutes
Complexity: Intermediate

1 cup	black-eyed beans
3-4 cups	water
2 cups	onions, diced
2	garlic cloves, minced
1 can (28 oz)	tomatoes, diced
1 cup	zucchini, diced
2 cups	carrots, grated
1 can (28 oz)	tomato sauce
½ tsp	cumin powder
½ tsp	ginger powder
1 tsp	basil, crushed
½ tsp	salt to taste

1. Boil beans in water until tender.
2. In a large nonstick frying pan, simmer onions, garlic, and diced tomatoes for approximately 10 minutes.
3. Add remaining ingredients to pan. Continue to simmer until vegetables are tender. Add cooked beans.
4. Serve hot over prepared brown rice, baked potatoes, or cooked quinoa.

CHEF'S TIP:

- Black-eyed beans are also known as black-eyed peas or "cow-peas."

Serves: 8

PER 1-CUP SERVING:	145 Calories	7 g Prot (19%)	29 g Carb (77%)	1 g Fat (4%)	9 g Sugar
	7 g Fiber	179 mg Sodium	0 mg Chol	87 mg Calcium	

BURRITO BEANS

Preparation Time: 10 minutes
Complexity: Easy

6 cups	water
3 cups	pinto beans
½ tsp	salt
1 tsp	garlic powder
	or
1	clove garlic, minced
1 tsp	onion powder
	or
1	medium onion, chopped

1. Rinse beans using a colander.
2. Place water and beans in a Crock-Pot. Turn on "high" temperature.
3. Allow cooking time of 6 hours or until beans are soft and most of the water is soaked up.
4. Mash beans with a potato masher until very smooth.
5. Mix in salt, garlic, and onion.

CHEF'S TIPS:

- Serve on tortillas or on the side with brown rice.
- Freeze extra and use instead of canned refried beans.

Serves: 12

PER ¼-CUP SERVING:	165 Calories	10 g Prot (24%)	31 g Carb (73%)	1 g Fat (3%)	1 g Sugar
	12 g Fiber	97 mg Sodium	0 mg Chol	62 mg Calcium	

CABBAGE ROLLS (see p. 126)

Preparation Time: 45 minutes
Complexity: Intermediate

1	**cabbage, green, large head**
1½ cups	**onions, finely chopped**
3	**garlic cloves, minced**
6 cups	**brown rice, cooked**
2 cups	*Gluten* (p. 128)
	or
1 pkg	**commercial Yves Ground Round vegetarian burger**
1-2 tbsp	**beeflike seasoning of your choice, to taste**
1 can (28 oz)	**tomato sauce**

1. Wash cabbage and cut most of core from bottom.

2. Place cabbage core, side down, in 1 inch of water in a large pot. Cover and simmer until cabbage is softly steamed.

3. Remove cabbage from pot, and then peel off each cabbage leaf. Allow leaves to cool slightly. Cut excess core out of middle leaves, if needed.

4. Saute onions and garlic in a little water until soft.

5. Mix together cooked rice, burger, onions, garlic, and beeflike seasoning.

6. Pour a little of the tomato sauce in the bottom of a large glass casserole dish.

7. Place 1-2 tablespoons of rice mixture in the center on a cabbage leaf. Roll up tightly, folding in sides as you roll.

8. Place cabbage roll, seam side down, in dish with tomato sauce.

9. Repeat process until rice mixture and cabbage leaves are used up.

10. Pour remaining tomato sauce over rolls. Cover dish.

11. Bake at 350° F for 45 minutes.

Variations:
- Use a variety of grains in place of the rice. Spelt would be a good choice.
- To make Lazy Cabbage Rolls: Alternate layers of chopped raw cabbage and burger mixture in a lightly oil-sprayed casserole dish. Pour tomato sauce or tomato soup over the top. (Add a little water if desired.) Bake at 350° F for 45 minutes.

Makes: 16 Rolls

PER 1 LARGE ROLL:	143 Calories	7 g Prot (20%)	28 g Carb (75%)	1 g Fat (5%)	5 g Sugar
	5 g Fiber	90 mg Sodium	0 mg Chol	48 mg Calcium	

TOFU-MILLET BURGERS

Preparation Time: 30 minutes
Complexity: Intermediate

½ cup	millet
1 pkg (16 oz, 454 g)	tofu, medium/firm (lite)
½ tsp	salt
1 tsp	poultry seasoning or
½ tsp	sage
1-2 tbsp	beeflike seasoning of your choice
1 tsp	garlic powder
2 tbsp	nutritional yeast flakes
1 tbsp	Bragg's All Purpose Seasoning
1 cup	onions, finely chopped
2 cups	oats, quick
⅓ cup	pecans, ground fine

1. In a small pot, simmer millet in 2 cups of water until done, about 15 minutes, or until water is absorbed. Place in a mixing bowl.

2. Blenderize tofu, salt, and seasonings until smooth. Pour into mixing bowl with cooked millet.

3. Add onions, oats, and pecans and mix well. Let stand 5 minutes.

4. In a preheated nonstick frying pan, drop batter by spoonfuls and form into the shape of a burger.

5. Fry both sides of burger until golden brown.

6. Let sit about 5-10 minutes before serving, to allow them to "firm up."

7. Serve warm on a bun with lettuce and tomato, or as an entree with gravy.

Makes: 12

PER 1 BURGER:	128 Calories	6 g Prot (18%)	18 g Carb (55%)	4 g Fat (27%)	1 g Sugar
	3 g Fiber	235 mg Sodium	0 mg Chol	30 mg Calcium	

COOKED LENTILS

Preparation Time: 15 minutes
Complexity: Easy

3 cups	water
1 cup	brown lentils
1	medium onion, chopped
½ tsp	garlic powder
1 can (10½ oz)	condensed tomato soup (dairy-free), reduced salt

1. Combine water, lentils, onion, and garlic powder in a medium-sized pot.
2. Simmer until lentils are slightly tender.
3. Add tomato soup and continue to simmer until lentils are cooked but not mushy. Add salt to taste if desired.

Chef's Tips:
- Serve over brown rice, or use in *Rice Stacks* (p. 125).
- Substitute tomato soup with tomato sauce.

Serves: 7

PER ½-CUP SERVING:	118 Calories	8 g Prot (28%)	21 g Carb (70%)	0 g Fat (2%)	5 g Sugar
	9 g Fiber	15 mg Sodium	0 mg Chol	23 mg Calcium	

CASHEW RICE ROAST

Preparation Time: 25 minutes
Complexity: Intermediate

1 cup	cashew pieces
1 cup	onions, finely chopped
2 cups	soft bread crumbs, finely ground (whole-grain)
2 cups	nondairy milk
2 cups	brown rice, cooked
2 tbsp	Bragg's All Purpose Seasoning
1 tsp	poultry seasoning or ½ tsp sage
2 tbsp	parsley flakes

1. Grind cashews until very fine. Place in a mixing bowl.
2. Add remaining ingredients to bowl and mix well.
3. Lightly oil spray a 9" x 13" baking dish. Pour mixture into baking dish.
4. Bake at 350° F for 50-60 minutes, or until golden brown.

CHEF'S TIPS:
- Use a blender or food processor to grind cashews and bread crumbs finely.
- Serve with gravy and cranberries as an entrée.

Serves: 10

PER ⅒ RECIPE:	220 Calories	8 g Prot (13%)	31 g Carb (59%)	7 g Fat (28%)	2 g Sugar
	3 g Fiber	141 mg Sodium	0 mg Chol	75 mg Calcium	

"CHICKEN" CACCIATORE

Preparation Time: 30 minutes
Complexity: Intermediate

3 cups	soy veggie "chicken," cubed
3 cups	onions, chopped
1	garlic clove, minced
1 tbsp	olive oil
1 can (6 oz)	tomato paste
½ cup	apple juice, unsweetened
1 cup	water
1-2 tbsp	chickenlike seasoning of your choice, to taste
½ tsp	basil, crushed
½ tsp	rosemary
½ tsp	oregano
3 cups	bell pepper, green, sliced
2 cups	mushrooms, sliced
1 can	stewed tomatoes (28 oz, 784 g)

1. In a large frying pan, sauté diced "chicken," onions, and garlic in olive oil until "chicken" has browned.
2. Add tomato paste, juice, water, and seasonings. Simmer 10-15 minutes.
3. Add peppers, mushrooms, and tomatoes. Simmer another 10 minutes.
4. Serve hot over brown rice or whole wheat pasta noodles of your choice.

CHEF'S TIPS:
- Substitute extra-firm tofu in place of veggie "chicken."
- There are a variety of soymeats on the market. The brand names "Cedar Lake," "MGM," or "Yves" are some of the healthier choices.

Serves: 8

PER 1¼-CUP SERVING:	176 Calories	11 g Prot (26%)	24 g Carb (54%)	4 g Fat (20%)	10 g Sugar
	4 g Fiber	218 mg Sodium	0 mg Chol	60 mg Calcium	

FALAFELS

Preparation Time: 30 minutes

Complexity: Intermediate

2 cans (14 oz, 392 g)	garbanzo beans, cooked and drained (3½ cups)
½ cup	garbanzo liquid or cooking water
1 cup	yellow split peas, cooked
⅓ cup	sesame seeds, unhulled
2 tbsp	onion flakes
2	garlic cloves, minced
2 tbsp	Bragg's All Purpose Seasoning
¼ cup	wheat germ
2 tsp	cumin
½ tsp	salt
1 tbsp	parsley flakes
2 tbsp	lemon juice
½ cup	dry bread crumbs, whole-wheat

1. Blend until smooth in food processor or blender: garbanzo beans, ½ cup juice from garbanzos, split peas, and sesame seeds. Place in a mixing bowl.
2. Add remaining ingredients except bread crumbs. Mix well.
3. Add bread crumbs slowly while mixing. Stir in just enough crumbs so that mixture holds together.
4. Using your hands, roll mixture into balls 1½ inches in diameter. Arrange balls on a lightly greased (using a nonstick spray) baking sheet.
5. Bake at 400° F for 20-30 minutes or until golden brown. Turn occasionally during baking to brown evenly.
6. Serve as an appetizer with tahini sauce or in pita bread with *Hummus* (p. 63) and shredded lettuce.

Serves: 8-10

PER 2 FALAFELS:	158 Calories	9 g Prot (23%)	26 g Carb (66%)	2 g Fat (11%)	2 g Sugar
	9 g Fiber	256 mg Sodium	0 mg Chol	43 mg Calcium	

MEATLESS PATTIES

Preparation Time: 25 minutes

Complexity: Intermediate

2 tbsp	yeast, dry active
½ cup	water, warm
1 tsp	honey
4 cups	oats, quick
1 cup	wheat germ
2 cups	onions, diced small
6 tsp	Ener-G Egg Replacer powder (dissolved in 8 tbsp water)
1 tbsp	Bragg's All Purpose Seasoning
2 tsp	sage
½ cup	walnuts/pecans, finely chopped
½ tsp	salt
1 tsp	garlic powder
3 cups	nondairy milk

1. Combine yeast, water, and honey in bowl; let stand 10 minutes.
2. Add remaining ingredients and mix well.
3. Form into patties and fry in a nonstick skillet or bake in oven.
4. Place in a baking dish and cover with gravy.
5. Bake in oven at 350° F 20-30 minutes or until gravy bubbles.

Makes: 12 patties

PER 1 PATTY:	235 Calories	11 g Prot (19%)	32 g Carb (54%)	7 g Fat (27%)	3 g Sugar
	6 g Fiber	185 mg Sodium	0 mg Chol	42 mg Calcium	

CURRIED CHICKPEAS

Preparation Time: 20 minutes
Complexity: Easy

3 cups	onions, thinly sliced
3	garlic cloves, minced
2 tbsp	brown sesame seeds
1 tbsp	curry powder
4 cups	chickpeas (garbanzos), cooked
3 tbsp	lemon juice
1 tbsp	Bragg's All Purpose Seasoning
⅓ cup	parsley, finely chopped

1. Saute onions and garlic, using a little water in a large covered nonstick frying pan, until soft.
2. Stir in sesame seeds and curry powder. Cook uncovered for a couple of minutes.
3. Add chickpeas, lemon juice, Bragg's seasoning, and parsley. Cook for about 5 minutes over medium heat, stirring often, until heated through.
4. Serve hot over rice or pasta.

Serves: 4

PER 1½-CUP SERVING:	350 Calories	16 g Prot (19%)	58 g Carb (68%)	5 g Fat (13%)	10 g Sugar
	15 g Fiber	169 mg Sodium	0 mg Chol	124 mg Calcium	

CURRIED STIR-FRY

Preparation Time: 30 minutes
Complexity: Easy

1 cup	soy curls, dry
4 cups	cauliflower, cut into bite-sized pieces
1 cup	onions, sliced into rings
1 cup	bell pepper, red, cut into strips
4 cups	cooked pasta, brown rice, or whole wheat
2 cups	garbanzos, cooked
3 tbsp	Bragg's All Purpose Seasoning
1 tsp	curry powder, to taste

1. Place soy curls in a bowl, cover with hot water, and let sit for 10 minutes.
2. In a large nonstick frying pan, saute, in a little water, cauliflower, onions, and red pepper, until tender.
3. Drain soy curls, and add to veggies in frying pan.
4. Add pasta, garbanzos, and seasonings to frying pan. Saute for about 5-10 minutes until heated through.

Chef's Tips:

- Goes well over cooked brown rice or cooked quinoa.
- This recipe can easily be cut in half.

Serves: 12

PER 1-CUP SERVING:	175 Calories	6 g Prot (15%)	34 g Carb (77%)	2 g Fat (8%)	3 g Sugar
	5 g Fiber	167 mg Sodium	0 mg Chol	26 mg Calcium	

DR. DIEHL'S LASAGNA

Preparation Time: 30 minutes
Complexity: Intermediate

8 cups	marinara sauce
1 lb	ground meatless burger (Kellogg's MorningStar Farms)
2 cups	condensed tomato soup, reduced sodium
3 tbsp	beeflike seasoning, of your choice
⅓ cup	onion flakes
½ tsp	garlic powder
1	bell pepper, green, finely chopped
2	celery stalks, finely chopped
1 tsp	Italian seasoning
1 lb	whole-wheat lasagna noodles (8-10 noodles)
2 pkg (12 oz)	tofu, silken, firm (lite), mashed
⅓ cup	parsley, finely chopped

1. In a medium-sized pot, combine all ingredients except noodles, tofu, and parsley. Bring to a boil, reduce heat, and simmer for 40 minutes.
2. Place noodles in boiling water and cook until tender.
3. Layer, in a 9" x 13" pan, hot tomato sauce mixture, then first layer of noodles; then sprinkle with tofu. Repeat sequence until pan is nearly full.
4. Bake at 350° F for 45 minutes.
5. Garnish with fresh chopped parsley.

CHEF'S TIPS:
- For less salt, use a low-sodium meatless burger. Yves Ground Round is a good choice.
- Sliced mushrooms are another nice added ingredient to this dish.

Serves: 8

PER 3" x 3" SERVING:	475 Calories	32 g Prot (27%)	80 g Carb (67%)	3 g Fat (6%)	18 g Sugar
	9 g Fiber	441 mg Sodium	0 mg Chol	59 mg Calcium	

PASTA STIR-FRY (see p. 114)

Preparation Time: 30 minutes
Complexity: Easy

1½ cup	soy curls, dry
2 cups	broccoli, cut into bite-sized pieces
2 cups	string beans, green, fresh
2 cups	asparagus, diagonally sliced
2 cups	carrots, diagonally sliced
1 cup	celery, diagonally sliced
2 cups	zucchini, diagonally sliced
¾ cup	natural plum sauce
6 cups	pasta noodles, cooked, whole-grain (any variety)
3 tbsp	Bragg's All Purpose Seasoning, or to taste
1 tbsp	garlic powder
	or
1-2	cloves fresh garlic, minced

1. Place dry soy curls in a bowl, cover with hot water, and let stand for 10 minutes.
2. In a large frying pan, sauté veggies in a little water until crisp-tender.
3. Drain water off soy curls and add to frying pan.
4. Add cooked pasta and seasonings. Stir well. Sauté until heated through.

CHEF'S TIPS:
- Use a variety of vegetables to create new flavors!
- Nice served with or on cooked brown rice or quinoa.

Serves: 10

PER 2 CUPS:	252 Calories	12 g Prot (20%)	47 g Carb (75%)	1 g Fat (5%)	4 g Sugar
(does not include rice)	5 g Fiber	268 mg Sodium	0 mg Chol	48 mg Calcium	

LENTIL ROAST

Preparation Time: 20 minutes

Complexity: Easy

2 cups	lentils, brown, cooked
¾ cup	finely ground pecans
1¾ cups	soy milk
1 cup	onions, finely chopped
1 tbsp	Bragg's All Purpose Seasoning
½ tsp	sage
½ tsp	garlic powder
1½ cups	crushed cornflakes (sweetened with fruit juice)

1. Mix all ingredients together well.

2. Pour into a lightly sprayed (using a nonstick spray) 9-inch-square casserole dish.

3. Bake at 350° F for 1 hour.

CHEF'S TIP:

- Nature's Path is a good brand of commercial cereal that is sweetened with fruit juice.

Serves: 8

PER ¾ CUP:	233 Calories	10 g Prot (17%)	28 g Carb (48%)	9 g Fat (35%)	3 g Sugar
	6 g Fiber	106 mg Sodium	0 mg Chol	45 mg Calcium	

RICE STACKS

Preparation Time: 25 minutes

Complexity: Easy

6 cups	brown rice, cooked
4 cups	lentils, cooked
6 cups	lettuce, shredded
3 cups	tomatoes, diced
3 cups	cucumber, diced
1 cup	green onions, chopped
1 cup	bell pepper, red, chopped
1 cup	bell pepper, green, chopped
6 tbsp	*Tofu Mayonnaise* (p. 56) or *Tofu Sour Cream* (p. 67)

1. Prepare each food item and place in individual serving bowls.

2. Each person prepares his or her own "rice stack" by layering each food item in the order listed to make a "stack."

3. Top off with 1 tablespoon of the *Tofu Mayonnaise* or *Tofu Sour Cream* and other optional ingredients, such as sliced olives, grated carrots, etc.

CHEF'S TIPS:

- Enjoy toppings such as guacamole (p. 66), salsa (p. 64), and almond cheese (p. 54).
- Serve with whole-grain garlic toast.

Serves: 6

PER 2-CUP SERVING:	272 Calories	11 g Prot (17%)	49 g Carb (73%)	3 g Fat (10%)	4 g Sugar
	10 g Fiber	58 mg Sodium	0 mg Chol	56 mg Calcium	

SHEPHERD'S PIE

Preparation Time: 30 minutes
Complexity: Easy

1½ cups	onions, chopped small
2 cups	gluten or commercial vegetarian burger
4 tbsp	flour, unbleached or whole-wheat
3 cups	water
1-3 tbsp	beeflike seasoning of your choice, to taste
4 cups	frozen peas
7 cups	potatoes, peeled and diced (5 medium potatoes)
½ cup	soy milk
	salt to taste
	paprika (for color)

1. In a large frying pan, saute onions in a little water until soft.

2. Add burger, then continue to saute for a few more minutes.

3. Sprinkle flour over burger and onions; stir and cook for another minute.

4. Add water and seasonings. Simmer until thickened.

5. Spread mixture evenly in a 9" x 13" baking dish.

6. Layer peas evenly over the burger mixture in baking dish.

7. Cook potatoes. Mash with soy milk and salt to taste.

8. Spread potatoes evenly over the peas. Spread smooth. Sprinkle with paprika for color if desired.

9. Bake at 350° F for 40 minutes or until heated through.

CHEF'S TIP:

• Serve with a fresh salad for a complete meal.

Serves: 8

PER 2 CUP SERVING:	206 Calories	18 g Prot (35%)
	32 g Carb (62%)	1 g Fat (3%)
	8 g Sugar	11 g Fiber
	74 mg Sodium	0 mg Chol
	70 mg Calcium	

1. Cabbage Rolls, *p. 119*
2. Mock Chicken-Asparagus Risotto, *p. 132*
3. Nut Loaf, *p. 133*
4. Gravy, *p. 58*
5. Cranberry Sauce, *p. 59*

GLUTEN

Preparation Time: 30 minutes
Complexity: Intermediate

3 cups	**gluten flour**
½ cup	**Minute Tapioca**
⅓ cup	**flour, whole-wheat**
2 tbsp	**nutritional yeast flakes**
1-3 tbsp	**chickenlike seasoning of your choice**
2 tbsp	**Bragg's All Purpose Seasoning or low-sodium soy sauce**
2¾ cups	**water**

Broth:

10 cups	**water**
1 can (28 oz, 784 g)	**tomato sauce, low sodium**
1-2 tbsp	**beeflike seasoning of your choice**
1 tbsp	**Bragg's All Purpose Seasoning**
1 tsp	**instant coffee substitute, optional**
1 tsp	**onion powder**
½ tsp	**Italian powder**
1 tsp	**garlic powder**

Breading:

1 cup	**bread crumbs, finely ground, dry**
2 tbsp	**nutritional yeast flakes**
1 tbsp	**parsley flakes**
½ tsp	**garlic powder**
½ tsp	**onion powder**
¼ tsp	**paprika**

1. In a large stockpot, combine all ingredients for the broth. Bring to a boil, then reduce to a simmer.

2. In a large bowl, combine gluten flour, tapioca, whole-wheat flour, nutritional yeast and seasoning. Mix well. Make a "well" in the center and add the Bragg's seasoning and water. Mix together at once quickly. (You may need to use your hands.) Do not knead, or gluten will become "tough." Shape dough into a roll about 3-4 inches in diameter (see Chef's Tips below).

3. With a sharp knife, slice each piece about ¼ inch thick.

4. Drop slices one at a time into the simmering broth. Gently stir the mixture, then do so periodically. Place lid on pot and simmer for 1 hour or until gluten is the desired texture. (A longer cooking time will increase tenderness.)

5. Remove gluten pieces from broth. Reserve broth to make a vegetable soup, or freeze to use for the next batch of gluten. (Just add some water and/or tomato sauce to increase its volume.)

6. Dip each piece of gluten in seasoned bread crumbs. Fry both sides in a nonstick skillet with a little olive oil as needed.

CHEF'S TIPS:

- If gluten mixture appears too dry, add tablespoons of water, one at a time, until it mixes easily. If it's too dry, mixing it will only make the gluten tough. If gluten appears too wet, roll gluten dough in a clean dish towel to absorb the excess moisture before slicing.

- Gluten freezes well. You may choose to grind it into burger or dice into cubes for various recipes. (Avoid step 6 in this case.)

- Freeze "broth" to use the next time you make Gluten, or add water and vegetables to make a delicious soup!

Makes: approximately 16 large gluten steaks or 16 cups ground burger

FOR GLUTEN (based on plain gluten, does not include breading)				
PER 1 STEAK:	136 Calories	20 g Prot (59%)	14 g Carb (40%)	0 g Fat (1%)	0 g Sugar
	2 g Fiber	80 mg Sodium	0 mg Chol	3 mg Calcium	

FOR BROTH (broth only when used as a soup base)				
PER SERVING:	25 Calories	1 g Prot (15%)	5 g Carb (80%)	0 g Fat (5%)	3 g Sugar
	1 g Fiber	69 mg Sodium	0 mg Chol	13 mg Calcium	

GLUTEN PATTIES

Preparation Time: 30 minutes
Complexity: Easy

1 cup	gluten flour
1 cup	oats, quick-cooking
2 tbsp	nutritional yeast flakes
¼ cup	flour, whole-wheat
1-2 tbsp	beeflike seasoning of your choice, to taste
½ tsp	thyme
½ tsp	poultry seasoning or sage
1 tsp	garlic powder
1 cup	onions, diced fine
1½ cup	water
2 tbsp	Bragg's All Purpose Seasoning

Broth:

3 cups	water
1-2 tbsp	beeflike seasoning of your choice, to taste
¾ tsp	garlic powder
1 tbsp	Bragg's All Purpose Seasoning

1. Combine all dry ingredients in a bowl. Mix well. Make a "well" in the center.

2. Pour the wet ingredients into the "well." Again, mix very well.

3. Let mixture stand 5 minutes.

4. Combine broth ingredients in a 9" x 13" glass baking dish.

5. Form mixture into patties or burgers and fry (using nonstick frying pan) until golden brown on each side.

6. Place cooked burgers into broth in baking dish. Using a spoon, scoop broth up over each patty.

7. Cover the baking dish and bake in oven at 350° F for 1 hour.

Serves: 8

PER 1 PATTY:	112 Calories	12 g Prot (42%)	14 g Carb (50%)	1 g Fat (8%)	1 g Sugar
(large, with gravy)	2 g Fiber	244 mg Sodium	0 mg Chol	20 mg Calcium	

MEATLESS MEATBALLS

Preparation Time: 40 minutes
Complexity: Easy

½ pkg (16 oz, 454 g)	tofu, medium/firm
2 cups	brown rice, cooked
¾ cup	pecans, finely ground
3 cups	oats, quick
¼ cup	soy milk
2 tbsp	Bragg's All Purpose Seasoning
1 tbsp	lemon juice
¾ tsp	garlic powder
2 cups	potatoes, hot mashed
2 tsp	Ener-G Egg Replacer powder (dissolved in 1 tbsp water)
2 tbsp	onions, finely chopped
3 tbsp	wheat germ
2-4 tbsp	beeflike seasoning of your choice, to taste
2 tbsp	nutritional yeast flakes

1. Mash tofu with a fork.

2. Add remaining ingredients. Mix well.

3. Form mixture into balls the size of a golf ball, then place on a lightly oil-sprayed baking sheet.

4. Bake at 350° F for 20 minutes. Turn balls over and bake for an additional 10 minutes.

5. Serve in a brown gravy (p. 58), a sweet-and-sour sauce (p. 55), or tomato sauce for spaghetti.

Chef's Tips:

- These "meatballs" are perfect for preparing before needed and then freezing.
- Reheated leftover potatoes work well in this recipe.

Serves: 16

PER SERVING: (3 meatballs)	169 Calories 3 g Fiber	7g Prot (14%) 123 mg Sodium	22 g Carb (54%) 0 mg Chol	6 g Fat (32%) 82 mg Calcium	1 g Sugar

MEXICAN TORTILLA LASAGNA

Preparation Time: 20 minutes
Complexity: Easy

1 cup	onions, chopped
1 tsp	basil, crushed
½-1 tbsp	chili powder
1½-2 cups	kidney beans, cooked
1½ cups	bell pepper, green, chopped
4 cups	spinach, chopped fresh
½ cup	salsa, mild
2 cups	zucchini, cubed
3 cups	tomato sauce, low sodium
1 cup	tomato sauce, low sodium
12	corn tortillas

"Cheese" Sauce:

¾ cup	cashew pieces, raw
¼ cup	nutritional yeast flakes
1 tbsp	Bragg's All Purpose Seasoning
1	garlic clove
⅓ cup	bell pepper, red, roasted
½ cup	water, or as needed
3 tbsp	lemon juice
¼ cup	onion, chopped

1. Place ingredients for "cheese" sauce in blender and blend until very smooth. Set aside.

2. In a large pot, saute onions until translucent.

3. Add seasonings, kidney beans, green pepper, spinach, salsa, zucchini, and 3 cups tomato sauce. Simmer until vegetables are soft.

4. Pour 1 cup tomato sauce into a 9" x 13" glass baking dish. Swirl sauce around to cover the bottom of the baking dish.

5. Place a layer of 6 corn tortillas in the baking dish overlapping each other.

6. Pour half of the cooked vegetable mixture over the corn tortillas.

7. Spread half the "cheese" sauce over vegetable mixture.

8. Layer another 6 corn tortillas in baking dish, followed by the remaining vegetable mixture, and topped with the remaining half of the "cheese" sauce.

9. Bake at 350° F for 25 minutes. Let stand 5-10 minutes at room temperature before serving.

10. Cut into squares.

CHEF'S TIPS:

- Serve with freshly baked *Corn Bread* (p. 45) and *Quinoa Salad* (p. 93).
- Roasted red pepper is known as pimiento (unpickled). You can make it easily yourself.
- Substitute chili powder with 1 tsp Spanish paprika and ½ tsp of mace.
- Add 2 cups of frozen corn. It works well.

Serves: 10

PER 2" x 3" SERVING:	220 Calories	8 g Prot (15%)	36 g Carb (65%)	5 g Fat (20%)	7 g Sugar
	8 g Fiber	183 mg Sodium	0 mg Chol	102 mg Calcium	

MOCK CHICKEN-ASPARAGUS RISOTTO (see p. 126)

Preparation Time: 50 minutes
Complexity: Intermediate

2 cups	**diced soy chicken**
2 cups	**onions, chopped**
2 cups	**mushrooms, fresh, diced**
1 tbsp	**olive oil**
3 cups	**rice, brown, short-grain**
¼-½ cup	**chickenlike seasoning of your choice, to taste**
8-9 cups	**water**
3 cups	**asparagus, fresh**
3 tbsp	**coconut milk, light**
2 tbsp	**minced fresh parsley or**
1 tbsp	**parsley flakes**

1. In a large frying pan, sauté diced soy chicken, onions, and mushrooms in 1 tablespoon olive oil until chicken has browned and the mushrooms and onions are soft. Set aside.
2. In another large frying pan, add dry, uncooked rice. Cook for 2-3 minutes, stirring constantly, over medium heat.
3. Stir chickenlike seasoning into water to make a broth. Add 2 cups of this broth mixture into the rice in frying pan each time the broth is absorbed by the rice. Simmer rice covered.
4. Cook rice until it is soft and tender, about 60 minutes.
5. Add soy chicken, onions, and mushrooms.
6. Wash and trim bottom ends of asparagus. Slice the asparagus in half lengthwise, then slice the thicker pieces in half widthwise. Add to rice. Cover and let cook 5 minutes.
7. Mix in coconut milk, and salt to taste if desired. Add parsley. Serve immediately.

CHEF'S TIP:
- When choosing a soymeat product, be sure to choose those low in salt, fat, and preservatives. (MGM of Cedar Lake brand is a good choice.)

Serves: 12

PER 1-CUP SERVING:	275 Calories	14 g Prot (20%)	47 g Carb (68%)	4 g Fat (12%)	3 g Sugar
	5 g Fiber	218 mg Sodium	0 mg Chol	30 mg Calcium	

SAVORY DRESSING/STUFFING

Preparation Time: 25 minutes
Complexity: Easy

5 cups	**bread crumbs, whole-wheat**
1 cup	**carrots, grated**
1½ tsp	**poultry seasoning or**
1 tsp	**sage**
¼ tsp	**salt**
¾ tsp	**garlic powder**
2 cups	**brown rice, cooked**
½ cup	**celery, thinly sliced**
¾ cup	**onions, finely chopped**
¼ cup	**olive oil**
⅔ cup	**water**
⅓ cup	**sunflower/sesame seeds** (optional)

1. Mix all ingredients together in a 2-quart casserole dish. Cover.

2. Bake at 350° F for 30-40 minutes until celery and onion are tender.

3. Serve as a side dish or use in *Stuffed Squash* (p. 113).

CHEF'S TIPS:
- To add some color, especially for festive occasions, add ⅓ cup dried cranberries.
- To make fresh bread crumbs, grind up slices of fresh whole wheat bread in a food processor to make needed amount.

Serves: 6

PER 1-CUP SERVING:	342 Calories	9 g Prot (12%)	56 g Carb (65%)	9 g Fat (23%)	3 g Sugar
	8 g Fiber	285 mg Sodium	0 mg Chol	127 mg Calcium	

NUT LOAF (see p. 126)

Preparation Time: 20 minutes
Complexity: Intermediate

1 cup	**cashew pieces, ground**
2 cups	**ground *Gluten*** (p. 128) (or use Yves ground burger or Cedar Lake Vegeburger)
1 cup	**onions, finely chopped**
⅓ cup	**celery, finely chopped**
1 cup	**bread crumbs, whole-wheat, dry**
¾ cup	**soy milk**
2 tbsp	**cornstarch**
1 tbsp	**Bragg's All Purpose Seasoning**
1-2 tbsp	**chickenlike seasoning of your choice, to taste**
1 tbsp	**parsley flakes**
1 tsp ½ tsp	**poultry seasoning, or sage**

1. Combine all ingredients and mix well.

2. Oil-spray 1 large or 2 small loaf pans. Pour mixture into pan(s) and spread evenly.

3. Bake at 350° F for 45-60 minutes or until brown on top.

4. Remove from oven and let sit 10 minutes before serving. Serve with gravy (p. 58)

CHEF'S TIPS:

• Loaf is more firm if prepared the day before serving. Reheat loaf and tip out onto a platter. Slice into ½-inch slices. Garnish with fresh parsley and cherry tomatoes.

• This loaf can be used on such occasions as Christmas or Thanksgiving in place of a turkey.

• Freezes well. Ideal sandwich filler, especially with pita (pocket) bread.

Serves: 10

PER ½-INCH SLICE:	160 Calories	10 g Prot (25%)	15 g Carb (38%)	7 g Fat (37%)	1 g Sugar
	3 g Fiber	130 mg Sodium	0 mg Chol	38 mg Calcium	

VEGETARIAN LASAGNA

Preparation Time: 30 minutes
Complexity: Intermediate

8	lasagna noodles, whole-wheat
1 pkg (12 oz, 340 g)	tofu, firm
1 can (28 oz)	tomatoes, diced
1 can (14 oz)	tomato soup
1 can (5.5 oz)	tomato paste
1 pkg	Yves Ground Round burger
	or
2 cups	ground *Gluten* (p. 128)
4 cups	spinach, chopped, lightly steamed
1 tsp	garlic powder
1 tsp	Italian seasoning
½ tsp	oregano
¼ cup	onion flakes
1 tbsp	parsley flakes

Optional:
Almond Cheese (p. 54)
or
commercial soy cheese

Garnish:
fresh parsley, chopped

1. Cook lasagna noodles until tender in boiling water. Rinse under cool water, set aside.

2. Mash tofu with a fork to make a "cottage cheese" texture. Place in a medium-large pot.

3. Add remaining ingredients to pot. Simmer for 10 minutes to blend flavors.

4. Lightly oil-spray a 9" x 13" glass baking dish.

5. Lay 4 lasagna noodles over the bottom of the baking dish, overlapping them.

6. Pour half of the sauce over the noodles.

7. Layer 4 more noodles over the sauce, again overlapping them.

8. Spread the remaining sauce over the noodles.

9. Sprinkle with grated *Almond Cheese* or soy cheese if desired.

10. Bake in a 350° F oven for about 30 minutes until heated through. Garnish with fresh chopped parsley.

CHEF'S TIP:

• If prepared ahead and then reheated before serving, the lasagna will hold its shape better.

Serves: 9

Analysis does not include the use of soy or low-fat cheese.

PER 3" x 3" SERVING:	324 Calories	21 g Prot (26%)	50 g Carb (62%)	4 g Fat (12%)	7 g Sugar
	5 g Fiber	74 mg Sodium	0 mg Chol	289 mg Calcium	

POTATO PIE

Preparation Time: 25 minutes
Complexity: Intermediate

1 cup	**onions, chopped**
3 cups	**carrots, shredded**
1½ cups	**TVP, rehydrated**
1¼ cups	***Condensed Celery Soup*** (p. 71)
1½ cups	**green beans, cut, cooked**
4 cups	**mashed potatoes**
⅓ cup	**soy milk, or as needed**
1 tsp	**garlic powder**
½ tsp	**onion powder**
½ tsp	**salt**
¼ tsp	**paprika**

1. In a large nonstick frying pan, saute onions and carrots in a little water until soft.

2. Add *Condensed Celery Soup* and green beans.

3. Place mixture in a large casserole dish.

4. Mash potatoes until light and fluffy.

5. Add garlic and onion powder, and salt to potatoes. Mix well.

6. Spread potatoes over filling. Sprinkle with paprika.

7. Bake at 375° F for 20 minutes or until heated through.

CHEF'S TIPS:

- Serve with a nice fresh salad for a complete meal.
- To rehydrate TVP: Place TVP in a bowl, pour hot water to cover TVP well. Allow to soak for 5 minutes or until water is absorbed. Drain off excess water before using.
  Serves: 4

PER 2-CUP SERVING:	235 Calories	19 g Prot (31%)	41 g Carb (66%)	1 g Fat (3%)	11 g Sugar
	13 g Fiber	291 mg Sodium	0 mg Chol	87 mg Calcium	

PECAN-RICE PATTIES

Preparation Time: 25 minutes
Complexity: Easy

⅔ cup	**pecans, finely ground**
1 cup	**brown rice, cooked**
1⅓ cups	**bread crumbs, whole-wheat, finely ground, dry**
1 tbsp	**soy flour**
1 tbsp	**parsley flakes**
½ tsp	**salt**
1 cup	**onions, finely chopped**
1 cup	**soy milk**

1. Combine all ingredients in a mixing bowl.

2. Shape mixture into patties or bite-sized croquettes. Place on a lightly sprayed (using a nonstick spray) baking sheet.

3. Bake at 350° F for about 30-40 minutes, or until golden brown.

4. Serve with chicken-style gravy (p. 58).

Serves: 8

PER 1 PATTY:	192 Calories	6 g Prot (13%)	24 g Carb (50%)	8 g Fat (37%)	2 g Sugar
	4 g Fiber	207 mg Sodium	0 mg Chol	78 mg Calcium	

SPAGHETTI SAUCE

Preparation Time: 25 minutes
Complexity: Easy

1 cup	onions, chopped
3	garlic cloves, minced
½ pkg	tofu, firm (diced into ½-inch squares)
(12 oz, 350 g)	
4 cups	tomatoes, diced, low sodium
1 can (6 oz)	tomato paste, low sodium
1 cup	tomato sauce, low sodium
¾ tsp	basil, crushed
½ tsp	oregano
¼-½ tsp	Italian seasoning
½ tbsp	parsley flakes
½ tsp	salt, to taste
½ tbsp	sugar (optional)

1. Using a nonstick spray, spray a medium-sized pot or large nonstick frying pan. Sauté onions, garlic, and tofu until golden brown.
2. Add remaining ingredients.
3. Simmer for about 10 minutes, stirring occasionally.
4. Serve hot over whole-grain spaghetti.

CHEF'S TIP:

- You may choose to omit the tofu, but it is a simple idea instead of making "meatballs."

Serves: 6

PER 1 CUP SERVING:	102 Calories	8 g Prot (19%)	17 g Carb (74%)	1 g Fat (7%)	6 g Sugar
	5 g Fiber	245 mg Sodium	0 mg Chol	127 mg Calcium	

SAVORY TOFU ROAST

Preparation Time: 20 minutes
Complexity: Easy

Tofu can be frozen to prolong freshness or to change its texture. Here is a great recipe for your frozen tofu.

1 pkg	tofu, firm, frozen and thawed
(16 oz, 454 g)	
1 cup	Nutty Rice or Grape-Nuts (commercial cereals)
3 tbsp	Bragg's All Purpose Seasoning
2 tbsp	nutritional yeast flakes
1 tbsp	parsley flakes
1 cup	onions, finely chopped
1½ tbsp	cornstarch
2 tbsp	olive oil
⅓ cup	soy milk
1 tsp	garlic powder
1 tsp	poultry seasoning or
½ tsp	sage
1 tbsp	Ener-G Egg Replacer powder

(dissolved in 1/4 cup water)

1. Thoroughly squeeze liquid out of frozen tofu. Crumble into a bowl (should be dry and crumbly).
2. Add remaining ingredients. Mix well.
3. Lightly oil-spray a 9" x 9" glass baking dish. Spread mixture into dish. Press down firmly.
4. Bake at 350° F for 1 hour, or until nicely browned on top. Allow to stand 10 minutes before serving.

CHEF'S TIPS:

- Serve with *Gravy* (p. 58).
- When freezing water-packed tofu, freeze entire package, unopened.

Serves: 9

PER 3" x 3" SERVING:	143 Calories	6 g Prot (15%)	18 g Carb (55%)	5 g Fat (30%)	3 g Sugar
	3 g Fiber	300 mg Sodium	0 mg Chol	39 mg Calcium	

SWEET-AND-SOUR TOFU

Preparation Time: 30 minutes
Complexity: Easy

2 cups	bell peppers, green, diced into 1-inch pieces
1 cup	onions, diced into 1-inch pieces
2	garlic cloves, minced
2 cups	celery, diced diagonally
¼ cup	water
4 tbsp	lemon juice
1 can (14 oz)	pineapple tidbits and juice
1 can (5.5 oz)	tomato paste
2 tbsp	Bragg's All Purpose Seasoning
1 tbsp	honey
1 tbsp	cornstarch
2 tbsp	cold water
2 cups	tofu, extra-firm, diced into 1-inch cubes

1. In a large nonstick frying pan, sauté green peppers, onions, garlic, and celery in a little water until tender.
2. Add lemon juice, pineapple and juice, tomato paste, Bragg's seasoning and honey. Stir well.
3. Dissolve cornstarch in 2 tablespoons of cold water, and add to pan.
4. Cook until sauce becomes clear. Add tofu cubes.
5. Heat through. Serve over rice.

Serves: 8

PER 1 CUP:	144 Calories	7 g Prot (20%)	20 g Carb (55%)	4 g Fat (25%)	11 g Sugar
	3 g Fiber	199 mg Sodium	0 mg Chol	133 mg Calcium	

VEGGIE FAJITAS

Preparation Time: 30 minutes
Complexity: Intermediate

4 cups	soy curls, dry
2 cups	red onions, thinly sliced
½ cup	bell peppers, green, sliced into strips
1 cup	bell peppers, red, sliced into strips
1 cup	bell peppers, yellow, sliced into strips
1 cup	bell peppers, orange, sliced into strips
2 tbsp	Bragg's All Purpose Seasoning (or to taste)
¼ cup	plum sauce
2 tsp	garlic powder
8	tortillas, whole-wheat or multigrain

1. In a bowl, cover soy curls with hot water and soak for about 10 minutes.
2. In a large nonstick frying pan, sauté onions and peppers in a little water until slightly tender.
3. Drain soy curls, add to contents in frying pan. Add Bragg's seasoning, plum sauce, and garlic powder. Stir and sauté for 3-4 minutes.
4. Serve warm in a tortilla with your choice of salsa and Tofutti sour cream or *Tofu Sour Cream* (p. 67), if desired.

Serves: 8

PER 1 TORTILLA:	284 Calories	12 g Prot (17%)	44 g Carb (63%)	6 g Fat (19%)	3 g Sugar
	5 g Fiber	172 mg Sodium	0 mg Chol	27 mg Calcium	

WHOLE-WHEAT PIEROGIES

This is a Canadian favorite, especially of those from the Ukraine.

Preparation Time: 60 minutes
Complexity: Advanced

Dough:

4 cups	flour, whole-wheat
2 cups	soy milk, or as needed
4 tsp	Ener-G Egg Replacer powder

(dissolved in 4 tbsp water)

1. Mix together all ingredients in a mixing bowl. Add enough flour or soy milk to form dough into a ball that is not sticky.
2. Roll dough out to 1/8 inch. Cut circles using a drinking glass.
3. Place 1 full teaspoon or so of filling in the center of each dough circle. (See *Pierogi Fillings* below.)
4. Fold dough in half over filling. Press edges together firmly.
5. In a large pot, bring 8 cups of water to a boil. Add 2 tablespoons olive oil.
6. Drop 8 pierogies into the water. Boil 8 minutes, then remove pierogies with a slotted spoon. Place in a dish. Repeat until all pierogies are cooked.
7. Warm up pierogies as they are, or fry with diced onion until lightly browned on each side. Serve with *Tofu Sour Cream* (p. 67) or Tofutti sour cream.

CHEF'S TIPS:

- To make a lighter dough, substitute some unbleached white or spelt flour for some of the whole wheat flour.

Makes: minimum 2 dozen

PIEROGI FILLINGS

Potato "Cheese"

1 tbsp	pimiento, chopped
¾ cup	cashew pieces
¼ cup	nutritional yeast flakes
1½ tbsp	lemon juice
1	clove fresh garlic
¼ cup	onions, chopped
⅔ cup	water
½ tsp	salt
3 cups	mashed potatoes

1. Place all ingredients except potatoes in blender. Blend until very smooth.
2. Mix "cheese sauce" into mashed potatoes.

PER 2 PIEROGIES:	249 Calories	10 g Prot (16%)	41 g Carb (66%)	5 g Fat (18%)	1 g Sugar
	8 g Fiber	124 mg Sodium	0 mg Chol	36 mg Calcium	

Potato Onion

4 cups	cooked potatoes
½ cup	soy milk
1½ cups	onions, red, finely chopped
½ tsp	salt, to taste

1. Mash hot cooked potatoes with soy milk until "fluffy."
2. Saute onions in a little water until soft.
3. Mix salt and red onions into potatoes.

PER 2 PIEROGIES;:	226 Calories	9 g Prot (16%)	43 g Carb (76%)	2 g Fat (8%)	1 g Sugar
	8 g Fiber	130 mg Sodium	0 mg Chol	38 mg Calcium	

Potato Spinach

1½ cups	onions, chopped fine
2	garlic cloves, minced
1 cup	spinach, cooked, finely chopped
3 cups	mashed potatoes
½ tsp	salt

1. In a nonstick frying pan, saute onions and garlic in a little water until soft.
2. Add spinach, potatoes, and salt. Saute until mixture is heated through.

PER 2 PIEROGIES;:	218 Calories	8 g Prot (15%)	42 g Carb (77%)	2 g Fat (8%)	2 g Sugar
	7 g Fiber	125 mg Sodium	0 mg Chol	58 mg Calcium	

Blueberry

2 cups	blueberries, frozen
2 tbsp	honey
2 tbsp	cornstarch
½ cup	water, cold

1. Place blueberries and honey in a pot. Dissolve cornstarch in cold water. Add to blueberries.
2. Bring blueberry mixture to a simmer over medium heat. Simmer until thickened and clear blue in color.

CHEF'S TIP:

• Serve blueberry pierogies warm with *Creamy Whipped Topping* (p. 144) as a dessert, or for a light supper or breakfast.

PER 2 PIEROGIES:	202 Calories	7 g Prot (14%)	39 g Carb (77%)	2 g Fat (9%)	5 g Sugar
	6 g Fiber	25 mg Sodium	0 mg Chol	31 mg Calcium	

Desserts

Banana-Strawberry Sherbet

Basic Piecrust

Apple Crisp

Banana-Oatmeal Cookies

Blueberry Pie

Creamy Whipped Topping

Lemon Pie Filling

Oatmeal-Raisin Cookies

Fruit and Nut Dessert

Fruit Soup

Carrot Pie

Pumpkin Pie

Raspberry-Peach Crumble Cake

Banana Cream Dessert

Strawberry "Yogurt"

Diehl-ight Banana Ice Cream

Diehl-ight Banana Split

Christmas Fruitcake

No-Bake Cookies

Pumpkin Cheesecake

Oriental Lychees With Pineapple

Pastry Crust

Pecan-Raisin Pie

Tropical Cheesecake

• Tropical Cheesecake, *p. 155*

BANANA-STRAWBERRY SHERBET

Preparation Time: 15 minutes
Complexity: Easy

3   **frozen bananas**

6   **frozen strawberries**

1. Place frozen fruit in food processor.

2. Blend until smooth. (Avoid blending too long, or it will begin to melt.)

3. Serve immediately.

Variation:

- Try substituting a variety of frozen fruit.

CHEF'S TIPS:

- Add a little soy milk if needed to make processing easier.
- Garnish with a fresh strawberry half.

Serves: 4

PER 1-CUP SERVING:	108 Calories	1 g Prot (4%)	24 g Carb (90%)	1 g Fat (6%)	13 g Sugar
	3 g Fiber	1 mg Sodium	0 mg Chol	8 mg Calcium	

BASIC PIECRUST

Preparation Time: 20 minutes
Complexity: Easy

2 cups   **whole-wheat pastry flour**

½ tsp   **salt**

2 tbsp   **wheat germ**

½ cup   **boiling water**

½ cup   **olive oil**

1. Combine dry ingredients in a mixing bowl. Mix well, then form a "well" in the center.

2. Pour in water and oil. Mix together, using a fork.

3. Divide dough in half. Shape each half into a ball.

4. Roll each piece of dough out between wax paper to make a thin piecrust. Place into a pie plate. (Makes two bottom crusts, or one double crust for a 10-inch pie.)

5. If prebaking, poke holes in the bottom of the crust using a fork.

6. Bake at 350° F until golden brown (approximately 10-15 minutes).

CHEF'S TIPS:

- If prebaking, press an empty pie plate or round cake pan on top of piecrust while baking, to help avoid "shrinkage."
- Dough freezes well if you wish to make ahead to have on hand, or if you choose to freeze half of the recipe amount.
- Try replacing whole grain spelt flour for the whole-wheat pastry flour for a nice change.

Makes: 1 double crust or 2 single crusts

Analysis based on a single crust.

PER 2-INCH SLICE:	114 Calories	2 g Prot (6%)	11 g Carb (38%)	7 g Fat (56%)	0 g Sugar
⅛ of pie	2 g Fiber	71 mg Sodium	0 mg Chol	6 mg Calcium	

APPLE CRISP

Preparation Time: 30 minutes
Complexity: Easy

6	apples, medium
½ cup	raisins
2 tsp	cinnamon
3 tbsp	olive oil
1 cup	oats, quick-cooking
¼ cup	maple syrup
½ cup	whole-wheat pastry flour

1. Peel and core apples. Slice apples ¼-inch thick into a 9" x 9" pan.

2. Sprinkle raisins and cinnamon over apples.

3. Mix together oil, oats, maple syrup, and flour. Crumble over top of apples.

4. Bake at 350° F for 40 minutes, or until topping is golden brown.

CHEF'S TIP:

- Serve warm or cold. Nice served for a dessert or for a light supper. Delicious topped with *Creamed Pears Topping* (p. 35) or *Creamy Whipped Topping* (p. 144).

Serves: 9

PER 3"X3" SQUARE SERVING:	214 Calories	3 g Prot (6%)	37 g Carb (70%)	6 g Fat (24%)	22 g Sugar
	5 g Fiber	3 mg Sodium	0 mg Chol	30 mg Calcium	

BANANA-OATMEAL COOKIES

Preparation Time: 20 minutes
Complexity: Easy

1 cup	oats, quick-cooking
¾ cup	whole-wheat pastry flour
⅓ cup	honey
½ cup	raisins
½ tsp	baking powder
3 tbsp	olive oil
⅔ cup	mashed bananas

1. In a medium mixing bowl, combine all ingredients. Mix well.

2. Prepare a cookie sheet using a nonstick spray.

3. Drop cookie dough by large tablespoonfuls onto prepared cookie sheet.

4. Bake at 350° F for 10-15 minutes until golden brown.

Makes: 1 dozen

PER 1 COOKIE:	164 Calorie	3 g Prot (7%)	29 g Carb (70%)	4 g Fat (23%)	13 g Sugar
	3 g Fiber	2 mg Sodium	0 mg Chol	20 mg Calcium	

BLUEBERRY PIE

Preparation Time: 30 minutes
Complexity: Intermediate

Crust:

1 cup	dates, chopped
⅓ cup	water
¾ cup	Grape-Nuts cereal
½ cup	oats, quick-cooking
¼ cup	pecans, finely ground

Filling:

2 cups	blueberries, frozen
1 cup	grape juice, frozen concentrate, undiluted
¼ cup	Minute Tapioca
1 tsp	vanilla extract
1 tbsp	lemon juice

Crust:

1. Place dates and water in a small pot. Bring to a boil. Simmer until dates are soft. Mash dates.
2. Place dates into a mixing bowl. Add remaining ingredients and mix well with a fork.
3. Press into a pie plate on the bottom and up the sides.
4. Bake at 350°F for 12 minutes. Cool to room temperature.

Filling:

1. Place grape juice and tapioca in a medium-sized pot. Let stand 5 minutes.
2. Bring pot to a boil, then reduce heat to simmer for 5 minutes.
3. Add blueberries, lemon juice, and vanilla to pot. Simmer for another 5 minutes, or until tapioca granules turn clear in color.
4. Pour into crust in pie plate. Chill in refrigerator until firm.

CHEF'S TIPS:
- Nice served with *Creamy Whipped Topping* (below).
- Garnish with cream and a fresh mint leaf.

Serves: 8

PER 2-INCH SLICE: (⅛ of pie)	244 Calories 5 g Fiber	4 g Prot (6%) 56 mg Sodium	48 g Carb (79%) 0 mg Chol	4 g Fat (15%) 26 mg Calcium	22 g Sugar

CREAMY WHIPPED TOPPING

Preparation Time: 10 minutes
Complexity: Easy

1 pkg (12 oz, 350 g)	tofu, silken, extra-firm (lite)
1 tbsp	oil (optional)
¼ cup	soy milk
2 tsp	vanilla extract
⅓ cup	maple syrup, or to taste

1. Place all ingredients in a blender or food processor. Blend until very smooth.
2. Chill in refrigerator.

Serve as a topping on cakes, fruit salad, pancakes, etc.

CHEF'S TIP:
- Add a small banana and 1 teaspoon of lemon juice to ingredients in blender and blend smooth. This will make a tasty, thick sauce. Be sure to use immediately, or the cream may turn brown.

Makes: 2 cups

PER 1 TBSP:	17 Calories 0 g Fiber	1 g Prot (9%) 5 mg Sodium	3 g Carb (86%) 0 mg Chol	0 g Fat (5%) 6 mg Calcium	2 g Sugar

LEMON PIE FILLING

Preparation Time: 20 minutes
Complexity: Easy

½ cup	honey
	or
¾ cup	cane sugar
½ cup	cornstarch
1 tsp	grated lemon rind
½ cup	fresh lemon juice
3 tsp	Ener-G Egg Replacer powder
3 cups	cold water

1. Place all ingredients in a medium-sized pot.

2. Whisk well. Simmer over medium temperature until thickened and clear in color.

3. Pour into a prebaked piecrust or tart shells. Chill in the refrigerator.

4. Serve with *Creamy Whipped Topping* (p. 144).

Serves: 8

Analysis does not include piecrust or whipped topping.					
PER 2-INCH SLICE:	99 Calories	0 g Prot (1%)	26 g Carb (99%)	0 g Fat (0%)	18 g Sugar
(⅛ of pie)	0 g Fiber	4 mg Sodium	0 mg Chol	5 mg Calcium	

OATMEAL-RAISIN COOKIES

Preparation Time: 20 minutes
Complexity: Easy

1 tbsp	olive oil
⅓ cup	applesauce, unsweetened
½ cup	honey
1½ tsp	Ener-G Egg Replacer powder (dissolved in 2 tbsp water)
½ cup	nondairy milk
1 cup	spelt or unbleached white flour
¼ tsp	salt
1 tsp	baking powder
1 tsp	cinnamon or substitute
½ tsp	nutmeg or cardamon
1½ cups	quick oats
1 cup	raisins
¼ cup	coconut, unsweetened shredded

1. Mix together wet ingredients.

2. Add dry ingredients to wet mixture, then mix together well.

3. Drop by tablespoonfuls onto a lightly oil-sprayed cookie sheet.

4. Bake at 375° F for 10 minutes or until golden brown.

CHEF'S TIP:

• Do not overbake cookies, or they will be dry.

Makes: 2 dozen

PER 1 COOKIE:	115 Calories	3 g Prot (11%)	19 g Carb (66%)	3 g Fat (23%)	10 g Sugar
	2 g Fiber	37 mg Sodium	0 mg Chol	16 mg Calcium	

FRUIT AND NUT DESSERT

Preparation Time: 20 minutes
Complexity: Intermediate

1 can (18 oz)	pineapple, crushed
2 cups	frozen raspberries
1 tbsp	honey
3 tbsp	cornstarch
½ tsp	almond extract

Topping:

1 cup	whole-wheat pastry flour
1 cup	whole rolled oats
½ cup	shredded coconut, unsweetened
½ cup	pecans, finely ground
¼ tsp	salt
1 tbsp	honey
1 tsp	almond extract
½ cup	pineapple juice, unsweetened

1. Place pineapple along with its juice, raspberries, honey, cornstarch, and almond extract in a medium-sized pot. Mix well.

2. Cook over medium heat until mixture simmers, thickens, and turns a clear red color.

3. Using a nonstick spray, prepare a 9"x 9" glass baking dish. Spread fruit mixture evenly into the baking dish. Set aside.

4. Using a fork, mix together topping ingredients in a mixing bowl.

5. Spread the topping evenly over the hot fruit mixture in baking dish. Press down slightly to compact.

6. Bake at 350° F for approximately 30 minutes, or until golden brown.

CHEF'S TIP:

- Serve warm or cold. Nice served as a dessert, light supper, or even at breakfast! Serve plain or top with a soymilk or a soy, natural almond-flavored ice cream!

Serves: 9

PER 3" x 3" SERVING:	214 Calories	5 g Prot (9%)	35 g Carb (65%)	6 g Fat (26%)	14 g Sugar
	6 g Fiber	68 mg Sodium	0 mg Chol	30 mg Calcium	

FRUIT SOUP

Preparation Time: 25 minutes
Complexity: Easy

3½ cups	pineapple juice, unsweetened
1½ cups	grapes, seedless, sliced
3	bananas, sliced
3½ tbsp	Minute Tapioca
2	apples, small, diced
2 cans (14 oz)	peaches, diced
3 cups	strawberries or raspberries, sliced

1. Soak tapioca for 5 minutes in pineapple juice.

2. Cook juice and tapioca until thick.

3. Add fruits to thickened sauce.

4. Serve warm, or better yet: chill!

5. Garnish with fresh sliced banana and a mint leaf.

Serves: 8

PER 1¾-CUP SERVING:	215 Calories	2 g Prot (4%)	50 g Carb (92%)	1 g Fat (4%)	35 g Sugar
	6 g Fiber	5 mg Sodium	0 mg Chol	40 mg Calcium	

CARROT PIE

Preparation Time: 20 minutes
Complexity: Easy

1	**prepared pie shell** (p. 142)
1 cup	**dates**
2½ tbsp	**cornstarch**
½ tsp	**salt**
3 tbsp	**unbleached white flour**
1 tsp	**vanilla extract**
1 tbsp	**olive oil**
2 cups	**cooked carrots**
1½ cups	**soy milk**
1 tsp	**cinnamon or substitute**
¼ tsp	**ground cloves**
¼ tsp	**allspice**

1. Place all ingredients into a blender. Blend until very smooth.
2. Pour mixture into an unbaked pie shell.
3. Bake at 350° F for 35 minutes or until filling appears set.

CHEF'S TIPS:

- Any variety of squash or pumpkin can be substituted for the cooked carrots.
- Nice served with *Creamy Whipped Topping* (p. 144).
- The *Basic Piecrust* (p. 142) recipe is a nice one used for this filling.

Serves: 8

Does not include crust.

PER 2-INCH SLICE: (⅛ of pie)	139 Calories 4 g Fiber	2 g Prot (6%) 178 mg Sodium	26 g Carb (75%) 0 mg Chol	3 g Fat (19%) 43 mg Calcium	16 g Sugar

PUMPKIN PIE

Preparation Time: 20 minutes
Complexity: Easy

1	**prepared, unbaked pie shell** (p. 142)
1 pkg (12 oz)	**tofu, silken, firm** (lite)
1 can (14 oz)	**pumpkin**
⅓ cup	**honey**
1 tsp	**vanilla extract**
1½ tsp	**cinnamon or substitute**
¼ tsp	**nutmeg or cardamon**
¼ tsp	**allspice**
½ tsp	**salt**

1. Preheat oven to 350° F.
2. Place all ingredients in a blender. Blend until very smooth.
3. Pour mixture into an unbaked pie shell.
4. Bake 1 hour or until filling appears set.
5. Chill pie. Slice pie into 8 pieces.

CHEF'S TIP:

- Nice served with *Creamy Whipped Topping* (p. 144).

Serves: 8

Analysis does not include piecrust.

PER 2-INCH SLICE: (⅛ of pie)	80 Calories 1 g Fiber	3 g Prot (15%) 175 mg Sodium	15 g Carb (75%) 0 mg Chol	1 g Fat (10%) 30 mg Calcium	12 g Sugar

RASPBERRY-PEACH CRUMBLE CAKE

Preparation Time: 30 minutes
Complexity: Intermediate

2 cups	unbleached white flour, or your choice of flour
1½ tsp	baking powder
⅔ cup	raw cashew pieces
⅔ cup	honey
1 cup	water
1 tbsp	olive oil
1 tsp	vanilla extract
1 cup	raspberries fresh
1 cup	peaches, fresh sliced
1 cup	blueberries, fresh

1. Preheat oven to 350° F.
2. In a mixing bowl, combine flour and baking powder.
3. Blenderize cashews, honey, water, oil, and vanilla until smooth.
4. Pour blended mixture into dry ingredients. Mix gently.
5. Spread and press two thirds of mixture into the bottom of a lightly oil greased 9-inch springform pan.
6. Cover with raspberries, peaches and blueberries.
7. Spoon remaining third of mixture over fruit.
8. Bake 50-60 minutes until golden brown.

CHEF'S TIPS:
- Serve warm or cold. Very good served with *Creamed Pears Topping* (p. 35).
- Store cake in refrigerator

Serves: 8

PER 2-INCH SLICE: (⅛ of cake)	359 Calories 4 g Fiber	6 g Prot (7%) 5 mg Sodium	59 g Carb (66%) 0 mg Chol	11 g Fat (27%) 62 mg Calcium	27 g Sugar

1. Strawberry "Yogurt," *p. 150*
2. Oriental Lychees With Pineapple, *p. 153*
3. Pecan-Raisin Pie, *p. 154*
4. Raspberry Peach Crumble Cake, *above*

BANANA CREAM DESSERT

Preparation Time: 30 minutes
Complexity: Intermediate

Crust:

1 cup	**dates, chopped**
⅓ cup	**water**
¾ cup	**Grape-Nuts cereal**
½ cup	**oats, quick-cooking**
¼ cup	**pecans, finely ground**

Filling:

2½ cups	**bananas, fresh sliced**
3 cups	**soy milk, vanilla-flavored**
¾ cup	**dried pineapple pieces**
½ cup	**cornstarch**
1 tsp	**vanilla extract**

Crust:
1. Place dates and water in a small pot. Bring to a boil. Simmer until dates are soft. Mash dates.
2. Place dates into a mixing bowl. Add remaining ingredients and mix well with a fork.
3. Using a nonstick spray, lightly spray an 8" x 11½" glass baking dish.
4. Press mixture into the bottom of the baking dish.
5. Bake at 350° F for 12 minutes. Cool to room temperature.

Filling
1. Layer sliced bananas over the crust evenly.
2. Warm soy milk so that it is above room temperature, but not hot.
3. Place soy milk, dried pineapple, cornstarch, and vanilla into a blender. Blend until very smooth. Pour into a medium-sized pot.
4. Cook mixture over medium temperature stirring constantly until it thickens and begins to simmer. Remove from heat.
5. Pour filling over sliced bananas in baking dish. Spread evenly.
6. Refrigerate until chilled.

CHEF'S TIPS:
- Nice served with *Creamy Whipped Topping* (p. 144) following the Chef's Tip of using a banana.
- Replace crust recipe with your favorite graham crust recipe.
- Garnish with banana slices.

Serves: 9

PER 3"X3" SERVING:	320 Calories 6 g Fiber	6 g Prot (8%) 87 mg Sodium	63 g Carb (78%) 0 mg Chol	5 g Fat (14%) 46 mg Calcium	31 g Sugar

STRAWBERRY "YOGURT" (see p. 148)

Preparation Time: 10 minutes
Complexity: Easy

1 cup	**tofu, silken, firm** (lite)
2 cups	**strawberries, whole frozen**
1 tbsp	**honey**

1. Place tofu and strawberries in a blender and blend until very smooth.
2. Add honey. Blend well.
3. Serve in a bowl garnished with fresh sliced strawberries, or use as a topping over muesli or granola.

CHEF'S TIP:
- You may choose to substitute maple syrup for the honey.

Serves: 3

PER 1-CUP SERVING:	83 Calories 3 g Fiber	2 g Prot (11%) 27 mg Sodium	20 g Carb (85%) 0 mg Chol	0 g Fat (4%) 34 mg Calcium	12 g Sugar

DIEHL-IGHT BANANA ICE CREAM

Preparation Time: 10 minutes
Complexity: Easy

6	**peeled bite-sized banana pieces**
½ cup	**water** (or pineapple juice)
1 tsp	**vanilla** (or some almond extract)
1-2 tsp	**lemon/orange juice**

1. Freeze the 6 banana pieces (1 ripe banana) for at least 24 hours.
2. Put through Champion Juicer, or blenderize with water or pineapple juice.
3. Add vanilla or almond extract and either lemon or orange juice.
4. To thicken ice cream, add ice cubes and blend. For a change in flavor, add 1 cup of pineapple chunks and blend thoroughly.

Variation:

• Add some blueberries or raspberries. Top off with some Grape-Nuts cereal, and garnish with a mint leaf. Serve with a clear conscience.

Serves: 1

Does not include garnishing of fruit, etc.

PER RECIPE:	109 Calories	1 g Prot (4%)	26 g Carb (93%)	0 g Fat (3%)	15 g Sugar
	3 g Fiber	4 mg Sodium	0 mg Chol	9 mg Calcium	

DIEHL-IGHT BANANA SPLIT

Preparation Time: 15 minutes
Complexity: Intermediate

1	**banana, peeled, split lengthwise**
¾ cup	**pineapple chunks, with juice**
1 tbsp	**cornstarch, or as needed**
2 tbsp	**unsweetened coconut flakes**

Add fruit in season, such as:
some blueberries
cantaloupe balls
mandarin orange segments
cut-up slices of kiwi and honeydew balls

1. Thicken the unsweetened pineapple juice with some cornstarch or tapioca. Pour over pineapple chunks. Then bring to a quick boil. Stir in some coconut flakes. Let cool.
2. Place banana halves on bottom of a serving dish.
3. Add some or all of available favorite, colorful fruits in season, such as those suggested.
4. Pour thickening pineapple over the banana-fruit mixture.
5. Garnish with a few walnut halves and a mint leaf. Chill before serving.

Serves: 1

PER 1 RECIPE:	232 Calories	2 g Prot (4%)	47 g Carb (76%)	4 g Fat (16%)	28 g Sugar
	8 g Fiber	16 mg Sodium	0 mg Chol	64 mg Calcium	

CHRISTMAS FRUITCAKE

Preparation Time: 25 minutes
Complexity: Easy

¾ cup	pineapple juice, unsweetened
1 tsp	vanilla
1 cup	mixed raw nuts
	(brazil nuts, hazelnuts, almonds, pecans, walnuts, etc.)
1½ cups	mixed dried fruit
	(papaya, mango, pineapple)
½ cup	dates, chopped
½ cup	cranberries, dried
1 cup	raisins
1 tbsp	Ener-G Egg Replacer powder
	(dissolved in 3 tbsp water)
¼ cup	honey
½ tsp	cinnamon or substitute
¼ tsp	allspice
1½ tsp	baking powder
2 cups	spelt flour

1. Mix all ingredients together in a mixing bowl in the order given.
2. Pour dough into a 9-inch round or square glass baking dish or two small (3" x 7") loaf pans that have been lightly greased, using a nonstick spray.
3. Bake at 350° F for 45 minutes or until golden brown and an inserted toothpick comes out clean.
4. Cool cake before removing from baking dish.

CHEF'S TIPS:

- May substitute unbleached white or whole-wheat pastry flour for spelt flour.
- These cakes freeze very well.

PER 1¾" x 3" PIECE:	225 Calories	4 g Prot (7%)	41 g Carb (73%)	5 g Fat (20%)	27 g Sugar
	4 g Fiber	5 mg Sodium	0 mg Chol	19 mg Calcium	

NO-BAKE COOKIES

Time: 15 minutes
Complexity: Easy

½ cup	soy milk
1 tsp	vanilla extract
½ cup	honey
⅓ cup	carob powder
1½ cups	unsweetened coconut
1½ cups	quick oats

1. Combine soy milk, vanilla, and honey in a pot. Bring to a simmer over medium heat.
2. Add carob powder and coconut to pot. Stir well.
3. Add oats and mix well.
4. Drop by tablespoonfuls onto a piece of wax paper. Chill in refrigerator.

CHEF'S TIP:

- These are especially nice as a "chocolaty" treat for festive occasions.

Makes: 2 dozen

PER 1 COOKIE:	140 Calories	2 g Prot (6%)	14 g Carb (40%)	9 g Fat (58%)	7 g Sugar
	4 g Fiber	8 mg Sodium	0 mg Chol	14 mg Calcium	

PUMPKIN CHEESECAKE

Preparation Time: 30 minutes
Complexity: Intermediate

Crust:

1½ cups	graham cracker crumbs
1 cup	walnuts, ground fine
⅓ cup	olive oil
1 tbsp	honey

Filling:

2 pkg (12 oz, 350 g)	tofu, silken, firm (lite)
2 cups	pumpkin, cooked and mashed
1 cup	cane sugar
2 tsp	cinnamon
½ tsp	ginger powder
½ tsp	nutmeg
¾ tsp	salt
4 tbsp	cornstarch
1 tbsp	lemon juice
⅓ cup	carob chips

Crust:

1. Mix together crust ingredients in a mixing bowl.
2. Using a fork, press mixture into the bottom of a lightly oil-sprayed 12-inch springform pan.
3. Bake at 350° F for 10 minutes or until golden brown.

Filling:

1. Place filling ingredients in a blender. Blend until smooth. Pour over crust. Smooth nicely with flat spatula.
2. Bake at 350° F for approximately 1 hour or until filling is set and begins to brown on top.
3. Melt carob chips slowly by placing them in small bowl and setting the bowl in hot water.
4. Remove cake from oven. Drizzle with melted carob chips. Chill.

CHEF'S TIP:
• Nice served for Thanksgiving or at times you would normally serve pumpkin pie.

Serves: 12

PER 1-INCH SLICE: (¹⁄₁₂ of cake)	248 Calories 2 g Fiber	5 g Prot (8%) 199 mg Sodium	30 g Carb (48%) 0 mg Chol	12 g Fat (44%) 65 mg Calcium	17 g Sugar

ORIENTAL LYCHEES WITH PINEAPPLE (see p. 148)

Preparation Time: 10 minutes
Complexity: Easy

1 can (20 oz)	lychees, water-packed, drained
2 cans (16 oz)	pineapple chunks, drained
1 cup	raspberries, slices of kiwi, and/or blueberries for garnish

1. Mix together lychees and pineapple. Place in individual bowls.
2. Garnish each dish with raspberries, kiwi, and/or blueberries, and with mint leaf.
3. Serve chilled.

Serves: 8 cups
(16 ½-cup servings)

PER ½ CUP:	75 Calories 1 g Fiber	1 g Prot (2%) 10 mg Sodium	16 g Carb (98%) 0 mg Chol	0 g Fat (3%) 16 mg Calcium	17 g Sugar

PASTRY CRUST

Preparation Time: 20 minutes
Complexity: Intermediate

1 cup	oats, quick or whole, rolled
2 cups	flour (whole-wheat unbleached white, whole-wheat pastry flour, or combination)
½ tsp	salt
1 cup	walnuts
1 cup	water

1. In a blender, blend oats until fine as flour.

2. Pour oat "flour" into a bowl and combine with flour and salt.

3. Blend walnuts and water in a blender until smooth. Add to dry ingredients in bowl.

4. Mix together well. Add some additional cold water if needed until dough is soft enough to form into a ball with your hands.

5. Roll between sheets of wax paper. Press into a lightly oil-sprayed pie plate.

CHEF'S TIPS:
- Recipe makes two single crusts if desired.
- If prebaking pie shells, press an empty pie plate or cake pan in on top of crust while baking, to help avoid "shrinkage."

Makes: 1 8-inch double piecrust

PER 2-INCH SLICE: (⅛ of pie)	256 Calories 6 g Fiber	9 g Prot (14%) 144 mg Sodium	32 g Carb (48%) 0 mg Chol	11 g Fat (38%) 36 mg Calcium	1 g Sugar

PECAN-RAISIN PIE (see p. 148)

Preparation Time: 20 minutes
Complexity: Easy

1 cup	raisins
¾ cup	water
1½ tbsp	ground flaxseeds
¼ cup	dates, chopped
⅓ cup	cane syrup
1 tbsp	vanilla extract
½ cup	quick oats, ground fine
1 cup	raw pecan halves
1	unbaked prepared piecrust (p. 142 or p. 154)

1. In a saucepan, mix together raisins, water, flaxseeds, and dates. Bring to a boil and simmer for 4-5 minutes. Pour into a blender.

2. Add syrup and vanilla to blender. Blend mixture until smooth.

3. Add finely ground quick oats, and pulsate blender until well mixed.

4. Spread ½ cup of pecans evenly over the bottom of an unbaked prepared piecrust.

5. Pour blended mixture over pecans and spread smoothly.

6. Decorate the top with the last ½ cup of pecans.

7. Bake at 350° F for 20-25 minutes or until crust edge is golden brown.

8. Chill pie thoroughly. Serve with a low-fat nondairy topping, such as *Creamy Whipped Topping* (p. 144).

CHEF'S TIP:
- A thick cane syrup is ideal in this recipe. Corn syrup may be substituted.

Makes: 1 8-inch pie

Does not include piecrust or whipped topping.

PER 2-INCH SLICE: (⅛ of pie)	282 Calories 4 g Fiber	4 g Prot (6%) 6 mg Sodium	40 g Carb (57%) 0 mg Chol	12 g Fat (37%) 36 mg Calcium	30 g Sugar

TROPICAL CHEESECAKE (see p. 140)

Preparation Time: 25 minutes
Complexity: Intermediate

Crust:

¾ cup	pitted dates, chopped
¼ cup	water
¾ cup	Grape-Nuts cereal
½ cup	quick oats
3 tbsp	almonds, finely chopped

Filling:

2 cups	tofu, silken, firm (lite)
1 tbsp	lemon juice
1 tbsp	vanilla
1 can (20 oz)	pineapple, crushed (do not drain off juice)
3 tbsp	cornstarch
1	medium banana, peeled and cut into thirds
⅓ cup	honey

Topping:

1½ cups	frozen blueberries or strawberries
⅓ cup	water
2 tbsp	cornstarch

1. Bring dates and water to a boil. Reduce heat to low and simmer, covered, 5 minutes or until soft.

2. Add remaining crust ingredients to date mixture. Mix well.

3. Press mixture into the bottom of a lightly oil-sprayed 9-inch springform pan. Set aside.

4. Place tofu, lemon juice, vanilla, and half of pineapple into a blender. Blend until very smooth. Pour into a bowl.

5. Place the remaining pineapple, cornstarch, banana, and honey in blender and blend until very smooth. Pour into bowl with other half of mixture. Mix together well.

6. Pour mixture over crust.

7. Bake at 350° F for approximately 45 minutes, or until edge of cake is browned slightly and center is firm. Cool to room temperature.

8. In a small pot, mix together frozen berries, water, and cornstarch.

9. Cook over medium heat, stirring constantly until it has thickened and is clear in color.

10. Spread fruit mixture over the top of the cheesecake.

11. Chill before serving. Slice into 9 pieces.

CHEF'S TIPS:

- Garnish each slice with a fresh mint leaf and berry.
- For a more tropical taste, substitute frozen mango slices or pineapple pieces in place of the blueberry or strawberry topping.

Serves: 9

PER 2-INCH PIECE: (⅑ of cake)	284 Calories 5 g Fiber	5 g Prot (7%) 81 mg Sodium	59 g Carb (83%) 0 mg Chol	3 g Fat (10%) 56 mg Calcium	36 g Sugar

Drinks and Party Foods

Almond Milk

Cashew Milk

Cashew Rice Milk

Raspberry "Yogurt"

Strawberry "Yogurt" (p. 150)

Soy Milk

Banana Shake

Carrot Juice

Hot Carob Milk

Layered Bean Dip

Nachos

Crisped Tortilla Chips

Piña Colada

Popcorn

Refreshing Lemonade

Spinach Dip

• Spinach Dip, *p. 165*

ALMOND MILK

Preparation Time: 25 minutes
Complexity: Advanced

1 cup	**almonds, raw**
1 tsp	**vanilla extract**
⅛ tsp	**salt**
8 cups	**water, divided**

1. Boil 2 cups water with 1 cup almonds for about 1 minute.
2. Strain almonds in a strainer and rinse with cold water.
3. Pinch off almond skins.
4. Place almonds in the blender with 2 cups water, vanilla and salt. Blend until very smooth.
5. Pour almond mixture through a cheesecloth into a pitcher. Add another 6 cups of water.
6. Chill and serve.

CHEF'S TIP:

• Use leftover almond pulp in patties or cooked cereal.

Serves: 8

PER ¼-CUP SERVING:	53 Calories	2 g Prot (13%)	2 g Carb (15%)	5 g Fat (72%)	0 g Sugar
	1 g Fiber	24 mg Sodium	0 mg Chol	22 mg Calcium	

CASHEW MILK

Preparation Time: 15 minutes
Complexity: Intermediate

1 cup	**cashew pieces, raw**
1/8 tsp	**salt**
1 tsp	**vanilla**
1 tbsp	**honey** (optional)
7-8 cups	**water**

1. In a blender, place cashews, salt, vanilla, honey, and 2 cups of water. Blend until nice and creamy.
2. Add remaining 5-6 cups of water. Stir well.
3. Refrigerate. Shake well each time before serving.

Makes: 8 cups

PER ¼-CUP SERVING:	81 Calories	3 g Prot (12%)	7 g Carb (69%)	7 g Fat (69%)	1 g Sugar
	0 g Fiber	23 mg Sodium	0 mg Chol	8 mg Calcium	

CASHEW RICE MILK

Preparation Time: 25 minutes
Complexity: Intermediate

½ cup	**cashew pieces, raw**
1 cup	**brown rice, hot, cooked, unsalted**
1 tbsp	**vanilla extract**
1½ tbsp	**honey**
¼ tsp	**salt**
7-8 cups	**water**

1. In a blender, place cashews, rice, vanilla, honey, salt, and 2 cups of water. Blend until very smooth and creamy.
2. Pour into a jug. Add remainung 5-6 cups of water, to taste.
3. Chill in refrigerator. Shake well each time before serving.

Makes: 8 cups

PER ¼-CUP SERVING:	62 Calories	2 g Prot (10%)	4 g Carb (43%)	3 g Fat (47%)	2 g Sugar
	0 g Fiber	40 mg Sodium	0 mg Chol	6 mg Calcium	

RASPBERRY "YOGURT"

Preparation Time: 10 minutes
Complexity: Easy

1 pkg (12 oz)	**tofu, silken, firm** (lite)
1 cup	**raspberries, frozen, unsweetened**
1 tsp	**vanilla extract**
2 tbsp	**honey**

1. Place all ingredients into a food processor or blender. Process until very smooth.
2. Serve in small bowls garnished with a fresh raspberry, or use as a topping for granola.

CHEF'S TIP:

- Try substituting a variety of frozen berries such as blueberries, blackberries, strawberries, or a mixture of berries in place of the raspberries in this recipes.

Serves: 4

PER ¼ RECIPE:	80 Calories	6 g Prot (28%)	13 g Carb (62%)	1 g Fat (10%)	11 g Sugar
	2 g Fiber	73 mg Sodium	0 mg Chol	39 mg Calcium	

SOY MILK

Preparation Time: 30 minutes
Complexity: Advanced

1 cup	**soybeans, dry**
	water
½ tsp	**salt, to taste**
3 tbsp	**maple syrup**

1. Soak 1 cup soy beans in 6-8 cups of water for 12-15 hours; or bring 4 cups of water to a rolling boil. Add 1 cup soybeans. Cover and let stand for 2 hours.
2. Drain soaked soybeans and rinse with fresh water.
3. Place beans in a blender along with 2 cups of water. Blend for 2 minutes or until as smooth as possible.
4. Place 8 cups water in a large pot. Bring water to a rolling boil. Add blended bean mixture to pot along with an additional cup of water used to rinse out the blender.
5. Over medium/high temperature, bring mixture to a boil. Stir continuously to avoid boiling over. When it comes to a boil, remove pot immediately from hot burner. Allow to cool slightly.
6. In a large container or pitcher, strain hot mixture through a fine-mesh cheesecloth. Squeeze the milk from the soy pulp. Reserve the soy pulp or use in various baked goods.
7. Stir salt and maple syrup into hot milk. Taste and adjust seasoning. You may choose to add a little vanilla extract. Add additional water if desired.
8. Store in refrigerator. Milk will keep for approximately 1 week.

Makes: 12 cups

PER ½-CUP SERVING:	39 Calories	3 g Prot (42%)	4 g Carb (42%)	2 g Fat (33%)	1 g Sugar
	1 g Fiber	51 mg Sodium	0 mg Chol	25 mg Calcium	

BANANA SHAKE

Preparation Time: 10 minutes
Complexity: Easy

3	bananas, whole frozen (cut in 1-inch pieces)
4 cups	soy milk, vanilla-flavored
1 tbsp	honey (optional)

1. Place ingredients into a blender. Blend until smooth.
2. Serve immediately.

CHEF'S TIPS:
- For a thicker shake, add a fourth frozen banana.
- A variety of frozen fruit (strawberries, etc.) may be added.

Serves: 6

PER 10-OUNCE GLASS:	155 Calories	8 g Prot (20%)	24 g Carb (62%)	3 g Fat (17%)	14 g Sugar
	4 g Fiber	91 mg Sodium	0 mg Chol	65 mg Calcium	

CARROT JUICE

Preparation Time: 15 minutes
Complexity: Easy

6	carrots, medium
2	celery stalks, large
½	apple, medium

1. Wash carrots, celery, and apple well. Core apple, but do not peel; trim ends off of carrots and celery.
2. Put all ingredients through a juicer. Stir; then drink immediately for optimal nutrutional value.

CHEF'S TIPS:
- Add ¼-inch peeled fresh ginger. A good boost for your immune system!
- You like it cold? Just add a few ice cubes!

Serves: 2

PER 12-OUNCE GLASS:	93 Calories	2 g Prot (8%)	22 g Carb (88%)	0 g Fat (4%)	14 g Sugar
	1 g Fiber	106 mg Sodium	0 mg Chol	67 mg Calcium	

HOT CAROB MILK

Preparation Time: 10 minutes
Complexity: Easy

4 cups	soy milk, vanilla-flavored
2½ tbsp	carob powder
3 tbsp	maple syrup

1. Place all ingredients into a pot on the stove. Whisk to dissolve.
2. Bring to a simmer.
3. Serve hot.

Serves: 4

PER 8-OUNCE MUG:	152 Calories	7 g Prot (18%)	22 g Carb (58%)	4 g Fat (24%)	13 g Sugar
	3 g Fiber	123 mg Sodium	0 mg Chol	97 mg Calcium	

LAYERED BEAN DIP (see p. 162)

Preparation Time: 20 minutes
Complexity: Intermediate

4 cups	*Burrito Beans* (p. 118)
2-4 tbsp	**green chili peppers, canned, to taste**
½ cup	*Guacamole* (p. 66)
½ cup	*Tofu Sour Cream* (p. 67)
1 cup	**lettuce, finely shredded**
1 cup	**tomato, diced**
¼ cup	**green onions, chopped**
1 cup	**sliced black olives**
⅓ cup	*Almond Cheese* (p. 54), **grated**

1. Mix green chili peppers into burrito beans. Spread bean mixture in the bottom of a 9" x 9" dish.

2. Continue by layering other ingredients on top in the order given. Press down gently.

3. Serve with *Crisped Tortilla Chips* (p. 163).

CHEF'S TIPS:

- *Burrito Beans* may be substituted with canned vegetarian refried beans.
- This dish tastes best fresh and not used as leftovers.

Serves: 10

Analysis does not include chips.

PER ¾-CUP SERVING:	107 Calories	5 g Prot (16%)	13 g Carb (48%)	5 g Fat (36%)	1 g Sugar
	5 g Fiber	189 mg Sodium	0 mg Chol	45 mg Calcium	

NACHOS (see p. 162)

Preparation Time: 20 minutes
Complexity: Easy

12 cups	**baked, unsalted corn chips, or**
1 recipe	*Crisped Tortilla Chips* (p. 163)
2 cups	*Cheese Sauce* (p. 57), **hot and freshly made**

1. Layer optional ingredients on individual plates in order given, beginning with corn chips and cheese sauce.

2. Serve immediately with *Guacamole* (p. 66), *Salsa* (p. 64), and *Tofu Sour Cream* (p. 67) (or commercial Tofutti sour cream) on the side.

Optional:

2 ounces	**canned green chili peppers added to** *Cheese Sauce*
3 cups	**tomatoes, diced small**
1½ cups	**green onions, chopped**
4 ounces	**black olives, sliced**

Serves: 8

Analysis done using *Crisped Tortilla Chips*.

PER 2-CUP SERVING:	144 Calories	4 g Prot (11%)	20 g Carb (58%)	5 g Fat (31%)	1 g Sugar
	3 g Fiber	154 mg Sodium	0 mg Chol	76 mg Calcium	

CRISPED TORTILLA CHIPS

Preparation Time: 15 minutes
Complexity: Easy

12	**corn tortillas**
½ tsp	**garlic powder**
½ tsp	**onion powder**
	salt, optional

1. Arrange the tortillas in a stack.

2. Cut all 12 tortillas in half and then into quarters.

3. Lay these wedges on a nonstick baking sheet. Do not overlap.

4. Combine garlic and onion powder.

5. Sprinkle tortilla wedges with garlic and onion powder mixture, and salt if desired.

6. Bake in a preheated 375°-400° F oven until the chips are crisp, stirring and turning to brown evenly. Remove the wedges as they are done.

CHEF'S TIP:

- If tortillas are dry before baking, spray lightly with water or olive oil to help seasonings stick to tortillas.

Serves: 12

PER 1 TORTILLA:	63 Calories	2 g Prot (13%)	12 g Carb (76%)	1 g Fat (11%)	0 g Sugar
	1 g Fiber	3 mg Sodium	0 mg Chol	46 mg Calcium	

1. Layered Bean Dip, *p. 161*

2. Piña Colada, *p. 164*

3. Nachos, *p. 161*

PIÑA COLADA (see p. 162)

Preparation Time: 15 minutes
Complexity: Easy

4 cups	**pineapple juice, unsweetened**
2 cups	**cold water**
2 cups	**ice cubes**
1 cup	**coconut milk, light**
½ tbsp	**honey, or to taste**

1. Combine all ingredients in blender and blend until smooth.
2. Serve immediately.

Variation:

- Omit the 2 cups water. After blending, add 2-4 cups sparkling mineral water.

Serves: 8

PER 8-OUNCE GLASS:	134 Calories	1 g Prot (3%)	19 g Carb (57%)	6 g Fat (40%)	16 g Sugar
	0 g Fiber	6 mg Sodium	0 mg Chol	28 mg Calcium	

POPCORN

Preparation Time: 15 minutes
Complexity: Easy

½ cup	**popcorn kernels**
3 tbsp	**olive or flaxseed oil** (you may choose to mix them)
1 tbsp	**nutritional yeast flakes**
½ tsp	**granulated garlic powder**
½ tsp	**Spike seasoning**

1. Pop popcorn in a hot-air popper.
2. Mix oil and seasonings together well.
3. Pour oil mixture evenly over popcorn and mix well. Sprinkle with salt if desired.
4. Serve immediately.

CHEF'S TIPS:

- By using flaxseed oil, you will increase your intake of essential fatty acids. However, flaxseed oil has a distinctive flavor, and getting familiar with the taste can take time. Mixing the flax oil and olive oil together will lighten up the flavor.

- To decrease the amount of fat in this recipe, spray the oil on the popcorn using an "oil pump," then sprinkle with seasonings.

Serves: 6

PER 2-CUP SERVING:	121 Calories	2 g Prot (6%)	13 g Carb (42%)	7 g Fat (52%)	0 g Sugar
	2 g Fiber	56 mg Sodium	0 mg Chol	2 mg Calcium	

REFRESHING LEMONADE

Preparation Time: 15 minutes
Complexity: Easy

1	**lemon, large** (or 2 small lemons)
6 cups	**water, cold**
½ cup	**maple syrup or honey** (to taste)
12	**ice cubes**

1. Squeeze all the juice out of each lemon. Place in a 2-quart pitcher.

2. Add cold water.

3. While stirring, pour in maple syrup. Dissolve well, then taste for sweetness. Adjust sweetener to taste.

4. Add ice cubes and serve immediately.

Makes: 8 cups
Serves: 8

PER 10-OUNCE GLASS:	54 Calories	0 g Prot (0%)	14 g Carb (100%)	0 g Fat (0%)	13 g Sugar
	0 g Fiber	7 mg Sodium	0 mg Chol	19 mg Calcium	

SPINACH DIP (see p. 156)

Preparation Time: 20 minutes
Complexity: Easy

1½ cups	**vegan mayonnaise** or *Tofu Mayonnaise* (p. 56)
2 cups	*Tofu Sour Cream* (p. 67) or **Tofutti sour cream**
1 pkg	**Fantastic* vegetable dehydrated soup mix** (to taste)
1 can (8 oz)	**water chestnuts, drained and chopped**
3	**green onions, chopped** (very fine)
1 pkg (10 oz)	**spinach, frozen chopped, thawed, and drained**

1. Mix all ingredients together in a mixing bowl. Refrigerate for 2 hours.

2. Serve in a hollowed-out round multigrain bread.

3. Place pieces of bread torn from the center of the loaf, with raw vegetables around the edge, for dipping.

*Comment: Fantastic is a brand name that is usually low in sodium. Other brands will work well too.

Makes: 6 cups

Analysis using *Tofu Mayonnaise* and *Tofu Sour Cream*.					
PER 2-TBSP SERVING:	38 Calories	4 g Prot (33%)	5 g Carb (49%)	1 g Fat (18%)	0 g Sugar
	0 g Fiber	111 mg Sodium	0 mg Chol	54 mg Calcium	

Week One Menu Plan

	Sunday	Monday	Tuesday	Wednesday	Thursday	Friday	Saturday
BREAKFAST:	· Buckwheat-Oat Waffles	· Brown Rice Porridge with Soy Milk	· Scrambled Tofu	· Muesli	· Blueberry-Oat Pancakes	· Apples and Rice	· Muesli
	· Creamed Pears Topping	· Oatmeal Raisin Bread	· Honeydew Melon	· Banana Nut Bread	· Fruity Maple Syrup	· Fresh Sliced Peaches	· Whole-Grain Toast
	· Almond Butter	· Banana	· ½ Grapefruit	· Hot Drink	· Fresh Pineapple Wedges	· Fresh Plum	· Nut Butter
	· Fresh Strawberries	· Oranges	· Whole-Wheat Bagels				
	· ½ Grapefruit						
LUNCH:	· Tofu-Millet Burgers	· Cabbage Rolls	· Pecan-Rice Patties	· Chili	· Falafels	· Bean Salad	· Nut Loaf
	· Whole-Grain Bun	· Multigrain Bread	· Paella	· Corn Bread	· Hummus	· Potato Salad	· Mashed Potatoes
	· Ketchup	· Corn Butter	· Cooked Carrots	· Raw Veggies	· Pocket Bread	· Vegetable Platter	· Gravy
	· Tofu Mayonnaise	· Tossed Green Salad	· Steamed Broccoli	· Creamy Cucumber Dressing	· Carrot/Celery Sticks	· Cold Peas	· Cranberry Sauce
	· Oven-baked French Fries		· Bok Choy Salad		· Tabouli Salad	· Cornmeal Buns	· Baked Carrots
	· Raw Veggie Platter					· Corn Butter	· Coleslaw
	· Coleslaw						
SUPPER:	· Squash Stew	· Fresh Cantaloupe	· Fruit Salad	· Greek Salad	· Potato Soup	· Nachos	· Ron's Sweet Rolls
	· Oat Crackers	· Blueberry-Spelt Muffins	· Popcorn	· Pocket Bread	· Dark Rye Bread	· Banana Shake	· Watermelon
	· Hummus						

Week Two Menu Plan

	Sunday	Monday	Tuesday	Wednesday	Thursday	Friday	Saturday
BREAKFAST:	• **Tofu Crepes** • **Thickened Fruit** • **Creamed Pears Topping** · Herbal Tea	• **Dr. Diehl's Crock-pot Breakfast** · Fresh Blueberries · ½ Banana · Fresh-squeezed Orange Juice	• **Millet Pudding** · ½ Mango · Sliced Strawberries	• **French Toast** • **Fruity Maple Syrup** · ½ Fresh Pear · Fresh Apricot	• **Bran Muffin** · Fruit Salad · Walnut Halves	• **Granola** · Toast With Applesauce · Orange Wedges	• **Baked Barley With Apples** · ½ Grapefruit · Fresh Raspberries
LUNCH:	• **Rice Stacks** • **Cornmeal Breadsticks** (Brushed With Olive Oil and Sprinkled With Garlic Powder)	• **Scalloped Potatoes** • **Savory Tofu Roast** • **Bok Choy Salad** • **Cooked Beets** • **Rutabaga Puff**	• **Vegetable Stew** · Whole-Wheat Biscuits	• **Quinoa Salad** • **Pocket Bread** • **Hummus**	• **Curried Chickpeas** • **Brown Rice** • **Green Bean Almondine** • **Baked Acorn Squash** · Fresh Slices of Tomato and Cucumber	• **Veggie Fajitas** • **Salsa** · Corn Chips	• **Dr. Diehl's Lasagna** • **California Lettuce Salad** • **Italian Dressing** · Corn · Steamed Broccoli • **Spelt Bread** • **Corn Butter** With Garlic • **Lemon Pie**
SUPPER:	• **Apple Crisp**	• **Cranberry Orange Bread** · Honeydew Melon Slices	· Raw Vegetable Plate • **Onion Veggie Dip**	• **Diehl-ight Banana Split**	· Watermelon • **Banana Nut Bread**	• **Minestrone Soup** • **Potato Focaccia Bread**	• **Popcorn** · Fresh-cut Apples

Sectional Index of Recipes

BREAKFASTS AND BRUNCHES

Apples and Rice 28
Baked Barley With Apples .. 28
Baked Oatmeal 28
Blueberry-Oat Pancakes 29
Breakfast Potatoes 29
Brown Rice Porridge 30
Buckwheat-Oat Waffles 30
Cashew-Oat Waffles 35
Creamed Pears Topping ... 35
Dr. Diehl's Crock-Pot Breakfast 30
French Toast 31
Fruit Topping 34
Fruity Maple Syrup 34
Granola 33
Millet Pudding 34
Muesli 37
Multigrain Waffles 36
Scrambled Tofu 37
Tofu Crepes 31
Wheat-Oat Crepes 36
Whole-Wheat Pancakes 36

BREADS AND MUFFINS

Banana-Nut Bread 42
Blueberry-Spelt Muffins 43
Bran Muffins 41
Corn Bread 45
Cornmeal Buns & Breadsticks .43
Cranberry-Orange Bread 45
Dark Rye Bread 44
Mom's Homemade Bread .. 44
Multigrain Bread 47
Oat Crackers 50
Oatmeal-Raisin Bread 48
Pocket Bread 50
Potato Focaccia 48
Ron's Sweet Rolls 49
Spelt Bread 42
Whole-Wheat Bagels 51

SPREADS, SAUCES, AND CONDIMENTS

Alfredo Sauce 54
Almond Cheese 54
Apricot Jam 55
Bean Spread 66
Bruschetta 56
Cheese Sauce 57
Chik-style Salad 57
Corn Butter 58
Cranberry Sauce 59
Cream Cheese 61
Flaxseed Gel 62
Gravy 58
Guacamole 66
Hummus 1, 2 63

Ketchup 64
Mock Tuna 59
Mushroom Gravy 62
Salsa 64
Strawberry Jam 1, 2 65
Sweet-and-Sour Sauce ... 55
Tofu Eggless Salad 67
Tofu Mayonnaise 56
Tofu Sour Cream 67

SOUPS AND STEWS

Barley-Tomato Vegetable Soup 76
Borscht 74
Butternut Squash Soup 70
Chili 72
Condensed Celery Soup ... 71
Condensed Mushroom Soup 71
Corn Chowder 83
Cream of Broccoli Soup 73
Creamy Carrot Soup 73
Easy Lentil Soup 75
Hearty Mediterranean Soup .75
Minestrone Soup 77
Pasta Chilli 72
Potato Soup 70
Pumpkin Soup 83
Quinoa Soup 74
Spanish Gazpacho Soup ... 79
Split Pea Soup 1, 2 80
Squash Stew 76
Tuscan Bean Soup 82
Vegetable Stew 82
Zucchini Soup 1, 2 81

SALADS AND DRESSINGS

SALADS

Bean Salad 86
Black Bean Mexican Salad .87
Bok Choy Salad 87
California Lettuce Salad .. 88
Cauliflower Salad 89
Coleslaw 89
Greek Salad 1, 2 90
Mandarin Orange Salad ... 91
Pasta Veggie Salad 91
Potato Salad 94
Quinoa & Bean Sprout Salad .94
Quinoa Salad 93
Spinach Salad 95
Squash Slaw 88
Tabouli Salad 86
Vegetable Pasta Salad ... 95

DRESSINGS

Creamy Cucumber Dressing .96
French Dressing 96
Garlic Omega Dressing ... 97

Gourmet Salad Dressing ... 97
Greek Salad Dressing 96
Italian Dressing 98
Onion Veggie Dip 98
Thousand Island Dressing 99
Zestful Lemon-Dill Dressing .99

VEGETABLES

Baked Acorn Squash 104
Baked Brussels Sprouts ... 104
Baked Carrots 104
Baked Yams 105
Baked Zucchini 106
Chinese Stir-fry Vegetables .107
Cooked Beets 107
Green Bean Almondine ... 110
Oven-baked French Fries .. 111
Ratatouille 109
Rutabaga Puff 112
Scalloped Potatoes 112
Stir-fried Cabbage 105
Stuffed Bell Peppers 111
Stuffed Green & Red Peppers .110
Stuffed Squash 113
Sweet Potato Sticks 106
Zucchini Sauté 113

MAIN DISHES

Baked Beans w. Soy Curls ..116
Baked Brown Rice 116
Black Bean Enchiladas ... 117
Black-eyed Bean Topping .. 118
Burrito Beans 118
Cabbage Rolls 119
Cashew Rice Roast 121
"Chicken" Cacciatore 121
Cooked Lentils 120
Curried Chickpeas 123
Curried Stir-fry 123
Dr. Diehl's Lasagna 124
Falafels 122
Gluten 128
Gluten Patties 129
Lentil Roast 125
Meatless Meatballs 130
Meatless Patties 122
Mexican Tortilla Lasagna .. 131
Mock Chicken-Asparagus Risotto132
Nut Loaf 133
Pasta Stir-fry 124
Pecan-Rice Patties 135
Pierogi Fillings 138
Potato Pie 135
Rice Stacks 125

Savory Dressing/Stuffing .. 132
Savory Tofu Roast 136
Shepherd's Pie 127
Spaghetti Sauce 136
Sweet-and-Sour Tofu 137
Tofu-Millet Burgers 120
Vegetarian Lasagna 134
Veggie Fajitas 137
Whole-Wheat Pierogies ... 138

DESSERTS

Apple Crisp 143
Banana Cream Dessert ... 150
Banana-Oatmeal Cookies .143
Banana-Strawberry Sherbet 142
Basic Piecrust 142
Blueberry Pie 144
Carrot Pie 147
Christmas Fruitcake 152
Creamy Whipped Topping .144
Diehl-ight Banana Ice Cream 151
Diehl-ight Banana Split ... 151
Fruit and Nut Dessert 146
Fruit Soup 146
Lemon Pie Filling 145
No-Bake Cookies 152
Oatmeal-Raisin Cookies .. 145
Oriental Lychees w. Pineapple .153
Pastry Crust 154
Pecan-Raisin Pie 154
Pumpkin Cheesecake ... 153
Pumpkin Pie 147
Raspberry-Peach Crumble Cake149
Strawberry "Yogurt" 150
Tropical Cheesecake 155

DRINKS AND PARTY FOODS

Almond Milk 158
Banana Shake 160
Carrot Juice 160
Cashew Milk 158
Cashew Rice Milk 159
Crisped Tortilla Chips ... 163
Hot Carob Milk 160
Layered Bean Dip 161
Nachos 161
Piña Colada 164
Popcorn 164
Raspberry "Yogurt" 158
Refreshing Lemonade ... 165
Soy Milk 159
Spinach Dip 165
Strawberry "Yogurt" 150

Alphabetical Index of Recipes

lfredo Sauce 54
mond Cheese 54
mond Milk 158
ple Crisp 143
ples and Rice 28
ricot Jam 55

aked Acorn Squash 104
aked Barley With Apples . .28
aked Beans With Soy Curls 116
aked Brown Rice 116
aked Brussels Sprouts . .104
aked Carrots 104
aked Oatmeal 28
aked Yams 105
aked Zucchini 106
anana Cream Dessert . . .150
anana-Nut Bread 42
anana-Oatmeal Cookies . .143
anana Shake 160
anana-Strawberry Sherbet .142
arley-Tomato Vegetable Soup76
asic Piecrust 142
ean Salad 86
ean Spread 66
lack Bean Enchiladas . . .117
lack Bean Mexican Salad .87
lack-eyed Bean Topping .118
lueberry-Oat Pancakes . . .29
lueberry Pie 144
lueberry-Spelt Muffins 43
ok Choy Salad 87
orscht 74
ran Muffins 41
reakfast Potatoes 29
own Rice Porridge 30
ruschetta 56
uckwheat-Oat Waffles 30
urrito Beans 118
utternut Squash Soup 70

abbage Rolls 119
alifornia Lettuce Salad . . .88
arrot Juice 160
arrot Pie 147
ashew Milk 158
ashew-Oat Waffles 35
ashew Rice Milk 159
ashew-Rice Roast 121
auliflower Salad 89
heese Sauce 57
Chicken" Cacciatore 121
hik-style Salad 57
hili 72
hinese Stir-fry Vegetables .107

Christmas Fruitcake 152
Coleslaw 89
Condensed Celery Soup . . .71
Condensed Mushroom Soup .71
Cooked Beets 107
Cooked Lentils 120
Corn Bread 45
Corn Butter 58
Corn Chowder 83
Cornmeal Buns & Breadsticks .43
Cranberry-Orange Bread . . .45
Cranberry Sauce 59
Cream Cheese 61
Cream of Broccoli Soup . . .73
Creamed Pears Topping . . .35
Creamy Carrot Soup 73
Creamy Cucumber Dressing 96
Creamy Whipped Topping .144
Crisped Tortilla Chips 163
Curried Chickpeas 123
Curried Stir-fry 123

Dark Rye Bread 44
Diehl-ight Banana Ice Cream 151
Diehl-ight Banana Split . . .151
Dr. Diehl's Crock-Pot Breakfast 30
Dr. Diehl's Lasagna 124

Easy Lentil Soup 75

Falafels 122
Flaxseed Gel 62
French Dressing 96
French Toast 31
Fruit and Nut Dessert 146
Fruit Soup 146
Fruit Topping 34
Fruity Maple Syrup 34

Garlic Omega Dressing 97
Gluten 128
Gluten Patties 129
Gourmet Salad Dressing . . .97
Granola 33
Gravy 58
Greek Salad 1, 2 90
Greek Salad Dressing 96
Green Bean Almondine . . .110
Guacamole 66

Hearty Mediterranean Soup .75
Hot Carob Milk 160
Hummus 1, 2 63

Italian Dressing 98

Ketchup 64

Layered Bean Dip 161
Lemon Pie Filling 145
Lentil Roast 125

Mandarin Orange Salad . . .91
Meatless Meatballs 130
Meatless Patties 122
Mexican Tortilla Lasagna . .131
Millet Pudding 34
Minestrone Soup 77
Mock Chicken-Asparagus Risotto132
Mock Tuna 59
Mom's Homemade Bread . .44
Muesli 37
Multigrain Bread 47
Multigrain Waffles 36
Mushroom Gravy 62

Nachos 161
No-Bake Cookies 152
Nut Loaf 133

Oat Crackers 50
Oatmeal-Raisin Bread 48
Oatmeal-Raisin Cookies . .145
Onion Veggie Dip 98
Oriental Lychees w. Pineapple .153
Oven-baked French Fries . .111

Pasta Stir-fry 124
Pasta Chili 72
Pasta Veggie Salad 91
Pastry Crust 154
Pecan-Raisin Pie 154
Pecan-Rice Patties 135
Pierogi Fillings 138
Piña Colada 164
Pocket Bread 50
Popcorn 164
Potato Focaccia 48
Potato Pie 135
Potato Salad 94
Potato Soup 70
Pumpkin Cheesecake 153
Pumpkin Pie 147
Pumpkin Soup 83

Quinoa & Bean Sprout Salad .94
Quinoa Salad 93
Quinoa Soup 74

Raspberry-Peach Crumble Cake149
Raspberry "Yogurt" 158

Ratatouille 109
Refreshing Lemonade 165
Rice Stacks 125
Ron's Sweet Rolls 49
Rutabaga Puff 112

Salsa 64
Savory Dressing/Stuffing .132
Savory Tofu Roast 136
Scalloped Potatoes 112
Scrambled Tofu 37
Shepherd's Pie 127
Soy Milk 159
Spaghetti Sauce 136
Spanish Gazpacho Soup . . .79
Spelt Bread 42
Spinach Dip 165
Spinach Salad 95
Split Pea Soup 1, 2 80
Squash Slaw 88
Squash Stew 76
Stir-fried Cabbage 105
Strawberry Jam 1, 2 65
Strawberry "Yogurt" 150
Stuffed Bell Peppers 111
Stuffed Green & Red Peppers .110
Stuffed Squash 113
Sweet-and-Sour Sauce 55
Sweet-and-Sour Tofu 137
Sweet Potato Sticks 106

Tabouli Salad 86
Thousand Island Dressing 99
Tofu Crepes 31
Tofu Eggless Salad 67
Tofu Mayonnaise 56
Tofu-Millet Burgers 120
Tofu Sour Cream 67
Tuscan Bean Soup 82
Tropical Cheesecake 155

Vegetable Pasta Salad 95
Vegetable Stew 82
Vegetarian Lasagna 134
Veggie Fajitas 137

Wheat-Oat Crepes 36
Whole-Wheat Bagels 51
Whole-Wheat Pancakes . . .36
Whole-Wheat Pierogies . . .138

Zestful Lemon-Dill Dressing .99
Zucchini Sauté 113
Zucchini Soup 1, 2 81

To Your Good Health®

Bob Moore

Bob's Red Mill &
The Coronary Health
Improvement Project:

A Partnership
for Life.

Announcing Bob's Red Mill

Dear Friends:

For over 30 years, Bob's Red Mill has been committed to providing you with the finest "Whole Grain Foods for Every Meal of the Day." And it all boils down to the fact that there is simply no better or more healthful way to grind grains than the way we do it—100% stone ground.

It's about being healthy—today, and for the rest of your life.

Recently, my wife Charlee and I attended a seminar that had a profound effect on our lives. The seminar reinvigorated us on how our whole grain products can bring about a significant improvement in our own health and the health of others.

A long-time customer of our Whole Grain Store came in recently and asked me if he

> "It's about being healthy—today, and for the rest of your life."

could post some information about a health education program that was going on in town. This person explained that the Coronary Health Improvement Project (CHIP) encourages people to eat "foods-as-grown," especially whole grain foods because they are the most nourishing and healthful. Well, as you can imagine, this was music to my ears! Wanting first-hand knowledge, that very night, Charlee and I drove to Portland to attend the second night of what turned out to be a month-long adventure in health. It was not only about staying healthy, but also about stopping and reversing the progress of certain diseases like heart disease, diabetes and high blood pressure.

I have never experienced a "lifestyle" education like CHIP, filled with fundamental principles of health, backed up by both long-standing science and current research. There was hands-on learning, group interaction, food sampling, and the quality of the materials and the people involved was unmatched. Nothing to sell but knowledge—and based on what they were charging, they were pretty much giving that away! For food—my particular interest—here's what they do: they direct people to the general grocery stores! But the CHIP program arms people with the ability to understand food labels and recognize the nutritional value and

Find more recipes and order products at www.bobsredmill.com

13 Bean Soup

2 cups Bob's Red Mill 13 Bean Soup Mix
1 cup chopped onion
1 qt. tomatoes or 15oz. can tomato sauce

1-1/2 tsp. chili powder
2 cloves garlic (minced)
2-1/2 qts. water

Wash 2 cups Bob's Red Mill Soup Mix, then soak overnight. In the morning drain, rinse and bring 2-1/2 qts. water to boil with the beans. Reduce heat and simmer 3 to 3-1/2 hours. Add 1 cup chopped onion, one 15 oz. can tomato sauce or 1 qt. tomatoes, 1-1/2 tsp. to 1 Tbsp. chili powder, according to preference, and 2 tsp. garlic powder or 2 cloves of garlic minced. Simmer 30 minutes. Makes about 8 to 10 servings.

For more information visit www.bobsredmill.com or www.CHIPhealth.org

CHIP Alliance

Get started now with whole grains!

quality of the food they're purchasing. Let the label show you what's "real," not the packaging! (Just as our transparent packaging is designed to let you "see" what you're getting!)

At the end of our four-week CHIP adventure, the participants received their clinical report cards.

Take a look at my progress in just four weeks!

	Before	After	Change
Weight (lbs)	206	196	-10 lbs
Total Cholesterol (mg%)	203	158	-22%
LDL Cholesterol (mg%)	131	96	-27%
Triglycerides (mg%)	173	138	-20%

And my wife, Charlee, enjoyed similar changes. And the best thing—after only a week, my heartburn, which had bothered me for years, was gone—and my physician was able to take me off my medication!

Charlee and I were so impressed with the program, we invited the founder of CHIP to our home. Dr. Hans Diehl and his wife Lily joined us for three days, as we shared our life experiences and scrumptious CHIP meals. What we discovered is that each of us, in our own unique way, has been on the same mission—to bring better health and more joy to people.

Given the health challenges many of us are facing, it gives me great pleasure to introduce my new friend, Dr. Hans Diehl and the CHIP program to all of you!

To Your Good Health®,

Bob Moore

Here's how to begin!

We should all be striving to eat whole grain foods for every meal of the day. We've taken the guesswork out of it by creating the CHIP Starter Kit. It contains the eight wonderful whole grain products pictured above to make your breakfast, lunch and dinner simple, heart-healthy, and delicious. The kit is available directly from Bob's Red Mill by emailing Lori Sobelson at lori@bobsredmill.com.

For more information visit www.bobsredmill.com or www.CHIPhealth.org

To Your Good Health®

Bob Moore

For more information about ordering
Bob's Red Mill CHIP Starter Kits
email Lori Sobelson at
lori@bobsredmill.com

Learn more about the
Coronary Health Improvement Project visit:
www.CHIPhealth.org

Or contact CHIP personally at:
909-796-7676
info@CHIPhealth.org

Manufactoring Plant
Tours Monday - Friday, 10-11a.m.
Bob's Red Mill Natural Foods, Inc.
13521 SE Pheasant Court
Milwaukie, OR 97222
1-800-349-2173
www.bobsredmill.com

Store • Cooking School • Bakery
Bob's Red Mill Whole Grain Store
5000 SE International Way
Milwaukie, OR 97222
503-607-6455

it's time *to feel better.*

Giving people the tools they need to live longer, healthier lives is just one of the goals of the Coronary Health Improvement Project.

It's a goal we can feel good about, a goal we can support and just one more way we can help make it better for everyone we serve. To learn more, *itstimetofeelbetter.com*

it's time *to feel better*

CIGNA

READY TO TAKE THE NEXT STEP?

If you have just finished your CHIP program, then you'll want to take advantage of the monthly follow-up meetings offered for the CHIP graduates to anchor down your new lifestyle and to extend its clinical benefits.

If you are not yet one of the 50,000 CHIP alumni, then you'll want to look for the CHIP program nearest you — and enroll!

What's CHIP?

CHIP is an educationally intensive 30-day lifestyle intervention program. Founded by Dr. Hans Diehl, the clinical results have been reported in 13 articles published in peer-reviewed medical journals. Endorsed by the *Physicians' Committee for Responsible Medicine* and the *Center for Science in the Public Interest,* the Coronary Health Improvement Project (CHIP) focuses on markedly reducing coronary risk factors through the adoption of better health habits and wiser lifestyle choices.

What will it do for me?

Overweight? It will show you how to eat more and still lose all the weight you want. *Hypertension?* It will lower your blood pressure. *Diabetes (type 2)?* It will help you to lower your blood sugar and your medication requirements. *Cholesterol?* CHIP will bring your cholesterol down on average 10-20% without medication. *Heart Disease?* It will show you how to slow down, halt and reverse coronary artery disease. *Depression?* It will give you the lift and energy you've been looking for. *Medication requirements?* Your physician will often reduce them, sometimes even discontinue them.

Where can I find CHIP?

CHIP program are conducted in more than 350 locations in North America — in cities, corporations, and churches, as well as in Australia, New Zealand, and England. For more information, please call the Lifestyle Medicine Institute at: **909-796-7676**, or online at: **www.CHIPhealth.org**. We'll be looking forward to helping you with your new journey.